THE MIND OF HENRY FUSELI

THE MIND

OF

HENRY FUSELI

SELECTIONS

FROM HIS WRITINGS

WITH

AN INTRODUCTORY STUDY

BY

EUDO C. MASON

ROUTLEDGE & KEGAN PAUL

First published in 1951
by Routledge & Kegan Paul Limited
68 Carter Lane, London E.C.4
Printed in Great Britain
by Butler & Tanner Limited
Frome and London
Typography by Seán Jennett

CONTENTS

CONTENTS

CONTENTS

PART FIVE

NON-CLASSICAL IMPULSES BURSTING THROUGH THE CLASSICAL HUSK

PART SIX

THE OLDER FUSELI ON LITERATURE   339

ILLUSTRATIONS

9

(Plates 4, 6 and 7 have been selected partly with a view to illustrating the relationship between Fuseli and Blake.)

Note:

The principal Swiss Galleries where Fuseli's paintings and drawings can be seen are:

Kunsthaus, Zurich (where there is also a fine collection of Fuseli's drawings);

The Museum, Winterthur;

Öffentliche Kunstammlung, Basel.

'I will now introduce you to a most ingenious foreigner, whom I think you will
like; but if you wish to enjoy his conversation, you will not attempt to stop the torrent of his words by contradicting him'
(*Joseph Johnson's whispered warning before
introducing Bonnycastle to Fuseli in 1779*)

ACKNOWLEDGEMENTS

THE EDITOR wishes to express his gratitude to the Trustees of the British Museum, to the *Zürcher Kunstgesellschaft* and to Mr. R. Brinsley Ford for permission to reproduce drawings and paintings of Fuseli, and to the Warburgh Institute for supplying a photograph of the Horse-Tamer of Monte Cavallo. Amongst the many helpers who have patiently supplied him with advice and information and saved him from various pitfalls he would specially mention the names of Professor Paul Ganz, Dr. R. Wehrli, Dr. W. Wartmann, Dr. M. Pfister, Dr. Schlatter and Dr. Markus Meier in Switzerland, Mr. Edward Croft Murray and Mr. Geoffrey Grigson in London, and Miss A. Calderwood and Dr. R. A. Leigh in Edinburgh.

E. C. M.

INTRODUCTION

I

The only man that e'er I knew
Who did not make me almost spew
Was Fuseli: he was both Turk and Jew—
And so, dear Christian friends, how do you do?

THESE VERSES, written about 1809, probably stick in the minds of most of Blake's readers. But until quite recently the Fuseli thus commemorated seemed to very few a figure about whom there might be anything better worth knowing than about the Hayleys and Cromeks in whose company he appears in the Rossetti Manuscript. Very few knew that, throughout the sixty-odd years from his first emerging into notice, in the early 1760s, when the great revolutionary movement in literature and art was still in its beginnings, down to his death in 1825, when that movement had reached its final phase, Fuseli was widely recognised among the alertest leading minds of the day, both in England and on the continent—not only by Blake, but also by Goethe—as one whose extraordinary genius simply had to be taken into account, if not with eager enthusiasm, then with an uneasy respect amounting to awe. During the last forty years or so Fuseli has, indeed, after nearly a century of neglect, been rediscovered—first of all in Germany, then in his native Switzerland, and finally in England, the country where he spent the greater part of his long life and where—in St. Paul's Cathedral —he also lies buried. This Fuseli revival of our times has necessarily been concerned almost exclusively with his work as a

13

painter. It is on his paintings and still more on his drawings that his claims to greatness rest. He was, however, also a man of letters, and this circumstance was so important for his life and also for his art, that he can never be fully understood, unless his writings are also taken into account.

Johann Heinrich Füssli—he only adopted the spelling *Fuseli*[1] after many years spent abroad, for the benefit of foreigners who could do nothing with the original Swiss form of the name— was born in Zurich of a family of painters on 6 February 1741. His strong original bent for painting was overridden by his father, who decided to make a Zwinglian minister of him; and a Zwinglian minister he actually did become, being ordained in 1761 and exercising the preaching office for a year or more, until certain external events emancipated him from it for ever. That he had no decisive vocation to the ministry, and that sooner or later he would have come into serious conflict with the ecclesiastical authorities and with the rigours of Zwinglian morality, is certain. At the time, however, he seems to have submitted to the profession imposed upon him with surprisingly little resistance, sympathising with and borne along by a widespread movement among his mentors and fellow theological students to undermine the old orthodoxies from inside with a half-rationalistic, half-emotionalistic humanism. From this subversive angle he really was interested in theology, and continued to be interested in it for years after he had broken away from his preaching past; and throughout his life, down to his old age, he seems to have clung to certain quasi-orthodox ideas about the nature of God, the relationship of God to man, and the metaphysical reality of sin, evil and damnation, which prevent him from sharing the pantheistic *élan* of the typical Romantics. It is unthinkable that he should ever have said with Blake: 'God is man and exists in us and we in him.'

The Zurich in which Fuseli studied was the fountain-head from which the great revolutionary movement in literature, known to us, though not to the Germans themselves, as

---

[1] The many instances in which the name *Fuseli* occurs in complimentary poems of the day all show that it must regularly have been pronounced as three syllables by contemporaries.

Romanticism,[1] was already gradually beginning to spread over all the territories where German is spoken. Professor Bodmer, one of the chief inaugurators of this movement, and still its leader, was a teacher in whom Fuseli found every stimulus and encouragement his mind needed, and Fuseli himself was Bodmer's chosen favourite, the most promising among a group of brilliant students, some of whom are still great names in German literary history, his temperament passionate and audacious, his mind acute and restless, his wit dazzling and ruthless, a delight and a terror to all who knew him. He was an insatiate reader with a great natural gift for languages, not only a fine Greek and Latin, and an adequate Hebrew scholar, but also from his early years a fluent speaker of French, Italian and English as well as of German; in later life he certainly also taught himself Dutch; Cunningham says he also knew Danish and Spanish, but there is no other evidence on this.

It was one of the chief objects of the new literary movement with which Fuseli was so intimately associated at its very source, and of which he was also one of the principal hopes, to emancipate German literature from the rules, standards and models of French Enlightenment classicism. Bodmer was, more than any other, responsible for the setting up of English poetry as the great well-head from which German literature must renew itself. First Milton was discovered and imitated; upon this followed enthusiasm for the first timid Miltonian rebels against Pope and the heroic couplet, Thomson and Young; only then, but most important of all, came the recognition of Shakespeare. Fuseli grew up on Milton and Shakespeare, and remained faithful to them to the end. From the first he drew much, and already impressively, but only as a side-line. He regarded poetry as his true vocation, emulating Klopstock, the one eminent poet the new movement had so far produced, in grandiose unrimed odes.

[1] In German usage—and it is to Germany that we owe the term 'Romanticism' and the very conception of a Romantic movement—Romanticism is only the final, already somewhat decadent phase of the great literary awakening, and does not begin before 1795. Goethe is, in the German sense, not one of the Romantics at all, while in the looser way of using the word current in England, Goethe is the greatest of the Romantics.

It was possible for him to interpret his preaching office as in some way appertaining to his poetic vocation, since a liberalised pietistic theology still formed an integral part of the new literary movement's programme. Theologically, and also in the political radicalism which was another point of their programme, Bodmer and his followers again looked largely to the progressive thinkers in England as their natural prototypes and allies.

In 1763 Fuseli had to leave Zurich in consequence of a bold attack on corruption and oppression in high places, and after about a year spent in Germany, where he met most of the leading writers of the day including Klopstock, he came to London, in March 1764. Bodmer was at the back of this step. It was intended that Fuseli should act as a liaison officer between the English and the German-Swiss advanced literary movements. He was now twenty-three, and still regarded literature as his real profession. The following six years, except for the ten months from December 1765 to October 1766, when he went to France as tutor to young Lord Chewton, Fuseli spent in England, chiefly occupied with writing and translating. He plunged into the life of London with extraordinary intensity, familiarising himself with every aspect of the literary, artistic, religious, political and social activities of the day, meeting personally many of the eminent writers, including Smollett and Sterne, forming close and lasting friendships with Armstrong the poet, with the liberal booksellers and publishers Millar, Cadell and Joseph Johnson, with the kindly banker Coutts and others. He must have had a great talent for friendship, contriving to make himself not only admired, but also liked, in spite of an arrogant and aggressive manner which often exasperated his acquaintances and sometimes gave them real offence. During these early London years he divested himself of such puritanical inhibitions as still clung to him, and seems to have sowed his wild oats unsparingly. He had previously felt himself chiefly attracted by the 'enlightened spirit of British theology' (Letter to Lavater of 13 November 1763), but after a year in London he writes: 'For anyone with a soul the London theatre is alone worth the journey.' Theatre-going became and remained one of his great passions, and he knew some of the great actors and

16

actresses personally. By March 1768 he has left the gods of his early youth so far behind that he can airily say: 'I don't set much store by Klopstock; if he were a pagan, I would.'

In spring 1770 Fuseli left England for Italy, where he remained eight years. He had decided that his true vocation was after all painting, and now, in his thirtieth year, he was about to begin his life again, and to try to make up for the lost years in which he should have been undergoing a proper technical training. He had only just begun to try his hand in oils, and to the last he was never quite at ease with them. Two years previously Sir Joshua Reynolds, on seeing some of his drawings, had told him that all he had to do to become the greatest painter of the age was to spend a few years in Rome. He had probably also about the same time begun to doubt more and more whether he had it in him ever to become a great poet.

In turning his back on literature as a vocation in 1770 Fuseli also ceased, and it would seem, quite deliberately and stubbornly ceased, to take a whole-hearted interest in the new literary movement which had, up to then, been his central preoccupation. The year in which he did this was, however, curiously enough, the very year in which the German literary movement decisively passed from its merely preparatory, now only historically interesting phase to its first magnificent and permanently valuable fruition; it was the year in which the youthful Goethe met Herder, who, together with his eccentrically mystical friend Hamann, had outsoared the limitations still attaching to the conception of poetry cultivated by Bodmer, Klopstock and their English pre-Romantic contemporaries, and achieved an emotional intensity for which there are no parallels in the new English poetry until the appearance of Blake and Wordsworth; it was the year of Goethe's first great lyrics. Fuseli, who had carefully kept in touch with every new development in German literature so long as there was nothing of supreme importance to be observed, cut himself off from it just when things began to move at last. And having thus lost touch with what was most central and vital in the German literary revolution, he never found it again, never wanted to find it. Hamann, Herder and Goethe were all greatly interested in him; the two latter knew all about him through their Swiss friend, the voluminous sentimental writer Lavater, who had for years been more intimate with Fuseli than anybody else.

'Fuseli in Rome is one of the greatest imaginations,' Lavater writes in 1773, in reply to Herder's eager and repeated inquiries. 'He is everything in extremes—always an original; Shakespeare's painter—nothing but an Englishman and a Zuricher, a poet and a painter. . . . Some day I will send you his original letters—hurricane and tempest. . . . He despises everything and everybody. . . . His wit is unbounded. He seldom acts, except with pencil and brush—but when he does, he must have a hundred yards' room, or else he would trample everything to pieces. He has devoured all the Greek, Latin, Italian and English poets. His look is lightning, his word a thunderstorm; his jest is death, his revenge hell. At close quarters there is no enduring him. He cannot breathe a single common breath.'

And as Lavater wrote to Herder and Goethe about Fuseli, so also he wrote to Fuseli about Herder and Goethe, sending him in 1774 their newest books. But although the scene was set for Fuseli to enter into communication with Herder and Goethe, and so with the new and splendid phase of the German literary revolution, he never did it. He read and was impressed by the books Lavater sent him in 1774, and that was all.

Goethe never quite lost sight of Fuseli, recurring to him with mingled fascination and repulsion down to within a year of his death, but for Fuseli it is as though Goethe and everything in contemporary German culture that centred around Goethe did not exist. This has indeed been denied by one of the principal authorities on Fuseli, Ernst Wirz,[1] who writes: 'It is owing to Fuseli's influence that the *Analytical Review* (1788–98) devoted so much attention to German literature, in which he still took a lively interest.' The *Analytical Review* does indeed more than once deplore that German literature should be so 'shamefully neglected in this country' (April 1791, Vol. IX, p. 569), and takes steps to set this right by printing frequent criticisms of German poets, especially of Goethe and Schiller.

---

[1] In his unpublished dissertation, *Die literarische Tätigkeit des Malers J. H. Füssli*, 1922, typewritten manuscript in the University Library of Basle.

Fuseli had in 1769 been on the point of publishing a *History of German Literature* in English, the manuscript of which was destroyed by fire together with most of his belongings on 8 January 1770; he contributed regularly to the *Analytical Review*, and had, as an old friend of the publisher, Joseph Johnson, considerable influence on its editorial policy. What could at first sight seem more likely and natural than that Fuseli should, under these circumstances, have been the initiator and most active and eager participant, when, in the 1790s, the *Analytical Review* set out to do for contemporary German poetry, with Goethe and Schiller as principal figures, exactly what he had himself set out to do for it single-handed twenty years earlier, with Bodmer and Klopstock as principal figures? Careful examination shows, however, that amongst the numerous articles in the *Analytical Review* devoted to German literature not more than two or three at most can possibly, on grounds either of style or of contents, be attributed to Fuseli, while the rest are certainly not by him, nor by anybody who had ever been even remotely associated with the new German literary movement from the inside. The exertions of the *Analytical Review* on behalf of German literature turn out, in spite of all good intentions, to be inept, inadequate and ineffective—if a man of Fuseli's special qualifications had been behind them, or only guided them, they must have proved very much more impressive and to the point. The article on German literature in the *Analytical Review* that looks most like being Fuseli's work is a review of Goethe's *Stella* and *Clavigo*,[1] in which certain aspects of Goethe's genius are praised lavishly, floridly, but aptly enough, indeed, with far greater insight than any of the other articles on German literature display; there is, however, something belittling, something which, in view of this very insight, seems almost disingenuous, in the qualifying assertion that Goethe's real province is the 'simple and affecting story of domestic life'. When one considers what Goethe had at this date (August 1798) come to be recognised as, not only in Germany, but even in England (Wordsworth and Coleridge were preparing for their abortive journey to the land of Goethe and Schiller), this review must be regarded either as an extra-

[1] *See* excerpt on page 94.

ordinary mixture of penetration and blindness, or else as a skilful achievement in 'damning with faint praise'. *If* Fuseli was responsible for it—and he probably was—it is in keeping with all his other pronouncements on contemporary genius. After his disillusionment over Rousseau in 1767, he is never found praising any man of genius of his own age without strange reservations or double-edged phrases which reduce the work thus characterised to a lower status than that it lays claim to. Even in speaking of Blake, whom he praised more than any other contemporary, he picks out the 'familiar and domestic atmosphere' of his drawings as their outstanding merit and finds their 'picturesque wildness . . . often redeemed by taste, simplicity and elegance'. '*If you mean to reign dictator* over the arts of your times, assail not your rivals with the blustering tone of condemnation,' he writes in his 135th Aphorism; 'sap with conditional or lamenting praise; confine them to unfashionable excellence; exclude them from the avenues of fame.' This is evidently in the first place directed against other artists and critics, by whom Fuseli felt himself ill-treated, but it describes accurately enough the procedure he himself, probably more instinctively than deliberately, adopted. 'He could not bear to be eclipsed or put in the background for a moment. He scorned to be less than the highest,' says Godwin. This is borne out not only by the verdict of all who knew him, and by many anecdotes, but also by various utterances of his own: 'He who submits to follow is not made to lead,' he says in the *Aphorisms* and again: 'Genius knows no partner . . .'; and: 'He who could have the choice, and should prefer to be the first painter of insects, of flowers or of drapery, to being the second in the ranks of history, though degraded to the last class of art, would undoubtedly be in the first of men by the decision of Caesar.' The ruthless struggle for a place in the sun, for self-assertion at all costs, is by no means confined to the material, economic and political planes; it can be found and must be allowed for also in art and in the things of the spirit, especially in the modern world. The most convincing explanation for the way in which the older Fuseli ignores German literature and Goethe in particular is, that, like so many of the German Romantic poets themselves, he felt and could not endure the immense preponderance of Goethe's genius. Goethe was himself fully aware of this state of affairs: 'I was too powerful for them,' he remarked to Eckermann in speaking of the Romantics on 30 March 1824. A German poet could do nothing but face this overpowering genius of Goethe and struggle with it in his own way—German Romanticism is largely the manifestation of this struggle; Fuseli, however, was no longer a German poet; he was a painter living in England; he could afford to ignore Goethe and all that arose from him, and that is what he did.[1] He outlived the final phase of the

[1] It must have been after 1806 and from Fuseli himself that Knowles heard of Goethe having 'celebrated in a poem the proficiency in music' of Anna Landolt (see Part I, Section 8). Music plays a comparatively small part in Goethe's life, far smaller than in the lives of most German poets of the age. This is one of the things Goethe and Fuseli have in common. It is impossible to discover what poem of Goethe's Fuseli here had in mind, or what reasons he had for suspecting an allusion to Anna Landolt in it; probably Lavater had written something to him on the subject—but unfortunately Lavater's letters to Fuseli have disappeared. The important point is that Fuseli must have known something about Goethe's poetry after 1779, although he has nothing to say about the impression it made on him. In the 1941 Zurich Fuseli Exhibition a water-colour was shown as No. 158 with the title *Faust in Auerbach's Cellar*. This title is, however, conjectural. The same picture is reproduced as Plate 69 in Paul Ganz's *Hans Heinrich Füsslis Zeichnungen* (Bern-Olten, 1947), together with a companion picture (Plate 68) which is interpreted as another scene from Goethe's *Faust*. The date ascribed to the *Faust in Auerbach's Cellar* in the 1941 catalogue is 'about 1790'; in the 1947 volume of Ganz both pictures are dated about 1800. Chronological difficulties arise here. Goethe published his *Faust ein Fragment* in 1790 and very few recognised its importance at the time, or, indeed, down to 1808, when the completed first part of *Faust* appeared. It was not till 1808, in the completed first part, that the fight between Faust and Valentin, which is taken to be the theme of one of the Fuseli water-colours, saw the light; it is missing in *Faust ein Fragment* of 1790. It would certainly be in accordance with our sense of what ought to be, that Fuseli should in some way have taken notice of the great representative poetic work of his age, and it would specially satisfy us to find him doing so at an early date, before the rest of the world had realised the importance of that still uncompleted and only fragmentarily published work—though 1790 and even 1800 are such early dates that difficulties arise over them, especially if the scene with Valentin is to be brought in. Here one can regret that there is nothing more definite to connect the two water-colours with Goethe's *Faust*. They contain three devils, who tally closely enough with our conception of Mephistopheles, there are German

great German literary movement of which he had been the heart and soul in its beginnings, but gave no further signs after 1780 of knowing anything about it. It is interesting to note that in an article on him published in the *Monthly Mirror* in January 1801 we are told that 'the translation of some German dramas has been attributed to him, *without foundation*'. This article was clearly what would nowadays be called an interview, and based on information obtained from him by personal interrogation.

Fuseli remained in Italy from May 1770 till September 1778, spending most of this time in Rome. It was not the time of formal and technical study that he seems at first to have envisaged—he attached himself to no *atelier*, became nobody's pupil, and to the last he bears signs of being an autodidactic painter, especially in his use of oils. Knowles records him as having applied to himself 'with a considerable degree of complacency' the words of Glendower:

> *Where is he living, clipped in with the sea*
> *That chides the banks of England, Scotland, Wales.*
> *Which calls me pupil?*

Farington writes: 'Fuseli was in Italy 8 years, which He said was much too long. A great deal of his time was passed among students in eighteenth-century student costume, with long pipes, in the one picture—but there is no figure one could identify as *Faust*, unless it be the woman dressed as a man, and the females all look like prostitutes—including those who would have to be identified with *Gretchen*. Ganz takes the *Auerbach's Cellar* picture as really two pictures, one half being *Auerbach's Cellar*, the other *Frau Marthe's Garden*. But Fuseli detested such double pictures. It is conceivable that the pictures may only be fantastic presentations of a masquerade; Knowles records that Fuseli got into trouble with a fancy-dress devil, when attending a masquerade at the Opera House with Lavater's son and Mary Wollstonecraft in 1789. Another interesting suggestion has been made to connect Fuseli with Goethe. He exhibited at the Academy in 1805 a painting which has disappeared, and of which nothing more is known than the name: *The Corinthian Maid*. W. Wartmann suggests (1941 Catalogue) that this may have been a pictorial treatment of one of Goethe's ballads which is exceptionally attuned to Fuseli's macabre imagination, *Die Braut von Corinth*. It is, however, far more probable that it dealt with 'the amorous tale of the Corinthian maid, who traced the shade of her departing lover by the secret lamp', which Fuseli speaks of as 'deserving our belief' in his first Lecture. We are therefore still without tangible evidence that Fuseli saw and estimated Goethe as the Romantics did, or as posterity does.

books, instead of applying to the practice of art, which He thought at that time was attainable, in a sufficient degree, at will' (*Farington Diary*, 17 November 1797). His studies took the form chiefly of visiting galleries and churches, especially the Sistine chapel, and of drawing from antique statues, especially from the colossal Horse-Tamers of Monte Cavallo.

It was not till he came to Rome that Fuseli made Michelangelo his great hero and model, and developed his own characteristic Michelangelesque style of drawing. Up to then he had admired Michelangelo's rugged integrity of character, but considered, in conformity with the dominant taste of the age, that, as an artist, he 'bloated expression to grimace', and 'wasted his great talents'. In Rome, Cunningham tells us, Fuseli 'lived in a species of intoxication—affected the dress and mimicked the manners of Michael. . . . He loved to dream along the road—to follow the phantasies of an unbridled imagination —to pen sarcastic remarks—sketch colossal groups, and would call out ever and anon, when some strange thought struck him, "Michelangelo!" '. Knowles confirms this, and contributes the interesting anecdote, communicated to him certainly by Fuseli himself, that one of the Italian artists was 'so struck with some of his compositions, that, in reference to their invention, he immediately exclaimed, "Michelangelo has come again!" '.

It was really only modern literature that Fuseli ceased to take anything more than a sporadic interest in on going to Rome. Older poetry, especially Homer, he was more occupied with than ever. It was in these years that the sentimental instability of his youth hardened into the drastic and grotesque wilfulness of his later period. But at the very end of his Roman episode, and during the half year he spent in Switzerland before returning to London in April 1779, he went through one last, particularly effervescent relapse into the chaos of adolescence. The records of this, the only one of his innumerable, for the most part mercifully obliterated erotic escapades which can be picked out as showing him whole-heartedly in love with a woman, are of the greatest interest.

The rest of Fuseli's life, from his return to London at the age of thirty-eight in 1779 until his death at the age of eighty-four, on 6 April 1825, was uneventful.[1] He quickly established a position for himself as a painter in the grand style, and un-academic though he remained, both in his art and in his personal bearing, became not only an Academician (1790) but also Professor of Painting (1799) and Keeper of the Royal Academy (1804). His reputation seems to have grown steadily up to about 1795, and then to have declined. The clearest sign of this was the comparative failure of his Milton Gallery (1799-1800), on the pictures of which he had worked for ten years. He lived much in society, meeting most of the notable people of the day and holding his own both with his artist colleagues and with the aristocracy, in spite of bizarre and often outrageous manners, as a privileged and likeable eccentric of extraordinary genius, learning and wit. There must have been a vein of toughness and of shrewd Swiss common sense in him, otherwise he could never have stayed the course as he did, without being shipwrecked by the daemonic elements which always appeared to surround him. In his youth he seemed again and again to be on the brink of death or disaster: 'There is little likelihood of my living to grow old,' he wrote to Lavater in his thirtieth year (14 May 1770)—but he did live to a great age, with all his mental powers undiminished to the last. He seemed always to be in a rage, or on the point of flying into one, or just recovering from one. His letters to Lavater, in particular, the 'beloved of his soul', had always been splenetic or fractious in tone, whatever the theme was; thus, when Lavater writes to him of the death of their old friend Felix Hess, Fuseli casts his reply into the form of an abrupt, exalted, laconic snub: ' "Hess has been lying in his grave a month!" Son of Immortality, do you confound the integument of your friend with himself?' (6 May 1768). The language and the gestures of anger became for Fuseli more and more a convenient and stereotyped medium through which to communicate with the rest of the world, and with which, also, to keep it at arm's length; for those who knew him best all testify that he was in reality both diffident and shy. He was a notorious and picturesque swearer, and almost the only words addressed by him to his prosaic wife of which any

[1] *See* chronological table, Appendix I, p. 351.

record has come down to us are the Hotspur-like admonition: 'Sophia, my love, why don't you swear?—you don't know how much it would ease your mind.' Audacious antinomian though he was, he attached, as did two such firebrands of our own days as D. H. Lawrence and James Joyce, great importance to one social disciplinary ideal which we might at first be inclined to leave out of account in considering either him or them—the ideal of a gentleman.[1] He begins his anonymous review of his own anonymous *Remarks on Rousseau* by declaring that the author 'is evidently a gentleman' (*Critical Review*, May 1767), thereby provoking an incensed reviewer to retort two months later in the *Political Register*, 'that he is not a gentleman is plain from his ribaldry, indecency, profaneness and disturbing the public tranquillity" '. He praised one of Lawrence's paintings as being 'so refined that no one but a *gentleman* could have painted it' (*Farington Diary*, 29 April 1805), and dismissed Beckford as 'an actor, but no gentleman' (*Farington Diary*, 22 January 1797). It must have been rather on such grounds as these than for the sake of pure scholarship that he regretted not having had 'the advantage of the amalgamating tuition of a public school' (Knowles, p. 5). The fits of rage for which he was notorious, and which sometimes brought him into awkward situations,[2] would subside abruptly, and he is again and again found apologising with a certain *grandezza*, either by writing and at the prompting of his wife, or orally and of his own accord. Thomas Phillips, who seems really to have hated him, can see in this nothing but a combination of insolence and cowardice. Cunningham is certainly juster when he says: 'He was as placable as passionate.' Knowles writes: 'Notwithstanding this violence of disposition, when his anger was aroused even to a high pitch,

---

[1] Northcote, however, found Fuseli's manner 'more like that of a Swiss valet' than of a gentleman (*Conversations with J. Ward*, quoted by Ruthven Todd).

[2] Cp. Knowles, p. 354: 'At Lyons, when a young man (1766), he had a dispute with a person, which aroused his feelings to such a height, that in a momentary fit of passion he made use of that agility which he possessed in a considerable degree, and kicked his antagonist in the face. The man coolly drew his sword, and immediately inflicted a very severe wound upon the offending leg.'

a kind word or look appeased him in a moment.' Shortly before his death he was heard to say: 'I have been a happy man, for I have been always well, and always employed in doing what I liked' (Cunningham). Some who know Fuseli only from his more satanic paintings and drawings may find it surprising and also a little disappointing that he should ever have spoken such words as these, and that they should be substantially true.

II

In his early days, when he still regarded poetry as his true vocation, Fuseli must have written much that has not survived. He is known not only to have been one of the first translators of Shakespeare into German, attempting a version of *Macbeth* while still in his teens, but also to have embarked on one or two verse tragedies of his own. In his early letters there are references to a *Caesar*. At the age of eighteen he writes to Jakob Hess, an aspiring poet of his own age: 'God bless you, what are you engaged on now? What I need for my present job is a little thunder and a mouthful of storm-wind, also a few eyes as dark as midnight. And what are your requirements? Evening breezes or rain?' (summer 1768). No fragments of these early attempts in tragedy remain, nor is there any reason to suppose that he went on with them after leaving Zurich in 1763. What does survive, partly in print and partly in manuscript, is a considerable number of odes in imitation of Klopstock, most of them from the time of his first residence in England (1764–70), a few earlier and a few from the Roman and post-Roman years.

It is impossible to be impressed by these odes now, and the fact that some of them, on being published anonymously, were taken for the work of Klopstock himself, and thus produced a mild sensation in some circles, is at most of historical interest. Except for a few very occasional flashes, they are characterised by nothing but strained, often bombastic rhetoric. They must be studied in the original and with constant reference to their Klopstockian models, if they are to convey anything, and all they convey then is ultimately that Fuseli was here engaged on something that he would have done better to leave alone. For this reason, and because no translation can give any idea of what is here involved, they are practically unrepresented in the present volume.[1] The aptest comment on all these odes is what Fuseli himself said on the most ambitious of them, that to Bodmer of 1764, looking back on it a year and a half later: 'It has always been my fate to see my subject in a visionary light, and Jupiter has too often in anger puffed out my cheeks with wind' (Letter to Lavater, 6 December 1765). The danger of turgidity which Fuseli here recognises as threatening his style as a lyric poet is, indeed, his peculiar danger in everything he undertakes to the end of his life—it attends his prose too, and his painting and drawing, and the whole of his temperament and conduct. He is forever inflating himself till he just bursts and collapses. He can hardly have failed to realise how applicable to himself as well as to Michelangelo his 79th Aphorism was: 'The fear of not being understood, or felt, makes some invigorate expression to grimace.' All his most valuable achievements are carried out on the fine border-line, where intensification, carried a step further, would degenerate into bombast, and to the last he still sometimes does overstep this border-line. In the odes of his earlier period, however, he is forever overstepping it. His genius is too theatrical, too boisterous to be lyrical, except in rare moments, and one of the things that distinguishes him from the Romantics is that he responds less spontaneously to lyric poetry than to drama *as* drama, to epic *as* epic. In an age which tended to see all poetry in terms of lyric, he tended to see it in terms of drama and still more of epic. It must have been a sense of his own proclivities and limitations which gradually led him to abandon ode-writing. But instead of taking to *writing* poetic drama or epic, he was to *paint* it.

Much better adapted to the purposes of the present volume than Fuseli's Klopstockian odes, though poetically in themselves hardly more satisfactory, are the rhapsodies in rhythmical prose entitled *Complaints* or *Lamentations* (*Klagen*), in which he unlocked his heart to Lavater in 1763. With all their weaknesses of sentimentality and immaturity, they show us the quivering emotional vulnerability which preceded and to the end prob-

---

[1] One odd stanza, more felicitous than most, will be found on page 103.

27

ably still underlay that devil-may-care porcupinish insolence Fuseli chose to present to the world. Only in the two poems which he wrote in spring 1779, on the occasion of his love for Anna Landolt, did he achieve a pure lyric tone. And after that he seems to have written very little verse. We know, however, that he never ceased to regard himself as being, amongst other things, a lyrical poet, though almost certainly with an eye chiefly to what he had produced in his youth. The writer of the interview-like article on him in the *Monthly Mirror* for January 1801 certainly had Fuseli's own authority for saying: 'There is more reason to believe that he possesses a higher excellence in the rare powers of lyric poetry.' Amongst the unpublished Fuseli manuscripts in the Kunsthaus in Zurich there are at least two German odes in the Klopstock style, which are better than any of those printed by Federmann, one of them an elegy on a certain 'Maria' (possible Mary Wollstonecraft), and the other (which appears to be incomplete and evidently dates from the beginning of the Roman years) on art. It is certainly this latter poem that is referred to by the anonymous author of the *Memoir of Henry Fuseli, M.A.* (a pamphlet written between 1825 and 1829, preserved in the Bodleian Library) in the words: 'There is also a German poem on art, which Mr. Fuseli himself regarded as the best thing he ever wrote.' There are also among the Zurich manuscripts four fragments of what would appear to have been a Dunciad of Painting, written in the diction and heroic couplets of Pope. Possibly Cunningham had seen this poem or part of it. They are the only original English verses of the older Fuseli's so far known to survive, and fit in well enough with Cunningham's judgment: 'His attempts in English verse are rude and unmelodious—distinguished by harsh rugged vigour.' The *Analytical Review* for June 1791 contains 370 lines of Miltonic blank verse, translated by Fuseli from Klopstock's *Messiah*, while two shorter similar passages, one also from the *Messiah*, the other from Bodmer's *Noachide*, occur in letters of 1766 and 1770. The following specimen will serve to illustrate both the overstrained rhetoric which is fatal to Fuseli's German odes and also the competency with which he manages to reproduce the more superficial effects of Milton's verse:

> *The din of Hell*
> *They heard, where o'er Creation's utmost shore*
> *Howling, it died along the echoing stars;*
> *Eccentric up and down the turbid space*
> *Hell rolls, all anarchy; of swift or slow*
> *Regardless, huge.—To her detested chasm*
> *Paths lead not, but on either side the rocks*
> *Unfathomed slope and yawn with lambent fire*
> *Struck; pallid, shudd'ring, mute, with down-dash'd eye*
> *Horrour hangs o'er the brink.*[1]

The line 'Howling, it died along the echoing stars' might have found a place in Wordsworth's *Prelude* or in Keats's *Hyperion*, while the rest is nothing more than effective rhetoric. One short early original English poem of Fuseli's, interesting enough for its theme and also as an attempt to reproduce accentual classical ode-forms in our language, is given in this volume under the title *The Kings of Earth* on page 117.

It is not by his verse that Fuseli claims attention or high rank as a writer. In his curious, erratic prose he is far more impressive—there it was that his age accorded, and rightly accorded to him exceptional powers, peculiar mastery, provocative pungency, galvanising vehemence and above all, for good or for ill, an unmistakably individual style, an idiom entirely his own. It is always in occasional prose that Fuseli unfolds these stylistic qualities of his, in disputation, critical exposition, controversy, invective, satire on the times—and he can seldom speak for long, even on the most uncontroversial of subjects, without breaking out into contemptuous fury over something or somebody. His qualifications in the handling of prose are, indeed, such as to lend themselves only to occasional and controversial writing of the kinds indicated, and even in the days of his great literary ambitions he seems but once to have been able to extract from himself anything like a rounded, self-poised work

---

[1] Transcribed by Fuseli in a letter to Lavater of 14 June 1770; the translation was made for the *History of German Literature* and is all that survives of the manuscript burned in January 1770—*see above*, p. 19. The passage occurs in Klopstock's *Messiah*, Canto IX.

of art in prose, and that is the *Character of Nicodemo Tardi*,[1] a modest enough little performance in the manner of Addison, but one which Fuseli himself was very proud of.

Of Fuseli's prose writings in German very little that can be identified now remains, except a number of letters—for the *Complaints* (*Koagen*)[2] must be regarded as a kind of free verse, rather than as real prose. These German letters, however, which cover the important period from his twentieth to his fortieth year,[3] are very valuable and characteristic documents, for in English he is never able to express himself quite so spontaneously or directly as he can in the language he grew up with. He appears here as one of the most temperamental exponents of the Storm-and-Stress style employed at the same period by Hamann, Herder and the youthful Goethe, a style for which no analogies can be found in contemporary English literature, though some of the Elizabethans, particularly Nashe, have something not unlike it. It is a tumultuous prose, in which all the emotions, savage and delicate, ethereal and fleshly, burst out simultaneously and elementally, intermingled with fragmentary religious, philosophical, historical, literary and artistic theorisings and allusions, with fantastic personifications, similes and metaphors, with student slang and buffoonery, reducing syntax to a breathless whirl of parenthesis, in which hardly a sentence terminates as it might have been expected to terminate, and many never terminate properly at all. Such a style tends to be loose, swollen, sometimes even garrulous—adjective is piled upon adjective and free use is made of the cumulative principle, grotesque and whimsical phrases being strung together unexpectedly, pell-mell and without limit. The shirt-sleeve German

[1] Identified and reprinted in this volume for the first time. *See* pp. 112–13.

[2] *See above*, p. 27, and *below*, pp. 98–102.

[3] After 1779 Fuseli seems to have kept in touch with few of his old Swiss friends or relations, except Lavater, and with him only sporadically. After Lavater's death in 1801 he seems to have ignored Switzerland almost completely. There are hardly any records of his having spoken, written or even read a word of German after 1800 or so—and yet he said to Knowles: 'I always think in the language in which I write, and it is a matter of indifference to me whether it be in English, French or Italian; I know each equally well; *but if I wish to express myself with power, it must be in German.*'

30

prose of the younger Fuseli displays all these typical Storm-and-Stress features, but they are counteracted in his case by a tendency of the opposite kind, by an underlying and intermittent striving (to which he attaches much importance) after the pithy and laconic, after a maximum of condensation. In 1767 he asserts, not altogether appositely, that it is an outstanding merit of the exuberant Rousseau 'to reduce a book to one idea', and forty or more years later he said of himself to Knowles, when he had been charged with cultivating terseness to the point of ambiguity and obscurity: 'I endeavour to put as much information into a page as some authors scatter through a chapter.' He is, indeed, from one moment to the next, cryptically abrupt, where he might well have been more explicit, and extravagantly orotund; apophthegm and dithyramb jostle one another in his sentences. His is a prose that seems always on the point of becoming something else—though not necessarily poetry; it is anything but prosaic. But when the most has been made of all these strictures, they amount to little more than a registration of the fact that Fuseli does not write an academically correct style—a thing nobody would expect him to do; he would be far less interesting than he is, if he did. The feverish energy of his style and his ferocious eagerness to express what he has on his mind—usually it is something well worth listening to—make one ready to accept as brilliant and therefore licensed idiosyncrasy mannerisms and eccentricities which, in a less imposing personality, would find short shrift.

The younger Fuseli had scarcely arrived in London in spring 1764 before he set up as a professional writer in English. Cunningham says that he wrote 'nearly a hundred . . . translations, essays and critiques' for the London press[1]—probably an excessive estimate. The only original literary work of the younger Fuseli (as opposed to letters and translations) of any magnitude or great value that is known to survive is a pamphlet in English on the *Writings and Conduct of John James Rousseau*, published anonymously in connexion with the Rousseau-Hume quarrel

---

[1] The editor of this volume has succeeded in identifying a few contributions of Fuseli's, original and translated, in the *Universal Museum* (*see* Appendix II).

in April 1767. This work, somehow procured and enthusiastically admired by Hamann and Herder, reviewed favourably but with reservations by friends of the author—one of them probably Armstrong—in the *Universal Museum* and the *Monthly Review*, and very much more warmly commended by Fuseli himself in the *Critical Review*, ignored, contemptuously dismissed or ferociously damned by all the other magazines, and described by William Godwin as 'scarcely English, and scarcely common sense, yet with some striking things interspersed', is well worth reading, both as a passionate, penetrating and witty interpretation of the most revolutionary mind in contemporary literature and thought by one in whose daemonic personality exaltation was forever at war with an almost cynical shrewdness, and also as a unique specimen of Storm-and-Stress prose in the English language. It is clear now to everybody that up to 1770 or so Rousseau was a much more significant and prophetic figure than any the new literary revolution had thus far produced either in England or in Germany, even though that movement was in itself an Anglo-Germanic and anti-Gallican one, and it speaks for Fuseli's acuteness and sensitiveness that he so early recognised this, ascribing to Rousseau an entirely different kind of importance from that he ascribed to Thomson, Young (whose once so enthusiastically admired and imitated *Night Thoughts* he was in 1775 to dismiss as 'pyramids of dough'), Gray, Armstrong, Richardson, Klopstock or Bodmer. In dealing with the Rousseau-Hume quarrel he rises above the wretched and petty personal recriminations which engaged all the other pamphleteers of the day and sees the affair on the grand scale, in terms of the much greater and more fundamental conflict between the old spirit of the Enlightenment and the emotional and imaginative forces which were then struggling to emancipate themselves. As both elements, shrewd matter-of-factness as well as emotional exaltation, were present and more or less evenly matched in his own temperament, Fuseli was all along writing of himself and of his own inner conflicts, in dealing with the ugly situation between Rousseau as representative of emotion and Hume and Voltaire as representatives of rationalism. It is remarkable, too, that although his conscious

32

sympathies and his deliberate partisanship are all with Rousseau, he does not, in the end, help the heart to an easy victory over the intellect, or to any victory at all, as might have been expected, and that what he makes of his theme is something very different from and very much more interesting than a sentimental effusion.

The chief reason why Fuseli's *Remarks* were either ignored or dismissed with undeserved contempt by the readers of the day is undoubtedly the frequent uncouthness of the style, which leads to obscurity and a sense of strain, and is due in large part simply to the difficulties Fuseli still has in dealing with the foreign language he is employing. He cannot here develop his Storm-and-Stress *élan* as directly and unrestrainedly as in his German letters. He has had to do what nearly everybody under the disadvantages of writing in a foreign language has to do, irrespective of personal bent, to acquire a formal, abstract style. He writes Johnsonianly—and this extraneously imposed Johnsonianism acts as a drag on the erratic sallies and gambols of his spontaneous manner. It is still a Storm-and-Stress prose that he writes, but a discordant, sometimes comically discordant element of pomposity has come into it. It was suggested, when the *Remarks on Rousseau* appeared, that they bore stylistically some resemblance to the writings of Sterne. In reality they do nothing of the kind. Often, however, Fuseli's early English style does recall that of his great friend Armstrong in the *Sketches of Lancelot Temple* and the *Muncher's and Guzzler's Diary*. Fuseli is more likely to have allowed Armstrong than anybody else to go over his manuscripts, emending them and making suggestions.

From 1770 to 1788 Fuseli seems to have written very little for publication. But from 1788 till his death he was always engaged on some literary work or other. It is now, however, definitely as a critic of the fine arts and of literature, or as a classical scholar, occasionally also as an entomologist, that he writes. The piece of writing from this later phase which was conceived with the highest degree of purely literary ambition, the posthumously published *Aphorisms chiefly relative to the Fine Arts*, on which he was engaged intermittently from 1788 till 1818, neither is nor raises pretensions to be as much of a self-contained work of art as the *Remarks on Rousseau*, in spite of their ephemeral origins and their polemical intentions, can lay claim to being. In addition to the *Aphorisms*, Fuseli is known to have written between 1786 and 1825 an extremely free translation of a little work of Lavater's, with a preface of his own (1788), *Advertisements* for publications of Lavater and Blake, some eighty articles in the *Analytical Review*,[1] twelve elaborately worked-out *Lectures on Art* for the Royal Academy, substantial additions to Pilkington's *Dictionary of Painters* and a posthumously published *History of Art in the Schools of Italy*. It is probable that he also contributed reviews to other magazines, after the suppression of the *Analytical Review* in 1798. Comparatively few of his English letters of the later years seem to have survived,[2] and those which Knowles publishes show him as a much less picturesque letter writer than he had been when corresponding in German with his Zurich friends in his youth. It is specially to be regretted that his letters to Sir Thomas Lawrence cannot be traced, as Lawrence speaks of them with great enthusiasm. In the English style of the older Fuseli the disparate elements of his earlier style reappear, sufficiently toned down to coalesce into comparative unity. His command of the language is now assured, he no longer indulges in his old Storm-and-Stress cavortings, his Johnsonese has taken on a thoroughly personal tang, and he has found a way of adjusting his striving after condensation to his weakness for grandiloquent flourishes—a way which appears most clearly in the *Aphorisms*, where brief epigrammatic utterances are followed up with long, sometimes very long and florid 'Corollaries': 'An aphorism', he says, 'may be discussed, but ought not to contain its own explication' (Knowles, p. 160). He came to specialise in flamboyant appreciations of particular paintings or painters, which were much admired by his contemporaries, but will be found very sparingly represented in the present volume. A typical example of this habit is the following account of a

[1] The editor of the present volume has identified over sixty of these contributions to the *Analytical Review*. *See* Appendix II.

[2] It is difficult to estimate at present how many of Fuseli's later letters have survived. A voluminous series to one person, adorned with remarkable marginal drawings, is said to have changed hands in recent years.

painting of Carracci's in Lecture VI: 'Such is the Flagellation of Christ in the same church, whose tremendous depth of flesh-tints contrasts the open wide-expanded sky, and less conveys than dashes its terrors on the astonished sense.' He is happy in discharging double-barrelled blunderbusses of denunciation: 'the bloated excrescences of diseased brains'; 'chalcographic callus'; 'the ostentatious vehicle of puny conceits'; 'the specious ingredients of this technic panacea'; 'the purblind criticism of Richardson and the flimsy petulance of Falconet'; 'the culinary abominations of Sandro Botticelli'; 'the repulsive and meagre dryness of Johann v. Eyck and Quentin Matsys'; 'the monstrous incubations of dropsied fancy on phlegm run mad'. A typical example of the sandbagging sarcasm and wit for which he was famed and dreaded is the passage in his seventh Lecture, where, having dealt with two classes of Mannerists, he proceeds to the third and says that it, 'though perhaps not strictly chargeable with the absolute impropriety of the first and the lowness of the second class, must be content with what we can spare of disapprobation from either'.

Nearly everything the older, and much also that the younger Fuseli writes is concerned with art. It was almost as much a necessity for him to speculate, argue and lay down the law about every aspect of the arts, theoretical, historical and practical, as it was to draw and paint. His writings embody, not without certain strange contradictions and puzzling uncertainties, a sufficiently comprehensive and coherent account of what, according to Fuseli, art is and ought to be, and what it is not and ought not to be; of its relationship to empirical reality on the one hand and to transcendency (granting hypothetically that that term means something) on the other; of the relationship between poetry and the plastic arts; of the connexion between the practice of the arts and the various phases in the history of civilisation; of the comparative importance and absolute worth of particular ages and schools of art, and of certain great individual works of art and artists; of form, style and technique in all their aspects. It is one of the chief objects of the present volume to present the most telling and characteristic utterances of Fuseli on questions of this kind in such an arrangement, that the essential purport and implications of what he thought and felt about art and its connexion to life may appear as unambiguously and intelligibly as possible, without distortion or suppression.

It will be seen that there is hardly a question one can ask about Fuseli's views on any problem of art that he has not himself provided an answer to, hardly a hypothesis one can maintain about what his attitude must have been which cannot be tested by appeal to some statement of his own as to what his attitude actually was. Here it is, however, that difficulties arise. The aesthetic tenets to which Fuseli emphatically and circumstantially professes his allegiance are very different from those one would, in view of the fantastic wildness both of his pictures and of his personality, expect to find him maintaining; they are the tenets of classicism. There can be no doubt that he is in his own art not a classicist in any current sense of the word. He was not regarded as such by any of his contemporaries, neither by those who admired nor by those who disliked him and his works. The outstanding representatives of classical standards either rejected him downright, or accepted him only with reservations, as an exceptional case, for which special allowances must be made, and not as one of themselves. When Horace Walpole's demented nephew, Lord Orford, wanted a particularly Gothic painter to paint a particularly gruesome and uncanny Gothic picture for him, Cipriani, feeling himself quite unequal to the task, unhesitatingly recommended Fuseli as the best man for the job—and Fuseli performed it to Lord Orford's full satisfaction. Where he was most admired, it was always for anything but classical qualities and powers, and usually by men who were indifferent or hostile to classical standards. Thus Kirke White, in his poem to Fuseli, invokes the 'genius of horror and romantic awe' to confer on Fuseli the wand once wielded by Dante, as on the man of all other moderns best qualified to express its 'shuddering images'. Yet Fuseli himself, when he theorises about art, is the champion of classical standards. Admittedly he is found here wearing his classicism with a difference. Not only is he, in his pronouncements on some points, unfaithful to his central body of classical doctrine, often seeming

to contradict himself and sometimes quite unmistakably contradicting himself; not only does he assault and batter Winckelmann, the chief prophet of later eighteenth-century classicism,
whom he had formerly himself translated and idolised; the
classical nucleus of his views itself embodies non-classical
elements and indulges in unclassical gestures and accents. As a
thinker on art and an art critic he was no more acceptable
to the orthodox classicists of his day than he was as a practising
painter, and his *Lectures* were most unfavourably received by the
Edinburgh reviewers and by Goethe's friend J. H. Meyer, the
mouthpiece of Weimar classicism. None of these circumstances
can, however, justify us in simply leaving Fuseli's classicistic
declarations out of account. It is our business rather to find out
what the classical ideas he insists on meant to him, and *why*
they meant so much to him. It is certainly not so, that his mind
was sluggish, timid or conventional in dealing with abstract
theories and problems, that all his boldness and originality
evaporated when he held a pen instead of a brush or crayon
in his hand. He was never submissive to authority as such. He
had deliberated carefully on everything he speaks about, considering the pros and cons, and knows always what follows
from his assertions; whatever he rejects by implication, he means
to reject, even though it may be something which one thinks he
ought to have been devoted to. The peculiar and heterodox
brand of classical creed which he had worked out for himself
turns out, when allowances have been made for the contradictions it contains within itself, to be nothing like so inconsistent
with his actual practice in painting as it at first sight appears
to be.

However far Fuseli's creed departs from the principles of
classicism proper, it can still never, without grave falsification
and manipulation of the evidence, be interpreted simply as a
curiously disguised romanticism, a romanticism which mis-
understands itself and somehow blunders into saying the opposite of what it really means. Thus it would be easy to give a
much more romantic cast to Fuseli's writings on art, only by
translating his old-fashioned, outworn classical aesthetic terminology into the more dynamic and vital terminology which

had already established itself in these matters long before his death, and to say that thereby we were only replacing what he seems to say with what he really must have meant to say. But Fuseli himself had thought this very question out and stuck to the old terminology because he preferred it, not because he knew no better: 'My vocabulary of technic expression', he tells his listeners in his first Lecture, 'is almost the same as that of your late President'—that is to say, of Reynolds. And, when occasion arises, he gives a particular instance, explaining his reasons for preferring to speak of the artist as an 'inventor', and not as a 'creator' (*see* p. 201). His theory of art, however suspect its classicism may be, is deliberately non-Romantic, even anti-Romantic. That, more than anything else, is the reason and point of his insistence on certain central classical conceptions. That he does not attack Romanticism by name is due only to the circumstance that, during his and its own lifetime, it still had no name in this country. It fought its battles without any slogan. But Fuseli saw enough of it as a phenomenon to be in disagreement with it—not, indeed, to be in disagreement with it all along the line, but still at some points which seemed to him of decisive importance. This is what emerges from a careful study of Fuseli's writings—and it is likely to be disappointing and disturbing to those who have got into the habit of summing Fuseli up as a 'Romantic painter'. That seemed to be the ideal, the convenient formula for him. As early as 1873 Sidney Colvin dubbed him 'the first of the Romantics'. There are unquestionably many senses commonly given to that equivocal, much overworked and the-worse-for-wear term 'Romantic', in which it can be claimed that it fits Fuseli very aptly. But if we mean by a Romantic one who assents to such doctrines concerning the relationship between art and the universe, between poetry and life, between the artist and mankind, as are expressed in Wordsworth's *Prelude*, in Coleridge's *Lectures*, in Shelley's *Defence of Poetry* and in the *Fragments* of Friedrich Schlegel and Novalis[1]; if we mean by a Romantic one who is united by

[1] For our present purposes it can be disregarded that the Romantics differed strongly amongst themselves on some important questions—for example, Wordsworth and Coleridge on the relationship between mind and

sympathy and a sense of solidarity with the generation of poets and painters which came to the fore in the 1790s, then Fuseli is as little a Romantic as he is a true classicist. The main text of this volume contains the necessary evidence for examining the theoretical side of this problem. What must be considered here is the relationship of Fuseli to the English Romantic movement as an actual historical process going on around him, and above all his relationship to Blake. For Fuseli's friendship with Blake might alone seem to prove that he must after all have been a real adherent of the Romantic movement.

The significant and remarkable fact is that Fuseli and the Romantics—apart from his friendship with Blake, which must be dealt with specially—had hardly any contacts with one another. Fuseli continued to take an interest in the newest developments in English poetry until well on into the nineties; he knew all about Erasmus Darwin, whose *Botanical Garden* he helped to illustrate; he recognised, loved and thoroughly comprehended the genius of Cowper, with whom he corresponded, making some curious illustrations to his *Task*. But from then onwards, that is to say from the very moment when the Romantics proper began to publish their work, he became indifferent to what was happening in English poetry (just as he had dropped the new German poetry twenty years before), giving once as a reason that he 'did not yet know every word in Shakespeare and Milton'. Not that he failed to read the Romantics completely. There is a quotation from Southey's *Joan of Arc* in a review that may be by Fuseli in the *Analytical Review* for October 1798, and Farington records him as speaking indignantly of the *Edinburgh Review*'s treatment of Southey's *Curse of Kehama* on 23 May 1811. And of Byron we know from Knowles that Fuseli 'always read his writings as soon as they were published with great avidity'. With Byron he was also personally acquainted, and Byron admired his paintings. That a man with the strongly developed literary habits and awareness of Fuseli should have taken an interest in Southey and Byron and yet either have failed completely to read Wordsworth, Coleridge,

nature. We are concerned with those tenets and assumptions which are common to all the Romantics.

Shelley and Keats, or else been so little impressed by them that no record of it has been preserved, is really noteworthy. It is still more remarkable in view of the fact that he had many acquaintances, sometimes intimate acquaintances, in common with all these poets—Joseph Johnson, the publisher of Wordsworth and Coleridge; Godwin, the friend of both and the father-in-law of Shelley; Haydon, the friend of Wordsworth, Keats and Shelley; and many others. One asks oneself how he could have failed to run into them; if there had been any reciprocal attraction, they would certainly have come together. Coleridge he did indeed once see. Farington records on 26 March 1804, in speaking of Coleridge: 'Fuseli had met him at Johnson's and thought little of him.' Coleridge, in return, gave him the nickname 'Fuzzle' or 'Fuzzly' (*Richmond Papers*). Wordsworth knew Fuseli's paintings and expressed an opinion on them to Haydon in 1842, when Haydon told him that in Canova's opinion Fuseli had more flame (*fiamma*) and Raphael more fire (*fuoco*). 'He forgot the third,' said Wordsworth, 'and that is *il fumo*, of which Fuseli had plenty.' These are slight enough indications, but so far as they go, they certainly do not suggest that the Romantics had much instinctive sympathy for Fuseli or he for them. The two Romantic critics who specially concerned themselves with painting, Hazlitt and Hunt, both detested Fuseli's work and attacked it. Cowper, Erasmus Darwin and Kirke White had looked up to him and praised him, but the time when Romanticism proper becomes a force more and more to be reckoned with coincides with the rapid decline of such popularity as Fuseli had achieved in the eighties and early nineties. He was no obscure, easily overlooked figure, like Blake. He was still very much there, larger than life, waiting to be acclaimed, and the Romantics were busy looking around them for figures they could hail as embodying their aspirations; but for some reason they passed over him or rejected him. One can set against this that he praised Turner highly, and that he was admired by the little group of young late-Romantic painters who followed in Blake's footsteps, especially by Samuel Palmer, and also by his pupil, the poisoner Wainewright. But nineteenth-century taste as a whole, which was essentially a perpetuation of Romantic standards, only found him ridiculous. Sidney Colvin says of him in 1873: 'Fuseli is by the younger generation laughed at or forgotten.'

III

The friendship between Fuseli and Blake was certainly of great importance to both, but especially to Blake, who feels about Fuseli, the only man 'who did not make me almost spew', as he does about no other acquaintance. Fuseli seems also to have been the only close friend Blake never had a serious quarrel with—for a real quarrel between two such firebrands as Blake and Fuseli, if it had taken place, would have been bound to leave some traces behind it. There was, moreover, a strong sense of solidarity between Blake and Fuseli—each felt that the cause of the other was also his own cause, each felt that he had in some important respects only the other to appeal to and rely on as corroborator, abettor and ally. This is most clearly shown by the fact that each did for the other what it is unthinkable that he should ever have done for any contemporary artist else—issued a signed appeal on his behalf to the public: Fuseli for Blake in the *Advertisement* for the illustrations to Blair's *Grave* in 1805, Blake for Fuseli in his letter to the *Monthly Magazine* of July 1806.

In addition to these two major documents there is a little further direct evidence on the relationship between the two painters to be found in Blake's letters, occasional poems and odd jottings, and also in the anonymous *Advertisement* to the illustrations for Young's *Night Thoughts* of 1797, which is usually attributed to Fuseli.[1] For the rest one must depend on a number of anecdotes and oral declarations, some of them spectacular and perhaps for that reason far more often quoted than the printed words of 1805 and 1806. The most reliable chronicler here is Joseph Farington, who in his diary recorded conversations at which he had himself been present, within a few hours of their taking place. J. T. Smith, writing in 1828 in his *Nollekens*

---

[1] It probably is by Fuseli, but if it is, he is writing with his tongue very much in his cheek most of the time.

and his Times, and Allan Cunningham, writing in 1829 in his *Lives of the Painters*, were both by their age and circumstances in a position to obtain their information, if not at first-hand, at least from reliable sources; both were conscientious enough in such matters by the standards of the day; and both had, like Farington, no axe to grind, where Fuseli and Blake were concerned. More problematic is the case of Frederick Tatham, who, born in 1805 and writing in 1832, could indeed speak authoritatively about Blake on the strength of his three years of intimacy with him (1825–8), but was, owing to his youth, in a very different position when he reported the conversational utterances of Fuseli. Nevertheless he must, as a sculptor, have been a pupil at the Royal Academy, though hardly before 1819 at the earliest, and presumably picked up a certain amount of gossip and more reliable information about Fuseli there. Still more problematic is the case of Alexander Gilchrist, who, born in 1828, the year of Blake's death and three years after Fuseli's death, and too much a disciple of Carlyle to be troubled over pedantic accuracy, is, in his life of Blake (not embarked upon till after 1855 and published posthumously in 1863), our earliest and sole source for the most striking utterances on Blake by Fuseli of which there is any record. As a rule he simply makes his assertions without naming his informant. In one specially interesting case, however, where he does mention 'Mr. Tatham' as his source, it proves chronologically impossible that either Frederick Tatham (who is certainly intended) or his father, the architect Charles Heathcote Tatham (1772–1842), could really have been an eye-witness of the scene he is represented as having been present at; apart from the unlikelihood that Tatham would ever have omitted so striking an incident from his own biography of Blake thirty years earlier. Sometimes it looks as though Gilchrist's fertile imagination may simply be reduplicating, amplifying and improving on passages in Blake's letter in defence of Fuseli in the *Monthly Magazine* of 1806 or in J. T. Smith's *Nollekens and his Times*. If he has independent sources of information, they can only be reports at second or third hand from John Linnell (born 1792), Samuel Palmer (born 1805), Frederick Tatham (born 1805) or from others who were also too young ever to have been on intimate terms with Fuseli. All this anecdotal material which appears for the first time thirty-five years after Fuseli's death in Gilchrist's *Blake* implies, in one way or another, that Fuseli looked up to Blake as his superior and master in art, an assumption Tatham had already timidly hinted at in 1832, but which Gilchrist boldly takes for granted. It is in the light of Gilchrist's anecdotes, and of the assumption underlying them, that Fuseli's *Advertisement* and the other contemporary and better authenticated evidence are still usually interpreted, so far as they are seriously examined at all. The point of departure tends to be Gilchrist's 'Blake is d——d good to steal from', or his 'What! you here, *Meesther Blake?* We ought to come and learn of you, not you of us.' For purposes of discussion, however, it is desirable and justifiable to treat as authentic all these oral declarations regarding Blake ascribed to Fuseli only by Tatham and Gilchrist; they are not out of keeping with what is otherwise known about Fuseli and his conversational manner; there is probably some element of fact at the back of them, whatever transformations it may have undergone; and they are anything but detrimental to Fuseli, if they are true. But they must be examined in the light of the less problematic contemporary evidence, and until this has been done, one must suspend one's judgment on the question, whether Fuseli really looked on Blake as his superior and master.

Gilchrist says: 'Of Fuseli Blake . . . was wont to declare, "This country must advance two centuries in civilisation before it can appreciate him!" ' This is freely adapted from Samuel Palmer's letter to Gilchrist of 23 August 1855: 'Fuseli's picture of *Satan building the Bridge over Chaos* Blake ranked with the grandest efforts of imaginative art, and said we were two centuries behind the civilisation which would enable us to estimate his *Aegisthus.*' With this one may compare the not dissimilar expression Blake employs in his letter of 1806 to the *Monthly Magazine*: 'A gentleman who visited me the other day said: "I am very much surprised at the dislike which some connoisseurs show on viewing the pictures of Mr. Fuseli; but the truth is, he is a hundred years beyond the present generation." Though I am startled at such an assertion, I hope the contemporary taste will shorten the hundred years into as many hours. . . .' J. T. Smith records Fuseli similarly prophesying that posterity will do justice to Blake: 'The predictions of Fuseli and Flaxman may hereafter be verified—"That a time will come when Blake's finest works will be as much sought after . . . as those of Michelangelo are at present." ' Tatham improves on this as follows: 'Fuseli and Flaxman both said that Blake was the greatest man in the country, and that there would come a time when his works would be invaluable.' Gilchrist, on the other hand, takes over Smith's words just as they stand, only embellishing them by saying that Fuseli and Flaxman *were in the habit of declaring with unwonted emphasis* that the time would come etc.' and by making Flaxman sometimes add: 'And ah! Sir, his poems are as grand as his pictures'—words modestly dramatised from Palmer's letter already quoted above. Flaxman does not concern us here —in fact, his presence is a disturbance to us, since we only want to know what Fuseli said. But one remarkable point does here arise: there is no direct evidence whatsoever for Fuseli ever having said a word about Blake's poetry or so much as known that he was a poet, still less for the assertion of Ganz (1947) that 'Fuseli valued Blake's poetry'. He must have known it, of course. But if he had attached any importance to it, some word about it would surely have come down to us. Objecting as he did on principle to mysticism and esotericism in all poetry, Fuseli is not likely to have been able to enjoy Blake's poetry. It is surely significant that anyone for whom poetry is one of the main interests in life should be able to be an intimate friend of Blake's for many years and yet virtually ignore him as a poet, seeing him only as a painter and an engraver.

The most important point that arises from a dispassionate survey of all the evidence is that from 1810 onwards, that is to say for fifteen years before Fuseli's death, and probably from a much earlier date, Fuseli and Blake, though they were both living in London, hardly ever met, that the old intimacy between them had quite ceased. Knowles, who was from 1805 onwards Fuseli's constant companion, who makes a special point of recording all Fuseli's friendships, and certainly bears

Blake no grudge, seems quite unaware that the two had ever been friends, speaks of the *Advertisement* for the Blair illustrations as though it had been a service rendered to a comparative stranger, and was evidently never brought together with Blake by or through Fuseli. Blake's letters tell the same story of a gradual drifting apart about or soon after 1800. 'Fuseli was given to me *for a season*' he says in his verse-letter to Flaxman of 12 September 1800. He had, indeed, just been separated from Fuseli by his move to Felpham. But this was not only an external separation. 'I find on all hands,' he writes on 10 January 1802, 'great objections to my doing anything but the mere drudgery of business, and intimations that if I do not confine myself to this, I shall not live. . . . This from Johnson *and Fuseli* brought me down here [i.e. to Felpham] and this from Mr. Hayley will bring me back again.' These words make intelligible the line in the verse-letter written ten months later:

> *And Butts shall give what Fuseli gave,*
> *A dark black Rock and a gloomy Cave.*

Blake would seem to have had more than one grievance against Johnson and Fuseli. On the one hand he had complained on 26 August 1799 that 'even Johnson and Fuseli have discarded my graver'. On his return to London in 1803 Blake was, however, given a commission to engrave two small plates from Fuseli's designs for Chalmer's Shakespeare. That Fuseli was no longer really satisfied with Blake's engraving and only put small, less important jobs in his way, for friendship's sake, seems probable. He had very exact ideas of what he wanted from an engraver, and from 1803 to 1819 had Moses Haughton living in his home and working under his direction. One has only to remember how Blake reacted when Schiavonetti was preferred to him as an engraver, to realise how hurt he is likely to have been at Fuseli's 'discarding his graver'. But Johnson and Fuseli had also tried to 'confine him to the mere drudgery of business'—and that looks as though they had discouraged him in his work on the prophetic books, and urged him to undertake booksellers' commissions instead—such as, for instance, the illustrations of Young or of Blair. We have Blake's own word for it that his life in Felpham was being poisoned for him by Hayley in just the same way as his life in Lambeth had been poisoned for him by Fuseli and Johnson—and how Hayley was poisoning his life in Felpham he explains to Butts in a letter of 6 July 1803, on the subject of his prophetic book *Milton*: 'But of this work I take care to say little to Mr. Hayley, since he is as much averse to my poetry as he is to a chapter of the Bible. He knows that I have written it, for I have shown it to him, and he has read part of it at his own desire. . . . But I do not wish to irritate by seeming too obstinate in poetic pursuits. But if all the world should set their faces against this, I have orders to set my face like a flint . . . against their faces, and my forehead against their foreheads.' It looks very much as though what Blake is going through in 1803 with Hayley and *Milton* he had already gone through before with Fuseli and the Lambeth books. Yet with all this there seems to have been no real quarrel. There are very few more references to Fuseli in Blake's letters or other writings after 1805, and none at all after 1810. Such references as do occur between 1806 and 1810 are all full of enthusiastic friendship and admiration. But meanwhile Fuseli had written the *Advertisement* for the illustrations to Blair, which was bound, among other things, to dispel any ill-feeling there may have been, and is quite likely to have been in part designed for that very purpose. There is only one recorded instance of Fuseli and Blake meeting again after 1810, or indeed after 1805; that is the well-known anecdote first communicated by Gilchrist in 1863 and already alluded to above; about 1815 Blake had to make a drawing of the *Laocoon* group for Rees' *Cyclopedia*[1] and went for that purpose to the Antique School of the Academy; Fuseli welcomed him with the words already quoted above: 'What! you here, *Meesther Blake*? We ought to come and learn of you, not you of us.' Gilchrist goes on: 'Blake took his place with the students, and exulted over his work, says Mr. Tatham, like a young disciple; meeting his old friend Fuseli's congratulations and kind remarks with cheerful, simple joy.' There is something fully convincing about this anecdote, apart from the fact that

[1] Blake's engraving of the *Laocoon* in Rees' *Cyclopedia* bears the date '1st October, 1815'.

46

Tatham was only ten years old at the time and cannot have begun to attend the Antique School till very much later, if he ever did so at all. He may, however, well have heard it from somebody a few years older than himself, who was then a student, or—a more interesting and also more likely possibility— he may have heard it from Blake himself. Be that as it may, the real point of the story, assuming it to be true, lies not in the particular phrasing of Fuseli's kindly and complimentary greeting, but in this being a meeting between two men who have not met for a long time, who are no longer in the habit of meeting,[1] whose paths have long since diverged from one

---

[1] There is no means of dating the anecdote in Gilchrist about Fuseli catching Blake dining on cold mutton and exclaiming: 'Ah! by God! this is the reason you can do as you like. *Now I can't do this.*' It may be after 1810; but Blake certainly dined on cold mutton and did as he liked long before that date. Seymour Kirkup (1788–1880), who, as a pupil in the Antique School and a friend of the Butts family, was from 1809 till 1816 in contact with both Fuseli and Blake, does not record ever having seen them together. 'I used to wonder at his [Blake's] praise of Fuseli and Flaxman, my two first masters,' Kirkup writes, 'for their tastes were so different to his, *which Fuseli specially disliked*, and he was a magnanimous fellow, though a sharp critic' (quoted by Mona Wilson in her *Life of Blake*, 1927, from one of the letters Kirkup wrote between 1864 and 1870 to Swinburne, W. M. Rossetti and Lord Houghton). Rev. Thomas Dibdin records that Blake, on his visit to him in 1816, professed not to remember Fuseli's painting of Lycidas 'asleep beneath the opening eyelids of the morn', but turned out really to have seen it and to consider it 'too tame' (Dibdin, *Reminiscences of a Literary Life*, 1836, quoted by Mona Wilson). There is one more relevant anecdote, this time again not datable, cited by Mona Wilson from the *Richmond Papers* (edited A. M. W. Stirling, 1928): 'Flaxman had complained of Fuseli's foul language and asked what Blake did when Fuseli swore. "What I do?" asked Blake. "Why, I swear again, and he says astonished, 'vy, Blake, you are swearing!' but he leaves off himself!"' Flaxman here being the informant, any date from 1794 onwards (the year of Flaxman's return from Italy) is possible. One further piece of evidence may be added for the sake of completeness. Samuel Palmer writes on 23 August 1855 to Gilchrist: 'Thus he [Blake] thought with Fuseli and Flaxman that the Elgin Theseus, however full of antique savour, could not, as ideal form, rank with the very finest relics of antiquity.' This judgment cannot have been delivered by Blake till after 1817, when the Elgin Marbles were made public—nor, indeed, till after 1824, when Palmer first met Blake. It was probably formulated in a very different way from that in which Palmer presents it, as classical antiquity

47

another. Fuseli would not be so startled and touched by seeing Blake on this particular occasion and at this particular place, if he were still in the habit of seeing him elsewhere and privately, if he were familiar with his present circumstances. This visit of Blake's to the Antique School led, however, not only to the commercial engraving of the *Laocoon* in Rees' *New Cyclopedia*, but also to Blake's own *Laocoon* sheet of aphorisms on art, a body of art doctrine utterly opposed to everything Fuseli stood for.

Tatham himself shows clearly enough in his summing up of what Blake had said to him variously about Fuseli between 1825 and 1828 that the relationship between the two had by no means been one of simple brotherly, give-and-take solidarity, and that there was a residue of sadness, quite unmixed with resentment or bitterness, in Blake's heart on account of these things. 'Fuseli was very intimate with Blake, and Blake was more fond of Fuseli than any other man on earth. Blake certainly loved him, and *at least Fuseli admired Blake* and learned from him, as he himself confessed, a great deal.' That is no happy, unclouded relationship, to be 'at least admired' by a person one loves more than anyone else on earth. The full story of the friction and tension between Blake and Fuseli will never be known, but that there was such friction and tension, and that it led to their seeing extremely little of one another from 1810 onwards, and probably from still earlier, may be taken as beyond doubt. We can be certain that the time when Fuseli and Blake were intimate with one another was from 1787 ('*When Flaxman was taken to Italy*, Fuseli was given to me : . .'—verse-letter of 12 September 1800) to about 1799; and those twelve years are the only ones we can be certain of. It does not look as though the friendly intercouse of the two was renewed, at least with the original warmth, after Blake's return to London in September 1803 from Felpham, whither he had fled, as he clearly enough implies, to escape from Fuseli's endeavours to

no longer meant to Blake what it had previously meant. The coincidence of opinion with Fuseli and Flaxman does not necessarily involve any exchange of views with either of them on the subject, though it leaves it open as a possibility. Moreover Palmer is mistaken about Flaxman, who ranked the *Theseus* 'above any male statues he knew'.

interfere with and supervise his work. In what way Fuseli must have tried to impose his will on Blake may be gathered from the passage in Farington's diary for 24 June 1796, where he is found declaring that Blake ought to devote himself to 'regular conceptions' instead of to 'singular shapes and odd combinations', or from that in the *Advertisement* to the Blair illustrations, where he shakes his head over Blake's tendency to overstep the 'verge of legitimate invention'. Everything points to Fuseli having regarded the prophetic books as an aberration, a misapplication of genius and labour, and tried to bully Blake into dropping them.

A single glimpse is enough to show that there is some special connexion between the pictorial work of Blake and of Fuseli. Those who know only one of them are convinced that there is nobody else like him, nobody he can be compared with; but on coming across the other, one immediately recognises that they are to a large extent partners in this particular kind of uniqueness, that, in differing violently from all the rest of their contemporaries, they strongly resemble one another. This startling resemblance does not, of course, apply to all the aspects of their art—in colouring, for instance, they are poles apart from one another. The point wherein they so closely resemble one another is, however, that which most strikingly distinguishes their art, which most startled their contemporaries and which to the present day still counts for most in our impression and estimation of their style; it is their peculiar way of employing, and charging with supernatural intensity, nude figures with wide-flung arms and remarkably long legs in fantastic straddling and crouching attitudes, in abandoned embraces, or swaying, hovering, soaring, flying at every possible angle, often head downmost, all this with over-emphasis of the audacious foreshortenings it necessitates, and with a tendency to give prominence to the knee, as though it were the most important and expressive part of the human body. For our present purposes it is unnecessary to speak of the precedents and models Fuseli and Blake may have found for this procedure in ancient art, in Michelangelo, especially in his *Last Judgment*, in *Giulio Romano* and elsewhere; nor need we go into the significant differences that can be observed between Fuseli and Blake in their handling of these pictorial principles whereby the human body is forever expanded and contracted beyond the ordinary limits of matter and gravitation. What concerns us is that they are so much together as they are in their isolation from current standards and practice. It is a resemblance which cannot be simply the result of coincidence, of two men hitting on the same thing by chance and quite independently of one another. The question of priority and influence, of leadership and discipleship, is here not extraneous, academic or invidious; it is essential and inevitable. We must ask whether it was Blake or Fuseli who was here the initiator, the pioneer. In this connexion the utterances vouched for by Gilchrist, 'Blake is d——d good to steal from', and 'We ought to come and learn of you, not you of us', take on a new importance. Closely involved in this question is also the other, which of the two, Fuseli or Blake, is the greater painter. The answer of the writers on Blake to these questions is that Blake is incomparably superior to Fuseli as a painter, that whatever is of value in Fuseli's work he has from Blake, and that he virtually admits as much himself. Thus Sidney Colvin writes: 'Yet they did not quite applaud the Swiss for nothing—he was far from a mere pretender to inspiration. He stood not quite without the sanctuary; and he had this sure sign of grace, that he knew and honoured the high priest. . . . Fuseli, in spite of his seniority, would have been the taker rather than the giver, as we may guess from the relative energies of inventive genius in the two' (*The Portfolio*, 1873). And A. G. B. Russell writes: 'It was under Blake's influence that his [Fuseli's] imaginative quality first began to develop itself, and that his style underwent a change in the direction of restraint and refinement'[1] (1906—*Footnote to Blake's Letters*). Similarly Mr. John Piper says: 'Fuseli was once heard muttering aloud about some angels that he was drawing: "They *shall* rise without wings." But he

[1] The present writer's attention has been drawn by Mr. Geoffrey Grigson to another similar judgment on Fuseli and Blake in Professor Anthony Blunt's 'Blake's Pictorial Imagination' (*England and the Mediterranean Tradition*, O.U.P., 1945): 'There are even cases in which we can say that Blake borrows from Fuseli, rather than vice versa.'

was not William Blake. His incantations were stage directions and his angels would not rise without wings. Blake's incantations were rules of life' (1942—*British Romantic Artists*). Cunningham, however, from whom Mr. Piper quotes these words of Fuseli's, and who has very much less affection for Fuseli than for Blake, speaks of 'the power which he [Fuseli] possessed above all men of giving aerial motion to his supernatural creations', and a good case can be made out for Fuseli being not only fully Blake's equal in preternatural aerobatics, but also the precursor from whom Blake acquired them. Blake's pictures will always make a strong appeal to certain types of poetry-lover. No approach to them is 'reasonable', according to Mr. Piper, 'but the approach of acceptance'. This would seem to have been Blake's own estimate of himself: 'My pictures', he writes, 'are equal in every part and superior in one to anything that has been done since Raphael' (to Butts, 22 April 1802). On that point it is better not to dispute. But where the question of reciprocal influence and priority between Blake and Fuseli arises, objective chronological data deserve to be taken into consideration. Fuseli was sixteen years older than Blake. When he returned from Rome and took up residence in London in 1779, he was a man of thirty-eight with all the decisive changes in his development behind him; his manner as a painter was already established, particularly in just those aspects in which he stands nearest to Blake. Innumerable examples might be cited. But one may compare Fuseli's drawing inscribed in Greek 'through the ambrosial night' and dated Rome, February 1778, where the spirit of a slain warrior, probably Sarpedon, is represented as being borne off through the air, with the sheet of Blake's *Europe* beginning with the words 'Enitharmon slept . . .'[1] Nothing could be more characteristic of Fuseli, nothing more characteristic of Blake than the soaring figure with the violently foreshortened right and the long-stretched left leg—yet it is essentially one and the same figure, and Fuseli drew it before he had heard of Blake and when Blake, not yet twenty-one

[1] Reproduced on the cover of Mr. Piper's *British Romantic Artists*. Fuseli's drawing is reproduced on Plate 50 of Federmann's *Fuseli* and also opposite p. 48 of Muschg's *Briefe Füsslis*. In the present volume, opposite p. 288.

years old, was still in his beginnings. But it is misleading to appeal to single cases only. Fuseli had fully anticipated that characteristic use of emancipated anatomy, without which Blake's art cannot be conceived of, by well over ten years, and Blake himself only gradually begins to develop it after he has become familiar with Fuseli and during the years of their intimate friendship, 1787–99. There is still very little trace of it in the *Songs of Innocence* (1789) and it can hardly have belonged to those 'primitive and original ways of execution' which Blake regrets having departed from, and talks of resuming, on 10 January 1802—in the same letter in which he complains of Fuseli. Contemporaries were in no doubt as to where Blake got his peculiar manner from. 'Stothard supported Blake's claim to genius, but allowed he had been misled in his art, *and He knew by whom*,' writes Farington in his diary for 12 January 1797, and it is certainly Fuseli who is here alluded to. Everybody regarded Blake as a follower of Fuseli—and not without grounds. It was as a follower of Fuseli's that he was attacked in the *Examiner* by Robert Hunt—and he was aware of it: 'Many people are so foolish to think that they can wound Mr. Fuseli over my shoulder,' he writes in his *Public Address* (about 1810). Cunningham says, 'He studied occasionally under Flaxman and Fuseli', and again: 'Though he was the companion of Flaxman and Fuseli, *and sometimes their pupil*, he never attained that professional skill, without which all genius is bestowed in vain.' Fuseli undoubtedly received much stimulus from Blake and stole an attitude or an idea from him here and there, and was ready enough to admit it, but it never entered into his head or Blake's head, or the head of anybody who knew them both, that Fuseli's debt to Blake was in any way comparable to that of Blake to Fuseli. Blake claims in one of his epigrams that he found Flaxman and Stothard blind and taught them how to see—but it is unthinkable that he should ever have made any such claim with regard to Fuseli. Anyone who likes can claim that Blake made something infinitely more valuable out of Fuseli's discoveries than Fuseli himself ever could, but there can be no doubt as to who the discoverer was. There are important elements in Blake's art which he has from himself alone, or from other sources than from Fuseli, particularly from Gothic monuments—but none of these did Fuseli take over from him; he took over at most modifications, experiments in and further developments of his own manner. The notion that Fuseli was 'the taker rather than the giver' first turns up in a very much more modest form in 1832, when Tatham writes: 'Before Fuseli knew Blake, he used to fill his pictures with all sorts of fashionable ornaments and tawdry embellishments.' The practice Tatham is here referring to Fuseli continued to indulge in long after he met Blake, in some types of picture, and the very different type of more heroic picture, in which he avoids it, occurs at the beginning of his permanent residence in London; in fact, it is a matter here of two different kinds of picture, which exist simultaneously in his work for whole decades, not of one style that ousts another under Blake's influence.

It was not, however, only in matters of painting practice that Fuseli contrived to gain and for some years maintain a certain ascendancy over the otherwise so untractable and rebellious Blake. Fuseli was a highly educated man, over-brimming with specialised knowledge in many fields, with powerful personal opinions and feelings about the things he knew, eager to talk about them too, and with great gifts as a conversationalist. Blake, with mental gifts of a subtler and more audacious order, was without any formal higher education, a self-taught man, and in his interchange of ideas with Fuseli it was inevitable that he should take over not only information, but also opinions and standards, some of which were not really congenial to him and were then later ejected. When we find him teaching himself Greek and later Italian, when we find him ready to worship Greek culture and Homer, we can safely assume that the contact with Fuseli is in a considerable measure responsible for it. So also, when we find him following up in a Rabelaisian poem certain opinions about Klopstock, of all people, which Fuseli had expressed as early as 1775; or when we find him referring to Dante as early as 1790, in the *Marriage of Heaven and Hell*; or when we find him in November 1802 declaring: 'So says Sir Joshua [Reynolds], and so say I'. In particular he took over from Fuseli many ideas about the theory and history of art, some

53

of them conformable with his natural bent, others hostile to it and later repudiated. But his mind is to the last a mind which Fuseli had a considerable share in furnishing. At the same time it is a very different kind of mind from Fuseli's. Half Blake's marginalia to Reynolds' *Discourses* are as though they had been written by Fuseli; but the other half, the more interesting, vituperative and characteristic half, might just as well have been written in the margins of Fuseli's *Lectures*, instead of in those of Reynolds' *Discourses*. Fuseli stood aggressively for much that Blake, on arriving at full intellectual autonomy, was to hate and attack with all his vigour. That they never violently quarrelled must be attributed to the affectionate veneration with which Blake always regarded Fuseli as an individual, and very likely also to Fuseli not being prepared to take Blake absolutely seriously in the intellectual field.

It is likely that Fuseli's admiration of Blake was not alone admiration of extraordinary natural genius, which he fully recognised, but also admiration of one whom he not altogether unjustifiably regarded as his own one great follower and disciple, of one whom he had for a time been able to advise, influence and direct and who, for his own good, ought to allow him to go on advising, influencing and directing him. This fits in far better with what Fuseli said of Blake in Farington's company and with what he wrote of him in the two *Advertisements*, than the assumption that he regarded him as his superior, or even as in every respect his equal. One can understand that Blake, greatly though he loved Fuseli, was far too independent, self-willed and conscious of his own genius, to be able to endure even from him such claims to supervise him. He felt that Fuseli was trying to condemn him to 'A dark black Rock and a gloomy Cave.' The friendship could only be maintained inwardly as a memory and an unappeasable longing. There is an anecdote given by Cunningham which throws some light on the character of the tension between Fuseli and Blake, and the way in which it may have worked itself out. 'When Blake, a man infinitely more wild in conception than Fuseli himself, showed him one of his strange productions, he said, "Now some one has told you this is very fine."—"Yes," said Blake, "the Virgin Mary appeared to me, and told me it was very fine: what can you say to that?"—"Say?" exclaimed Fuseli, "why nothing—only her ladyship has not an immaculate taste." ' Two men of genius appeal to the Virgin Mary and to the principle of immaculate taste, having anything but implicit faith in either, in order to express how little they are prepared to give way to one another's opinion.

If one turns from the actual practice to the doctrine of art, there are certain points on which one finds Fuseli and Blake in fullest agreement with one another—and often one has the impression that Blake has taken over some aggressive conception or formula from Fuseli, eliminated from it all the modifying clauses, all those more matter-of-fact ingredients which are present under the surface in Fuseli's wildest utterances, heightened it out of all recognisable resemblance to normal experience, and turned it into a sublimely irresponsible oracle—setting in fact the Virgin Mary or the Spiritual Sun or the Angel Gabriel or some other of his celestial visitants in the place of Fuseli's objective and universally valid 'Taste'. Such points of agreement between Blake and Fuseli are their championship of drawing and outline against colour; their doctrine that the truly great artist never draws from nature; their contempt for portrait-painting; their idolisation of Michelangelo and Raphael; and their hostility towards the Venetian, Flemish and Dutch Schools. Fuseli's writings can often prove a valuable help towards elucidating how Blake came to write as he did on some of these themes, and what he was getting at. It is instructive to compare the remarkable utterances on 'Venetian and Flemish Demons', on the 'most outrageous demon', Rubens, and the 'soft and effeminate, and consequently most cruel demon', Correggio, in Blake's *Descriptive Catalogue* (1809) with Fuseli's relatively much discreeter, better informed and more responsible strictures on the same painters in his 1801 and 1805 Lectures. Fuseli, whom many contemporaries regarded as quite demented, sometimes appears, by the side of Blake, sane and prudent to the point of insipidity. Fuseli was himself a visionary —'I see the vision of all I paint—and I wish to Heaven I could paint up to what I see,' Cunningham records him as saying;

but he evidently found that Blake let himself go too much in this matter of seeing visions.

The points of opinion on which Blake and Fuseli were in absolute disagreement are more numerous and of more fundamental importance than those on which they agree. Blake insists that art should be concerned only with the particular, Fuseli with the general. Greek art is for Fuseli alone valid, for Blake an abomination; Gothic is for the older Blake alone valid, for Fuseli at all times an abomination. That Fuseli values Reynolds' art while Blake hates it like poison is partly to be accounted for by extraneous circumstances. What is more interesting and revealing is that whereas Fuseli highly admires Turner, Blake feels no great enthusiasm for him, and that whereas Blake admires Constable, Fuseli ridicules him. All divergencies between Blake and Fuseli can, however, be traced back ultimately to the difference between their views on religion in its relationship to art. For Fuseli art is always something clearly distinguished in its origins, nature and functions from religion, while Blake's entire personality and work rest on a complete mingling or identification of these two elements. It was not only out of respect for the religion he no longer believed in—though that certainly also enters into it—it was primarily and more emphatically on account of what he regarded as the truest interest and the integrity of art, that Fuseli was opposed to all mystical and esoteric views of art, with everything that follows upon them. All Fuseli has to say on this theme is of the greatest interest, and it would be shortsighted to dismiss him as one who was too backward and limited to move with his own times or to understand their spirit. It is rather so, that he sees beyond his times, or in a certain sense sees through them, anticipating something of what was not to come till after 1900, when T. E. Hulme, for instance, was to write: 'Romanticism . . . confuses both human and divine things, by not clearly separating them'; when Jacques Rivière was to write: 'It is only with the advent of Romanticism that the literary act came to be conceived as a sort of raid on the absolute and its result as a revelation'. It is significant, too, that Fuseli, in his magnificent criticism of Klopstock of March 1775, anticipates the arguments

56

and the programme of Imagism. In speaking of the driving forces at the back of the artist's vocation, Fuseli does not shrink from assigning a decisive role to that ambition, that 'love of fame', the very mention of which in bald terms in this connexion had by 1800 and earlier become a bit of indecency. Never does he conform to the tendency of the age to wrap these things up in mystery and myth. There is no parallel anywhere in his writings to Blake's declaration that the Holy Ghost had come to him and said: 'Blake, be an artist and nothing else.' It is in keeping with this that Fuseli avoids representing God in his pictures, even in his *Creation of Eve* for the Milton Gallery, while Blake brings God into *his* pictures again and again. Something that follows from all this is that whereas Blake is forever thrusting out beyond Good and Evil—as, for example, when he says, 'What are called vices in the natural world are highest sublimities in the spiritual world'—nothing is more unthinkable or undesirable for Fuseli, than that this distinction should ever or anywhere lose its inflexible austerity. For him there can be no *Marriage of Heaven and Hell*. He wants his Hell undiluted. It is interesting to see how differently Fuseli and Blake react to Milton and Dante. The difference between the minds of the two men is brought out particularly clearly in the indications each gives as to what alienates him from orthodox Christian tradition. 'If Morality was Christianity, Socrates was the Saviour,' says Blake, while Fuseli, who had in his youth identified Christ with Socrates, finds that the divinity of Christianity is 'proved by its beautiful morality'.

IV

Fuseli's intimacy with Blake is therefore, when more carefully examined, very far indeed from proving that he was, after all, a Romantic in the sense of agreeing with, or even being substantially in sympathy with, those doctrines about art and life which characterise the advanced English and German poets who flourished from 1790 to 1820. The more one ponders on Fuseli's friendship with Blake, the more one will feel confirmed in the suspicions which arose from there having been so extremely few contacts—and those slight and seldom cordial

57

—between him and the other Romantics. It is also impossible to argue that he may never really have had a chance of seeing what Romanticism is at its highest and most typical, that he may only have come across inferior, uncharacteristic or unworthy representatives of it (such as, for example, Southey and Byron), that he never gave it a chance. He saw it for years at close quarters, in its purest form, represented by one of its very greatest men of genius; the circumstances could not have been more favourable for a *rapprochement*. He liked Blake, and Blake was the only Romantic proper who was near enough to him in point of age for no insuperable barrier to arise on that score. In analysing the differences between Fuseli's and Blake's attitude towards art and life, we have touched upon most of the points which made it impossible that Fuseli should ever have been an adherent of Romanticism. It may, however, here be added, that he had no use for the Romantic cult of ruins, and that he was a sworn hater of all 'superstition', from the old-fashioned belief in ghosts, a subject on which he felt equal to crushing Dr. Johnson in argument, to the new-fangled mania for 'animal magnetism'. Whatever his own artistic practice may have been—that is a separate question on which we shall touch briefly later—and in spite of his notorious eccentricity and wildness of tone and manner, Fuseli turns out in the face of Romanticism to be theoretically and in principle a champion of sobriety and common sense, an antagonist of the irrational. In the long run he proves to be a great deal more temperate in these matters than Goethe usually—though not always—is. What is found in Fuseli's writings, what the present volume aims at presenting in a palatable and digestible form, is anything but yet another variation on the familiar Romantic rhapsodies. Fuseli is the last writer one could recommend to anybody who simply wants to feel himself confirmed in the conviction that there is nothing to beat Romanticism—there was very much more of that sort of thing in Lavater, too much for Fuseli's liking. Nor are Fuseli's writings simply a rehashing of the old classical theories—if they were, no interest would attach to them at all. On some questions, indeed, he maintains views which are now irrecoverably superseded, and he takes over a surprising amount from Mengs, Winckelmann, Lessing and Reynolds. There one is sometimes tempted to dismiss him as conventional—but that he is even in such cases by no means conventional, in the sense of blindly submitting to the authority of established standards, is shown at once by the energy of his formulations, and by the new aspects he gives even to ideas which we can only regard as stereotyped and discredited. He belongs ultimately to a one-man party, to his own party, and what is classical, conservative or temperate in his programme is always, in part at least, individualistically acquired, deduced, proclaimed and defended. He salutarily challenges all our pigeon-holing habits, our hankering after neat symmetrical categories and types, where work, personality and *Weltanschauung* conform to pattern and fit in with one another like nuts and bolts, leaving no disturbing and inexplicable components over. He is often one of the most sensitive and acute critics in detailed points of meaning, form and style, both in literature and in the plastic parts. And he is, when at his best, a fine writer, witty, forceful, picturesque, and an excellent marksman in picking off elusive and tricky ideas. The spontaneous, urbane, graceful and leisurely had never been within his range, even when he wrote German, and are quite missing in his English. He is specially impressive when his sense of evil, of the 'rocks and whirlpools that endanger life', manifests itself. He has a flair for the sinister, though this manifests itself very much less in his writings than in his drawings—and it is remarkable that as a writer he always avoids satanic posturings, and however much he may have felt attracted by them in Byron, was critical of them in Beckford. It pleases him to find Dante calling woman an 'animal of beauty', and he is able to give Farington statistics about the various types of lunatics in Bedlam (*Farington Diary*, 2 April 1804).

Fuseli never felt himself in tune with his age—except for a brief period, immediately after the fall of the Bastille—or with the land of his birth, or with the land of his adoption, or, after 1770, with any existing group or movement. He was eight years older than Goethe and sixteen years older than Blake—though he liked to post-date his birth by four years—and was far too imperious to submit to the leadership of men younger than himself. The older he got, the more he detached himself from contemporary developments in poetry and painting alike, not knowing of anybody who was doing what really ought to be done, except himself, and possibly also Blake, if only Blake had had the sense to recognise what was good for him. Posterity necessarily sees Fuseli in connexion with the great efflorescence of genius in his times, partaking of it and contributing to it. He himself, however, would have been as little ready as Goethe to admit that he lived in a great age for art and literature, an age in every way worthy of him. He belonged, moreover, by the date of his birth, to the generation of Gibbon, Boswell and Tom Paine, and in parting company early with the main stream of the great cultural revolution, he went his own ways, retaining something of the old Enlightenment mentality to the last, and neither expecting nor perhaps desiring to find himself attached to a group, unless as its undisputed leader and dictator. It was a necessity for him to see the art not only of his own days, but also of the entire past and even of the future in such a light that the kind of things he felt the urge and power to perform, and the kind of man he felt himself called upon to make out of himself, should stand at the very centre and at the very top, with everything else far below. This is responsible for most of the eccentricities and distortions that mark his work as a critic —he foreshortens the philosophy and history of art in his writings as he does the limbs of the human body in his pictures. All great individualistic artists tend indeed to do something of the kind, when they set up as critics—and the strangeness of the results is one of the measures of their originality. The Romantics themselves were also engaged in re-interpreting the world's literature, and indeed the whole universe, in terms of their own personalities. The vision of these things that they stood for was, however, very different from that which Fuseli stood for—its central and topmost pinnacle was not reserved for Michelangelo and his legitimate successors, if there were any; it was rather, at least in Germany, reserved for Goethe, whom Novalis hailed as 'the true vice-regent of the poetic spirit on earth'. How different Fuseli's interpretation of the nature, destiny and history of mankind in their bearings on the arts was from the Romantic interpretation, the present volume will show.

The most original, interesting and valuable aspect of Fuseli's attitude towards art is that he repudiated, far more radically and on other grounds than Goethe himself in his classical phase, the dominant tendency of the new poetry to cultivate subjective impalpabilities, shadowy moods, intuitions of the infinite and abstract reflexions, at the expense of concrete, objectively presented images, figures and actions. This goes hand in hand with his distrust after 1770 or so of all ambiguity and vagueness on the philosophical as well as on the aesthetic plane, with his desire that all such great opposites, disparates or incommensurables as God and man, good and evil, ideal and reality, religion and art, should remain distinct, and not be blended or merged into one another by compromise or synthesis, by identity-postulates or by mystical intuitions. Thence also his dislike of 'mixed expression' in art. He comes more and more to demand of a work of art, plastic or poetic, that there should be a monumental structural principle operating in it centripetally, a maximum density and firmness of substance, clearness and incisiveness of outline. These qualities he found in Michelangelo and in certain antique statues, in Homer, Milton and also, by a certain subjective violence in his way of reading, in Shakespeare, but in hardly any contemporary writers or plastic artists; these qualities he cultivated in his own mature drawings and paintings, and also in his later writings. In dealing with the theory and history of art, it is these qualities that he sets above all others; instead of treating Michelangelo as an exceptional figure of colossal but abnormal genius, outside the main channel of art, which is what most contemporaries did,[1] Fuseli makes of him the central criterion by which all his predecessors and successors should be judged, relegating all non-heroic forms of painting—portrait, landscape, still life and *genre*—and all non-linear types of technique—pure colouring and chiaroscuro—together with the Venetian, Dutch and Flemish masters, who excelled in these things, to a lower rank. In dissociating himself

---

[1] *See* Martin Shee, *Elements of Art*, 1809: 'Buonarroti is a blazing star, too eccentric in its orbit to direct us safely in the navigation of art.'

more and more from the great literary and artistic movement of his day, Fuseli felt the lack in it of just that heroic concentration, unambiguity and monumental firmness which he had missed before 1770 in the poetry of Klopstock and Young, and in the character of Rousseau.

Where Fuseli most clearly parts company with the representative classicism of his day is in his insistence that expression is more important in art than beauty—a doctrine with which he flies in the face of Winckelmann, Lessing, Reynolds and the classical Goethe. This belief in 'Expression' is of the greatest importance to Fuseli, and very much follows from it. It means, amongst other things, that in rejecting realism and demanding that art should always idealise, Fuseli neither advocates nor practises that smoothness and tranquillity which make so much of the classicism of the age too elegant to be convincing; there is never any pretence in his work that life is not such a dangerous or terrible business after all—on the contrary, he seems, if anything, to exaggerate the treacherous and daemonic aspects of existence, which is a very unclassical thing to do. He is able to square this procedure with classical theory by giving a very liberal and extended interpretation to the idea of the sublime, which regularly alternates with that of beauty in the conservative aesthetic terminology of the day. But what Fuseli makes of the sublime has very little to do with what normal contemporary classicism understands by that term.

The discrepancy between Fuseli's peculiar form of classical aesthetic theory and his non-classical artistic practice is, then, not so great as it at first sight appears to be. Yet a discrepancy there still is. Since there can be no doubts as to his good faith in his theorisings about art, one can only assume that he was in his sustained creative exertions nearly always striving after something different not only in degree but also in kind from what he actually achieved, and furthermore that he usually tended to see his completed pictures as having qualities which nobody else has ever been able to recognise in them, that is to say, as conforming to a norm or as being adapted for acceptance as a norm, as standing for 'proportion' as opposed to 'hugeness', as exemplifying 'Propriety' and 'Immaculate Taste'. His theory is certainly intended to tally all along the line with the character and purport of his own work, at least with what he is consciously aspiring after in his work, and at many points this correspondence is clearly enough present—so when he speaks of *composition* (as opposed to grouping), of *line* (as opposed to colour), of *expression* (as opposed to beauty) and of *terror*. But much that is of central importance to his theory is almost entirely missing in his practice, and much that seems to us of the greatest importance in his work, much that for our feeling constitutes his chief claim to genius, is either hardly touched on at all in his theory, or utterly opposed to it.

To those who know Fuseli only from his paintings and drawings, he is above all the painter of dreams, particularly of horrible dreams, and thence by an easy transition also of the uncanny and macabre, of the night-side of things, of the irrational, the daemonic, the sinister, the pathological and the perverse. This has been the chief point of interest in the Fuseli revival of the last thirty years. Muschg makes a sharp distinction between those of his pictures which, showing a 'literary, mannered classicism', belong only to his own age, and his 'visionary dream-pictures and twilight hallucinations', which alone are of permanent value. Edmond Jaloux, going further, says of Fuseli that dreams were the 'principal preoccupation of his life', and speaks of his unfailing 'constancy to the exploration of the nocturnal world'. That is how we are bound to see him, but it is not how he saw himself, nor is it how those who were familiar with him during his lifetime tended to visualise his personality. The horrible in all its forms he touches on only as something that ought never to be admitted into art at all. There is one solitary reference in all his writings to dreams as 'one of the most unexplored regions of art', but it is followed up in a very meagre and disappointing way, quite different from what one would have expected from the painter of the *Nightmare*. For the rest, he never in his writings betrays any awareness that art can or should be concerned with anything but the ideas of the fully conscious and alert mind. Many of his acquaintances wrote of him at length and with extreme candour; all sorts of things emerge from their communications, much that is amusing, much that is mildly scandalous; but one searches in vain for what one expects. The nearest approach to it is Coutts's mention to Farington of 'a sort of distortion in his mind'. Haydon, calling on him for the first time at the age of nineteen, with 'mysterious awe' in his heart and his father's 'God speed you with the terrible Fuseli' in his ears, was relieved and a little disappointed at the sight of the 'little white-headed, lion-faced man in an old flannel dressing-gown, tied round his waist with a piece of rope, and upon his head the bottom of Mrs. Fuseli's work basket'. 'Well, well,' Haydon thought to himself, 'I am a match for you at any rate, if bewitching is tried.' Fuseli was full of oddities which could sometimes be alarming or exasperating, he flew into fearful tempers, he had long fits of depression, he could be extremely rude, he could be profane and indecent—but nobody seems to have felt any of these things as really sinister or uncanny. He neither inspired preternatural terrors, nor made the impression of being himself subject to them. When he was occasionally called mad, it was by those who only knew his pictures, or it was just a figure of speech, an exaggerated way of saying 'eccentric'. The most shattering crises of his life, the separation from Lavater and his love for Anna Landolt, discharge themselves, for all the hyperbolical language they release, still comfortably within the boundaries of sanity and solid realities. Fuseli never toyed with the belief that in real life insanity might be something ennobling and glorious—when he was forced to doubt Rousseau's sanity, he reluctantly dropped him, and it is likely that some similar considerations entered into his estrangement from Blake.[1] There are no indications of his ever having been addicted, or even tempted, to any practices likely to expose him to hallucinations or terrors—he lived abstemiously, and even the rumour that he ate raw pork chops to induce spectacular

[1] It is interesting to compare Blake's utterances on the insanity of Cowper (Note to Spurzheim's *Observations on the deranged Manifestations of the Mind, or Insanity*) with Fuseli's words to Farington on the same subject—Diary, 28 May 1803. Blake, who was certainly 'but mad north-north-west', at once applies Cowper's case to his own. Fuseli regards it quite objectively, as an external fact like any other. He was interested in insanity, but always in this way, as in one of the multiform phenomena of existence.

Fuseli in conversation with Professor Bodmer

dreams is demented by the not over-friendly Cunningham in a way that carries conviction. His bark was tremendous, but he did not bite at all. He laid the law down, indulged sometimes in crude humour and horseplay, joked about his familiarity with the devil, burst into tears from time to time, was vain, bragged, would neglect his evening duties at the Academy and go to the theatre instead—but with it all he impressed nobody as being haunted. He seemed to be a man with innumerable crotchets but still a man without a mystery. Yet a mystery he must have had. Whether his toughness was a consciously assumed manner, maintained with continual effort, or a natural growth, it was but a scaly carapace enclosing something much more sensitive and fantastic. Where does the horror in his pictures come from? Is it quite outside him, a phenomenon observed, conjured up, visualised by an act of the detached imagination, for the purposes of his art, and as easily cast off again? Or is it completely inside him, rising to consciousness and expression only in and through the act of painting, and otherwise dormant and unfelt? Is it just his sense of evil, of the 'rocks and whirlpools that endanger life'? Or were there some sensational facts which we have not yet discovered and may now never discover? Be that as it may, we cannot connect the most impressive and characteristic of his pictures with his personality, still less with his theories of art, in the way in which we feel that it should be possible to do so. Yet in one important respect his nocturnal visions do conform to his theoretical demands: they are presented in clear-cut, monumental outlines, without vagueness, without blur, without 'mixed expression'; therein lies the chief secret of their effectiveness, of their strangeness and horror. The problem remains, nevertheless, how such a master of nightmare and hallucination as Fuseli should have been so much at home and comparatively happy in the waking world as he seems to have been, how he should even have contrived to feel himself in his own way a sturdy advocate of sobriety and common sense.

The first object of the compiler of the present volume has been to bring together with a minimum of ballast all passages of special value and interest in Fuseli's writings, passages which display vividly his distinctive qualities as a personality, critic and writer. Most of these passages gain considerably through being detached from their original contexts, especially those from the *Lectures*, which, full though they are of admirable things, constitute in their totality rather a wearisome than a satisfactory book for the non-specialist. The scheme according to which the excerpts are arranged largely dictated itself, and is intended primarily to give a certain unity and perspicuity to the whole, and to provide the individual passage with a significant setting. Where Fuseli contradicts himself interestingly, as he often does, the passages in question are brought together, without the inconsistency always being expressly pointed out. Some of his conversational utterances are introduced by the side of his more formal written pronouncements on the same themes. Telling phrases which cannot stand by themselves, but are too characteristic to be omitted, have been woven into the Introduction and the editorial comments on the single sections. It has been furthermore one of the chief objects of the editor to indicate the relationship of Fuseli to the spiritual developments of his age, to outstanding contemporary minds and to such momentous events as the French Revolution and the discovery of the Parthenon marbles. Only in the case of some of the quotations from Blake and from the *Farington Diary* have the peculiarities of the original spelling and punctuation been consistently retained. To give the names of Shakespeare and Michelangelo spelt in seven or eight different ways seemed pointless, and without a certain modernisation of the punctuation, Fuseli's prose, especially in the earlier works, is unnecessarily obscure. In the few cases where the original text has been conjecturally emended, the original reading is always given in the footnotes. The editor is responsible for all translations from German and other languages, except where some other indication is expressly given. A considerable number of Fuseli's hitherto unidentified contributions to the *Analytical Review* and to other magazines have here been drawn on for the first time.

EUDO C. MASON

Edinburgh,
6 April 1949

66

SOME SPECIMEN OPINIONS
ON FUSELI

I

CONTEMPORARY IMPRESSIONS OF
HIS PERSONALITY

Lavater on Fuseli in letters to Herder

4 February and 16 November 1774.

GOETHE AND FUSELI—admirably paired with one another, and yet as different as possible. Goethe—more of a human being; he—more of a poet. He is the most original genius I know. Nothing but energy, profusion and calm! the wildness of the warrior—and the feeling of supreme sublimity! But inexorable to all pleadings—and yet led as easily as a child by looks and hints, which he greatly feels! His spirits are storm-wind, his ministers flames of fire! He goes upon the wings of the wind. His laughter is the mockery of hell and his love—a deadly lightning-flash. Jupiter's eagle! Belial, treading a whole coast into the abyss with a single kick! I am now sending him the '*Urkunde*', the '*Philosophie*',[1] '*Götz v. Berlichingen*', the glorious '*Leiden des jungen Werther*' and Klopstock's Odes. I hope thereby to get him interested in you and Goethe.

(Translated from the German)

---

[1] Abbreviated titles of two of Herder's works.

'That reptile Vanity'

IT MUST be acknowledged that Fuseli was fully sensible of his various acquirements, and never underrated his own powers, although apt to undervalue those of others. . . . Mrs. Wollstonecraft was alive to this weakness in Fuseli's character, and on one occasion emphatically exclaimed, 'I hate to see that reptile Vanity sliming over the noble qualities of your heart.'

(Knowles, *Biography*, p. 363)

Godwin on Fuseli's character

HE WAS the most frankly ingenuous and conceited man I ever knew. He could not bear to be eclipsed or put in the background for a moment. He scorned to be less than the highest. He was an excellent hater; he hated a dull fellow, as men of wit and talents naturally do; and he hated a brilliant man, because he could not bear another near the throne. He once dined at my house with Curran, Grattan and two or three men of that stamp; and retiring suddenly to the drawing-room, told Mrs. Godwin that he could not think why he was invited to meet such wretched company.

(From a letter of Godwin's to Knowles of 28 September 1826)

Northcote on Fuseli

NORTHCOTE . . . thinks . . . Fuseli . . . a butterfly—ingenious and fanciful and amusing, but has no strength of mind—timid, —capricious,—vain and affected.

(*Farington Diary*, 12 December 1797)

Coutts on Fuseli

MR. COUTTS[1] spoke to me of Fuseli and His eccentricities—of

[1] The banker Thomas Coutts (1735–1822) was one of Fuseli's oldest and most loyal friends and patrons. Without the financial help Coutts gave him, Fuseli would never have been able to go to Italy.

68

His dislike of particular persons, which wd. cause Him to run into the corner of a room on their appearance,—a sort of madness. I mentioned Rousseau as having something of the same kind of mind.—He said he knew Fuseli 40 years ago or more through Dr. Armstrong. . . . Dr. Armstrong . . . travelled to Italy with Fuseli, and two men more like children, in respect of management of worldly affairs, could not have been sent together.—Mr. Coutts sd. Fuseli had Shakespeare's work so completely in His memory as to be able to recollect any passage alluded to;—but with all His talent He still had a sort of distortion in His mind, something similar to what is seen more or less in all His pictures.

(Farington Diary, 24 February 1809)

2

CONTEMPORARY ESTIMATES OF FUSELI AS AN ARTIST

Herder on Fuseli in 1774

May 1774.

THERE IS living in Rome a noble German from Zurich, Henry Fuseli, a genius like a mountain torrent, a worshipper of Shakespeare, and now, Shakespeare's painter. As a master of the characteristic, though not of the ideal style, he is said to be far superior to Mengs.

14 November 1774.

IF YOU want to make the acquaintance of a young Michelangelo of the Germans, look at Fuseli's engraving in the *Noachide*.[1] He is now in Rome just such a prodigy as a painter of the characteristic as Mengs is of beauty. I have seen a drawing of his which tears its way through the soul, and am in hopes of getting

---

[1] The *Noachide*, an epic by Bodmer, for which Fuseli drew a frontispiece.

69

hold of another. He is the disciple of Shakespeare with every stroke of his pen.

(Excerpts from two letters to Hamann, quoted by Ganz in the notes to his *Hans Heinrich Füsslis Zeichnungen*, 1947)

Horace Walpole on Fuseli in his exhibition catalogue

1780—On *Satan starting from the touch of Ithuriel's spear*: 'Extravagant and ridiculous.'

1784—On *Lady Macbeth walking in her sleep*: 'Execrable.'

1785—On *The Mandrake*: 'Shockingly mad, madder than ever, quite mad.'

(Quoted in William T. Whitley's *Artists and their Friends*, London and Boston, 1928)

Dr. Erasmus Darwin on Fuseli's 'Nightmare'

'The daring pencil of Fuseli transports us beyond the boundaries of nature, and ravishes us with the charm of the most interesting novelty' (Darwin, quoted by Knowles)

so on his Nightmare, through the evening fog,
Flits the squab fiend o'er fen, and lake, and bog;
Seeks some love-wilder'd maid with sleep oppress'd,
Alights, and grinning sits upon her breast—
Such as of late, amid the murky sky,
Was marked by Fuseli's poetic eye;
Whose daring tints, with Shakespeare's happiest grace,
Gave to the airy phantom form and place—
Back o'er her pillow sinks her blushing head,
Her snow-white limbs hang helpless from the bed;
While with quick sighs and suffocative breath,
Her interrupted heart-pulse swims in death.

Dance on Fuseli's paintings

WHEN WE came away, Dance remarked on the pain of being with Fuseli with His pictures before Him,—a man of so much ability, but whose pictures it was impossible to speak to Him of in such a way as to cause Him to think they were liked.

(*Farington Diary*, 14 August 1809)

Allan Cunningham on Fuseli

AS A PAINTER, his merits are of no common order. He was no timid and creeping adventurer in the region of art, but a man peculiarly bold and daring—who rejoiced only in the vast, the wild, and the wonderful, and loved to measure himself with any subject, whether in the heaven above, the earth beneath, or the waters under the earth. The domestic and humble realities of life he considered unworthy of his pencil, and employed it only on those high or terrible themes where imagination may put forth all her strength, and fancy scatter all her colours. He associated only with the demigods of verse, and roamed through Homer, and Dante, and Shakespeare, and Milton, in search of subjects worthy of his hand; he loved to grapple with whatever he thought too weighty for others; and assembling round him the dim shapes which imagination called readily forth, sat brooding over chaos, and tried to bring the whole into order and beauty. . . . He had splendid dreams, but like those of Eve, they were sometimes disturbed by a demon, and passed away for ever before he could embody them. His main wish was to startle and astonish—it was his ambition to be called Fuseli the daring and the imaginative, the illustrator of Milton and Shakespeare, the rival of Michelangelo. . . . It cannot be denied, however, that a certain air of extravagance and a desire to stretch and strain is visible in most of his works. A common mind, having no sympathy with his soaring, perceives his defects at once, and ranks him with the wild and unsober—a poetic mind will not allow the want of serenity and composure to extinguish the

71

splendour of the conception; but while it notes the blemish, will feel the grandeur of the work. The approbation of high minds fixes the degree of fame to which genius of all degree is entitled, and the name of Fuseli is safe.

(*The Lives of the Painters*, 1829)

Hazlitt on Fuseli as conversationalist and as painter

MR. FUSELI'S conversation is . . . striking and extravagant. . . . He deals in paradoxes and caricatures. He talks allegories and personifications, as he paints them. You are sensible of effort without any repose—no careless pleasantry—no traits of character or touches from nature—everything is laboured or overdone. His ideas are gnarled, hard and distorted, like his features —his theories stalking and straddle-legged, like his gait—his projects aspiring and gigantic, like his gestures—his performance uncouth and dwarfish, like his person. His pictures are also like himself, with eyeballs of stone stuck in rims of tin, and muscles twisted together like rope or wires. Yet Fuseli is undoubtedly a man of genius, and capable of the most wild and grotesque combinations of fancy. It is a pity that he ever applied himself to painting, which must always be reduced to the test of the senses. He is a little like Dante or Ariosto, perhaps, but no more like Michelangelo or Correggio than I am. Nature, he complains, puts him out. Yet he can laugh at artists who paint ladies with iron lapdogs; and he describes the great masters of old in words or lines full of truth, and glancing from a pen or tongue of fire. . . .

[Fuseli's] . . . distortions and vagaries are German, and not English: they lie like a nightmare on the breast of our native art. They are too recondite, obscure and extravagant for us: we only want to get over the ground with large, clumsy strides as fast as we can; we do not go out of our way in search of absurdity. We cannot consider his genius naturalised among us, after the lapse of more than half a century; and if in saying this we do not pay him a compliment, we certainly do not intend it as a very severe censure. Mr. Fuseli has wit and words at will; and though he had never touched a pencil, would be a man of extraordinary pretensions and talents.

(From *On the old age of artists*, 1826, and from a review of Farington's *Life of Reynolds* in the *Edinburgh Review* for August 1820)

Leigh Hunt on Fuseli

... he was reckoned, I believe, not quite so bold as he might have been. He painted horrible pictures, as children tell horrible stories; and was frightened at his own lay-figures. Yet he would hardly have talked as he did about his terrors, had he been as timid as some supposed him. With the affected, impression is the main thing, let it be produced how it may. .... He was an ingenious caricaturist of ... Michelangelo, making great bodily display of mental energy, and being ostentatious with his limbs and muscles, in proportion as he could not draw them. A leg or arm was to be thrust down one's throat, because he knew we should dispute the truth of it. In the indulgence of this wilfulness of purpose, generated partly by impatience of study, partly by want of sufficient genius, and, no doubt, also by a sense of superiority to artists who could do nothing but draw correctly, he cared for no time, place or circumstances, in his pictures. .... He endeavoured to bring Michelangelo's apostles and prophets, with their superhuman ponderousness of intention, into the commonplaces of modern life. A student reading in a garden is all over intensity of muscle; and the quiet tea-table scene in Cowper he has turned into a preposterous conspiracy of huge men and women, all bent on shewing their thews and postures, with dresses as fantastical as their minds. One gentleman, of the existence of whose trousers you are not aware till you see the terminating line at the ankle, is sitting and looking grim on a sofa, with his hat on, and no waistcoat. Yet there was real genius in his designs for Milton, though disturbed, as usual, by strainings after the energetic. His most extraordinary mistake, after all, is said to have been on the subject of his colouring. It is a sort of livid green, like brass

73

diseased. Yet they say, that when praised for one of his pictures he would modestly answer: 'It is a pretty colour.'

(Lord Byron and Some of his Contemporaries, 1828)

Haydon's fluctuating judgments on Fuseli

(from his autobiography and journals)

'BEWARE OF FUSELI' was in everybody's mouth; but having higher authorities in the great Greeks and Italians, I was fearless. I adored Fuseli's inventive imagination, and saw his mannered style. In conveying his conception, he had all the ethereal part of a genius, but not enough of the earthly to express his ideas in a natural way.

My incessant application was soon perceived by Fuseli, who coming in one day, when I was at work and all the other students were away, walked up to me, and said in the mildest voice, 'Why when de devil *do* you dine?' and invited me to go back with him to dinner. Here I saw his sketches, the sublimity of which I deny. Evil was in him. . . . He said a subject should interest, astonish or move; if it did none of these it was worth 'noting by Gode'. . . . He was about five feet five inches high, had a compact little form, stood firmly at his easel, painted with his left hand, never held his palette upon his thumb, but kept it upon his stone, and being very near-sighted, and too vain to wear glasses, used to dab his beastly brush into the oil, and sweeping round the palette in the dark, take up a great lump of white, red or blue, as it might be, and plaster it over a shoulder or face. Sometimes in his blindness he would put a hideous smear of Prussian blue in his flesh, take a bit of red to deaden it, and then prying close in, turn round to me, and say, 'By Gode, dat's a fine purple! it's vary like Correggio, by Gode!' and then all of a sudden, he would burst out with a quotation from Homer, Tasso, Dante, Ovid, Virgil, or perhaps the *Nibelungen*, and thunder round to me with 'paint dat!' I found him the most grotesque mixture of literature, art, scepticism, indelicacy, profanity and kindness. . . . Weak minds he destroyed. They mistook his wit for reason, his indelicacy for breeding, his swearing for manliness, and his infidelity for strength of mind; but he was accomplished in elegant literature, and had the art of inspiring young minds with high and grand views. . . .

[Fuseli's art compared with one of Raphael's cartoons:]

THINK OF Fuseli's savage ferocity and abandoned women—the daughters of the bawds of hell, engendered by demons—and then bring to your fancy this exquisite, graceful, innocent creature dropped from heaven on a May morning. Think of Fuseli's men—the sons of banditti—and contrast them with the rapturous innocence of St. John. It can't be borne. The more I see of nature, the more I see of Raphael, the more I abhor Fuseli's mind, his subjects and his manner; let me root his pictures from my fancy for ever.

(Haydon's *Diary*, 27 April 1812)

[Thoughts on Fuseli's death—1825:]

HIS CONCEPTION of Adam and Eve for pathos, and Uriel contemplating Satan for sublimity, have never been excelled by the greatest painters of the greatest period of art either in Greece or Italy. With a fancy bordering on frenzy, as he used to say, the patience, the humility and calmness necessary for embodying your conceptions . . . angered and irritated him. His great delight was conception, not embodying his conceptions, and as soon as he rendered a conception intelligible to himself and others by any means, he flew off to a fresh one, too impatient to endure the meditation required fully to develop it. To such a temperament nature was an annoyance, because she is an irrefutable reproach to extravagance and untruth. She put him out, likely enough, and unable to bear the fatigue of investigating her perfections, he left her in anger because she disdained to bend herself to his own spasmodic conceits. . . . He was an intense egotist, as all mannerists must be. If you acknowledged the supremacy of his style, no man was more fatherly; if you disputed his infallibility, he heard you with irritation. On the

75

whole Fuseli was a great genius, but not a sound genius, and failed to interest the nation by having nothing in his style in common with our natural sympathies. . . . How many delightful hours have I passed with him in one continued stream of quotation, conception, repartee and humour. In his temper he was irritable and violent, but appeased in an instant. In his person small, with a face of independent, unregulated fire. I have heard he was handsome when young, and with women (when gratified by their attentions) no man could be more gentle.

Cunningham on Fuseli's drawings

THOSE WHO are only acquainted with Fuseli through his paintings know little of the extent of his genius; they should see him in his designs and drawings, to feel his powers and know him truly. The variety of these productions is truly wonderful, and their poetic feeling and historic grandeur more wonderful still. It is surprising too how little of that extravagance of posture and action which offends in his large paintings is present here; they are for the most part uncommonly simple and serene performances.

(*The Lives of the Painters*, 1829)

3

VICTORIAN ESTIMATES OF FUSELI AS AN ARTIST

Fuseli in Redgrave's 'Century of Painters' (*1866*)

BUT HOW much Fuseli needed that elementary training which had led Michelangelo into the full power of expressing his noble thoughts is evident to anyone examining the works of the Swiss painter. Grand in invention, revelling in the mystic and terrible, and with a wild energy of action that defies the charge of

76

being theatrical, bordering as it does on the fearful; having indeed a formal and marked style, he yet entirely fails to satisfy us. He has no refinement nor accuracy in drawing, many of his attitudes are impossible; his females are somewhat more than masculine, they are absolutely coarse and at times disgusting; while, as has already been said, his entire want of knowledge of the elementary laws of colouring and processes of painting not only hindered him from developing his innate sense of colour, but, from the imperfect methods he resorted to, have left us too often to contemplate fading ghosts and moribund canvasses. The only thing that can be said on the other side is, would not a sound elementary education have tamed down his originality and poetic feeling, while giving him the language in which to express it? . . . But then the painter is never commonplace; he always carries us away into a poetic region of his own—a region apart from the everyday world we live in; and if we cannot agree that it is the same that Shakespeare and Milton would picture to us, it is at least a dream-land in which we awaken to sublime thoughts and curious pleasures too often wanting in the works of those who are more literal or more faithful to their text.

Sidney Colvin on Fuseli in 1873

THE HOBGOBLINRY of the Teutonic genius . . . is in reality a stronger point in Fuseli than either the terrible or the graceful. . . . He was another instance of the lack in the most imaginative painters of that age, of a genius possessed by pictorial images as distinct from images of literature. . . . Where Fuseli, then, would be Michelangelo, he fails; . . . he succeeds where he lets himself be familiarly wild and grotesque.

(Portfolio)

Mrs. Mary Margaret Heaton on Fuseli in 1879

HE WOULD probably have been a better artist if he had not lain on his back day after day and week after week, studying Michelangelo. This has been the ruin of many a promising young artist. . . . His art . . . might have been fancifully original, but for his passion for the great Italian master. Few can walk on the heights with Michelangelo, and trying to do so filled poor Fuseli's brains with vain phantoms which he fondly imagined to be real living forms. . . .

(Footnote to Bohn's Cunningham)

4

PRESENT-DAY ESTIMATES OF FUSELI AS AN ARTIST

From Arnold Federmann's 'J. H. Füssli, Dichter und Maler' (Zurich 1927)

AS A LYRICAL poet Fuseli appears to-day in part as the precursor of the young Goethe, in part as his rival and equal. As an aphorist Fuseli is classic. As a painter and draughtsman Fuseli is the most important of all the Classicists and the precursor of the Romantics, whose movement only begins in his wake; in many respects, indeed, there is a hidden line of connexion between Fuseli's work and such masters as Rodin and Hodler. Blake's prophecy, that two centuries would have to elapse before Fuseli's value would be recognised, has been fulfilled. It has taken, indeed, not two centuries, but still almost one entire century, for Fuseli to be seen as what he was: as the third artist of genius at the turn of the century, together with his coeval, Goya, and his younger friend, Blake.

(Translated from the German)

The pioneer of modernism

TO-DAY, in the age of expressionism and surrealism, his importance as the pioneer of modernism is gradually becoming manifest. . . . If Fuseli allowed a specially large scope in his art to the conception of the unsubstantial and to the daemonic forces springing from an invisible world, he therein responded to the sense of crisis prevailing in those days in all classes; he knew the perturbation with which the approach of a social convulsion was watched by many people, once the inexorable course of events had begun to cast its shadows before it in two continents. . . . It was reserved to our age to appreciate Fuseli's art; we live under similar conditions of oppression and uncertainty, in a world churned up with passions, to those which obtained when the *Nightmare* and the *Witches* were painted and kindled the conscience of the people. . . . Fuseli is a Romantic genius employing classical modes of expression, and thereby achieving intensities and contrasts which, like those of surrealism, lead beyond the limits of nature and deep into the spiritual world, thus laying the foundations of the Romantic attitude. He depicts fright and horror in order to awaken *Fear* [in the existential sense]; he presents the power of evil, in order to strengthen belief in the good. . . . The goal he strives towards is the emancipation of mankind from the yoke of slavery and spiritual servitude. He was the first to succeed in expressing the agitation of the soul in the German language. . . . He created a new type of hero, the free man who gives full rein to his passions and is rewarded or punished for it by destiny, bearing his cross through joy and suffering. With this supreme spiritual exploit he shattered the fetters of sophistication and untruth, the rigidity of the old absolutism, contributing his share to pave the way for the modern spirit of enlightenment.

(Paul Ganz, from his *Hans Heinrich Füsslis Zeichnungen*, Bern-Olten, 1947—translated from the German)

Marcel Fischer on Fuseli's art

THE LIMITATIONS of his art are, however, determined by a certain one-sidedness and exclusiveness with which he devotes himself to the representation of abnormal feelings, not transcending these to give the great positive aspect of life . . . The things that

79

ascend from the creative depths of his imagination are principally murky appetites of the soul and emissaries of Satan,
whereas mankind seeks longingly in a work of art for the good
Daemon and the triumph of light; for this reason the works of
this artist are not easily appreciated.

(A study on Fuseli's Roman Sketch-book, *Neujahrsblatt der Zürcher
Kunstgesellschaft*, 1942)

Fuseli the follower of fashion and man of the world

HOW DIFFERENT is the high-flown Blake with his plethora of
genius from worldly-wise, acute-minded Fuseli with his clear-
cut imagination! . . . Fuseli is the man who says 'Yes!' to life,
who is bent on seeing and enjoying the world, who takes
pleasure in beautiful girls, indulges his passions, and yet holds
his own against his environment as a shrewd, witty man, master
of any situation. . . . Impetuous and self-confident he makes his
way through his age. It is delightful to see how he wears the
costume of the day, and how it always suits him. All storm-and-
stress, sentimental, exalted, tearful—that is the style of his
youthful German letters, in which he addresses his coeval
Lavater as his 'heart's darling'. But beneath the guise of the
passing fashion we divine the dilating contours of an individual
will, of a self-assertive body. The young man comes to England,
where the costume he wears is still for a time the fashion. But
then the majority of the educated begin to change their gar-
ments. The romantic attitude grows more manly and temperate, prouder and more harmonious. Fuseli, too, conforms,
changes his coat; his Academy Lectures and his later letters are
cast in pithy, elegant, fluent and correct English phrasing,
always straightforward and pregnant. His art followed a similar
course. . . . Even his romantic subjects, such as the Nightmare,
Puck, the Witches, Titania and Bottom, are full of the breath of
reality. Fuseli is also a great virtuoso, a master of technique—
and this sureness of eye and hand is matched by his sureness of
knowledge. Taking him all round, Fuseli remains, with all his

And with his head over his shoulder turned,
He seem'd to find his way without his eyes . . .
(Hamlet and Ophelia)

idealism, a man of the world, whom external success attended, though not, indeed, to the full measure of his wishes.

(Professor Bernhard Fehr in the *Neue Zürcher Zeitung*, 7 February 1926, reprinted in *Von Englands geistigen Beständen*, Frauenfeld, 1944—translated from the German)

Fuseli's 'Queen Mab' and 'Titania'

FUSELI'S FAIRY world is adorable and cruel; above all it is disturbing. Fuseli knows that fairies are wicked, or at least mischievous; he has also discovered that there is generally a kind of dangerous stupidity in them. His *Queen Mab* has something indefinably degenerate about her; her laughter is that of a demi-imbecile, her gaze is fixed and malicious. Some children are like that. . . .

On Fuseli's *Titania and Bottom*:

THE BITTER and sarcastic Zuricher infused into these images of liberty and poetry his own malice and venom, but also his latent schizophrenia, his escapism, everything that he lacked. The fairy queen is not so much in love with human stupidity as playing with it. . . . And yet one guesses that Fuseli is not altogether comfortable. Does this come from seeing so many ambiguous figures emerging from his imagination? Does it not come rather from gazing too long at these naked adolescent girls, with whom he feels vaguely in love, and who are his unsubstantial paramours?

(Edmond Jaloux, *Johann-Heinrich Füssli*, article in *Le mois suisse*, April 1942—translated from the French)

'This inexplicable note of the sinister and terrible'

THE ORIGIN of such dreams lies in the dark chambers of the mind. These are unexplored, and are more curious than things seen. The evidence for it . . . comes in the drawings of Fuseli, who, in them, attempted something that no one else has done. There is a body of his drawings, which, taken together, as they never have been, and never can be, would constitute the only witnesses. They may be few in number among his huge output of drawings, but they could be collected, none the less, into a series. We should then have a set of drawings, two or three dozens, it may be, which could be published, and a hundred, perhaps, or more, probably several hundreds, unpublishable, which would compare in quality of horror, but in nothing else, with the '*Caprichios*' of Goya.

(Sacheverell Sitwell, Splendours and Miseries, 1943)

5

OPINIONS ON FUSELI AS A MAN OF LETTERS, SCHOLAR AND STYLIST

'*The most extraordinary critic that I have ever heard of*'

I CALLED him an extraordinary person, and such he is. For he is not only versed in Homer, and accurate in his knowledge of the Greek to a degree that entitles him to that appellation; but, though a foreigner, is a perfect master of our language, and has exquisite taste in English poetry.

(Cowper in a letter of 4 July 1786 to Rev. Walter Bagot, with
reference to the help Fuseli gave him in the translation of Homer)

His many-sidedness

IT IS a singular spectacle, for those who love to contemplate the progress of the social arts, to observe a foreigner, who has raised himself to high rank in the arduous profession of a painter, correcting, and thanked for correcting, the chief poet of England, in his English version of Homer.

(Hayley, Life of Cowper, 1803)

West recommends Fuseli as Keeper to George III

THE KING . . . next took up that (paper) which had the name of *Fuseli* as *Keeper*. He advanced towards West and said, Fuseli is a man of genius.—West replied, He is a very able man.—The King then went towards the window and took a pen and coming back to West said, 'You think Fuseli is an able man.' West replied, He is not only an able man in his profession, but He is distinguished as a Literary Character, and known to all Europe. —The King then eagerly went to the table and signed it.

(Farington Diary, 28 December 1804)

The style of Fuseli's 'Remarks on Rousseau'

COME WE now to the style, which we frankly own is new and original; yet it is such as we hope will have but few imitators; and we confess also, that on some occasions we do not understand the writer, and are inclined to suspect he does not always understand himself. It is turgid with scarce an idea to support its swelling; it is figurative, after which [sic] no imagination can paint ideas. . . . Besides the above qualities, the style is extremely vulgar in many parts, devoid of every drop of humour which might give it relish; and sometimes libertine without one spark of wit to give it lustre: in fact, the subject on which this production pretends to treat, is not understood; it is one of those productions which speak the decline of literature in this age; it deserves not to be read in the present, and will never be heard of in the future.

(Political Register, May 1767)

The 'Edinburgh Review' on Fuseli's 'Lectures' (*July 1803*)

OUR AUTHOR has the peculiar talent of diffusing around the most commonplace ideas which a man can conceive such a glare of absurd expression, and of daubing over his sketches with such a violent and fantastic colouring, that it frequently requires a little reflection to recognise the most familiar object. . . . He has removed the meaning beyond the reach of *all*, by composing in such an unintelligible jargon, as no reader can hope to decipher, without an extravagant waste of time and attention.

83

Lawrence on Fuseli's style as a writer

LAWRENCE REMARKED that Fuseli's letters were written in an *Epigrammatic style,* in which much sense and knowledge was condensed in a small compass, That His manner of writing was not agreeable to those authors and readers of the present day, who are captivated by a stile woven out and very different from his. Were His *matter* expressed in the manner which suits their taste, they would be enchanted by it.

(*Farington Diary,* 13 February 1805)

Fuseli's prose style

NO UNIMAGINATIVE dauber ever hid his ignorance of anatomy under a redundancy of drapery more effectually than this remarkable man could veil ordinary thoughts under colossal words.

(1829—Allan Cunningham, in his *Life of Fuseli*)

Sidney Colvin on Fuseli's prose style

IT IS grandiloquent, it is Johnsonian; it errs by what I have called the gymnastic procedure of a pen conscious of insecurity, and determined to prove its footing by feats; but it is astonishing for a foreigner, and always personal, piquant and stirring.

(*Portfolio,* 1873)

Mrs. Mary Heaton on Fuseli's prose style (*1879*)

HIS STYLE of writing . . . was as exaggerated and distorted as his art. He could not express his thoughts in simple language, and tried to make them appear profound by involving them in dark speech. Much of his art criticism, when analysed, is found to be contradictory nonsense.

PART ONE

PERSONALITY

AND LITERARY ACTIVITY

OF THE

YOUNGER FUSELI

UP TO 1779

SECTION ONE

THE DISCIPLE OF BODMER[1]
AND THE EARLY HOPE
OF THE GERMAN LITERARY REVOLUTION

Bodmer in Retrospect

. . . a man whose aspect and manners were those of a patriarch; who, whether he be considered as a politician, historian, philosopher, critic or poet, deserved the most eager attention, and generally commanded the concourse of all whom emulation, taste or curiosity prompted to go in quest of excellence; a man whom the voice of his own country styled 'the Father of Youth' and that of all Germany 'the Restorer of Language and of Taste'.

> (*Analytical Review*, February 1790, review of Coxe's Travels in Switzerland, signed R. R.—VI, p. 154)

Gleim—the False and the True Friends of Klopstock

Fuseli writes to Bodmer from Berlin in March 1763 of his literary encounters in travelling through Germany.

FROM LEIPZIG we went direct to Magdeburg, meeting Gleim[2]

---

[1] For Bodmer and his importance, *see* Introduction, p. 15.

[2] *Ludwig Gleim* ('Vater' Gleim), 1719–1803, an Anacreontic poet and author of the *Preussische Kriegslieder von einem Grenadier* (1758); his 'office' was that of secretary to the cathedral of Halberstadt, where he also had the title of a canon.

and his niece at the house of Herr Bachmann, a nephew of Herr Sulzer. *Quantum diversus ab illo*, as I had imagined him from his works. I had pictured to myself a simple, nonchalant person, well-versed, indeed, at least theoretically, in voluptuousness, yet not entirely disrelishing the grave and severer aspects of life and art; and what I found was something midway between a well-nourished canon of Halberstadt, a lieutenant in the Prussian army and a squire of dames. I have never seen a face in which the most contradictory passions of the heart express themselves in such rapid succession, in which altogether such diverse violent emotions can dwell without utterly disfiguring the man. He has nevertheless the air of a man of discernment, and his taste is, so far as his own verse goes, admirable. But the curious figure he cuts, when he sets up in all earnestness for a critic of epic poetry and such things, for a judge of learning and for an arbitrator in the dispute between Uz and Wieland[1]—that really is worth hearing. He is, as everybody knows, a great friend of Klopstock's, and praises him, because he thinks it good policy to do so. . . . In a word, I cannot make head or tail of the man; as the poet of the *Songs of War* he commands my esteem. I took him to task for Klopstock's and his own remissness in writing, but he replied that he has an office to attend to, and that Herr Klopstock declares he has answered one letter. Rousseau is, in his opinion, a scatter-brain. 'I would undertake to turn out whole piles of trashy volumes like the *Nouvelle Héloise* every year without thinking about it', he said—if he had not an office to attend to. You cannot possibly imagine how many great projects this man would execute, if he had not an office to attend to. The fox spoke of you with tenderness and veneration; for Herr Gessner[2]

[1] *C. M. Wieland* (1733–1813) had as a disciple of the austere Bodmer in 1757 in his *Sentiments of a Christian* denounced the immorality of *Peter Uz* (1720–96), a friend of Gleim's and like him an Anacreontic poet. Shortly afterwards Wieland himself was to make himself notorious as an immoral poet with works very much more provocative than the harmless verses of Uz, thereby grievously disappointing and shocking the patriarch Bodmer.

[2] *Salomon Gessner* (1730–88), Zurich poet and painter, popular all over Europe through his *Idylls* and his *Death of Abel*. He was Fuseli's godfather. Fuseli regarded him as not much better than Gleim (*see below*, pp. 89 and 110–11).

he then and there wrote a little poem for me to deliver to him.
. . . But do you think, beloved Bodmer, that I could go and
stay away from my native country, perhaps for a long time,
without having once at least seen him who is near by—for what,
after all, are half a dozen leagues or so[1]?—him whom I long for
for his own sake, for your sake, for my sake, more than a bride-
groom for his bride? My beloved Klopstock, I will yet kiss you,
I will tell you with what love Bodmer loves you, and how I love
you—I will prove to you, if a sincere heart, and a tongue utter-
ing the feelings of that heart, can prove it, that those are not
your best friends, nor the worthiest of you, whom you have
known so far, that, unknown to you, there are hearts beating
for you worth more than the lot of them.

(30 March 1763—Muschg, pp. 61–4, German)

Salomon Gessner, Poet, Painter and Godfather *(1730–88)*

MR. GESSNER'S talent was to work in small: a decayed willow
overshadowing a rivulet, a brook glittering or lost beneath
luxuriant herbage, a mouldering cottage—whatever is strictly
called rural, represented in diminutive forms, was the province
of Gessner; but an attempt to treat in large the grander scenes
of nature on his plan, would much resemble an attempt to cross
the Atlantic in a river-boat. In oil he never painted; what harmony, what glow could be imparted to water-colours, he
obtained. His figures, if they exceed the size of an inch, or (for
that was his rage) pretend to something ideal, are always
execrable. . . . His address . . . unless a rival was praised . . .,
was not unlike that of Goldsmith.

> (*Analytical Review*, February 1790, review of Coxe's Travels in
> Switzerland, signed R. R.—VI, p. 155)

[1] Klopstock was at this time staying at Quedlinburg, his native town, over
thirty miles from Magdeburg, and about a hundred miles from Berlin,
where Fuseli wrote the present letter. Just a year later, in March 1764,
Fuseli broke his journey to England in Quedlinburg for three days, in order
to meet Klopstock.

Tragedy as it should be—hearsay accounts of Klopstock's 'Solomon'

YOU CAN form some idea of how tragic his 'Solomon'[1] is, when I tell you that he makes Solomon sacrifice a child to Moloch, and has a scene between him and the mother of the sacrificed child. Pharaoh's daughter is also one of the characters. Nothing pathetic and terrifying that has so far been known on the stage, they say, can equal the solemn, infernal horror of the sacrifice scene; the dismal, gruesome chanting of the priest of Moloch is said, like the arguments of the adversary with whom Dr. Luther had to contend, almost to sing the soul of the petrified listener, or rather spectator, out of his body. . . . I have found a letter here from Bodmer; he wanted to write to me again before I go to England! My God! he would like me to embrace Klopstock for him first. . . . For the rest, he reminds me once more for the last time of my fatherland, to lacerate my poor heart yet further. . . .

(Letter to Lavater, 26 October 1763—Federmann, p. 121, German)

Klopstock re-estimated after a year and a half in England

SINCE I HAVE been in England, German literature has ceased to exist for me. Klopstock wrote to me from Copenhagen . . . asking me for some drawings for his *Messiah*; I sent the drawings to his bookseller, and left his letter unanswered. I still look on him as the giant of the century, and Immortality has set her stamp on his Odes more than on anything else of that kind acclaimed as masterpieces by the ancients or moderns. In his *Messiah* he set out with the spirit of Homer: invention is the soul of his work, and the sublimest of all inventions in plan, episodes, figures, expression. But a religion—the most grotesque of all religions, quintessenced schoolman's jargon, the court idiom of

[1] Klopstock's *Salomo* (1764) is notoriously dull.

the pietist's heaven, the rigmarole of a brain fuddled with apocalyptic weeping, bursting bubbles with no more meaning than their own pop—these have inlaid the marble pyramid with pasteboard, with sugarloaf paper and with the jumbled tawdry of the tiring-house. That Homer degraded his Zeus to a king, Milton Jehovah to a pedagogue, Klopstock the Father to a prosecutor, inquisitor and judge, is not what exasperates me. The imagination of the Finite succumbs to Infinity, and whatever a sinner like Warburton may snivel, it is neither from Homer, Virgil nor Milton that we have to learn morality, politics and religion. Delight the imagination, paint mankind as they are, and the gods as best you can, seems to be the most universal law of epic poetry. But to seize hold of religion and murder the action of the entire work with it, to cripple Nature with Art and, when you possess the tongues of angels, every flight of fancy, every manly or tender feeling, every lofty image, the thunder of the Greeks, the persuasiveness of the Romans, the hues of Nature, to go and barter them all for Cramer's[1] mystical *sistrum*,[2] his tinkling handbell, for the lip-smacking of a Parisian *abbé*, for the lascivious allurements of Mohammedan houris, for the language of *terra Australis*—ἑκατόμβοι ἐννεαβοίων[3]—that is enough to make me despise the poet, if he were any other than Klopstock.

> (12–15 November 1765, Letter to Dälliker—Muschg, pp. 111–12, German)

---

[1] *Johann Andreas Cramer* (1723–88), Klopstock's great friend, pietistic poet and theology professor at Kiel.
[2] *Sistrum*—jingling instrument, used by ancient Egyptians in rites of Isis.
[3] 'Nine oxen for a hundred'—Homer.

The thirty-four-year-old Fuseli on Klopstock

'The principal beauties of poetry spring
from the force or elegance of its images.
. . . It is by the frequency and degree of
these beauties principally that an original
genius is distinguished. Metaphors are to
him what the eagle was to Jupiter or the
doves to Venus, symbols of his divinity,
and sure indications of majesty and beauty'
(from an anonymous article entitled *Critical Remarks on Genius* in the *Universal
Museum* for December 1768, possibly by
Fuseli)

THE GREATER part of Klopstock's sublime devotional odes may
God seize, and nearly all those on Teutonic mythology the
Devil. It is a lie, that the *longest* of David's psalms is poetic, and
that just for the very reason on which Klopstock bases the supposed superiority of his own poetry, and of Germany poetry in
general, to English poetry[1]: that is to say, because most of the
psalms derive from a private emotion, a locality or some other
sentimental fad. Who dares to tell me that such lenten stuff as
the 119th psalm or one of Klopstock's own eternal variations on
the invocation 'Lord! Lord!' is poetry? *Images*—the images
which you (not you personally, but the Germans as a whole,
and the Swiss too) despise, the images you cannot invent—are

---

[1] In his ode *Wir und sie* (1766) Klopstock, comparing English poetry with
German, had written:

> When did their bard fully touch the heart?
> It is only in images that he weeps.

The theme occurs also in *Die beiden Musen* (1752) and *Unsere Sprache* (1767).
It is to these poems that Blake refers in his Rabelaisian verses 'When Klopstock England defied . . .', and he certainly knew nothing more about them
than what he had heard from Fuseli in conversation. Swinburne's interpretation of the Klopstock lines, as occasioned by Hayley's Felpham readings
from the *Messiah* after Klopstock's death, in 1803, must be rejected. This is
material to the dating of the poems in the Rossetti manuscript.

what make Homer the Father of all poetry, Homer and also the Song of Solomon and the Book of Job; they it is that authenticate the value of emotions. A genuine, universal, vital emotion streams through the medium of an appropriate image into all hearts, while a spurious, merely local and private emotion will please only a few, and those only in special places and periods, and must bewilder and benumb everybody else. . . . The *facultas lacrimatoria*, that beauty-patch of German poetry from the heights of Klopstock down to Dusch,[1] the eyes turned to telescopes, the ineffable looks and all such theological hermaphroditism are more transitory rags than the rag-paper they are printed on.

(Letter to Lavater, March 1775—Muschg, pp. 171–3, German)

Klopstock in Retrospect

. . . since the lapse of so many ages the human race has acknowledged but three names whose claim to the epic palm has not been disputed. If, after the name of Milton, another were to be produced, perhaps that of the German, Klopstock, author of the *Messiah*, might merit our attention. He began, indeed, young; but the vigour of his life was dedicated to incessant meditation of his design, and his riper years were consumed in giving it the utmost polish; from thence, perhaps, and the subtilisation of sentiments arise its greatest blemishes. Had he contented himself to stand on the broad base of universal feelings, had he less refined language, such is his sublimity of conception, such the fertility of his invention, such the majesty and pathos of his diction, that his work, as it is nearest in extent and metre to the Iliad, would perhaps have been next to it in merit. He is unknown in this country . . .; for what idea can be obtained of his powers from an execrable prose translation, which can scarcely be said to convey the skeleton of his plan? But as a taste for German literature and German poetry is gaining ground amongst us, we presume that the communication of

[1] *Johann Jakob Dusch* (1725–87), eclectic poet of very little value.

a metrical translation of one or two fragments . . . will . . . be
highly acceptable to our readers. . . .

> (*Analytical Review*, June 1792, review of Cumberland's *Calvary*, signed
> R. R.—XIII, p. 130; the 370-odd lines of Fuseli's own trans-
> lation from the 2nd and 4th Books of the *Messiah* in Miltonic
> blank verse which follow have little to commend them)

The Genius of Goethe

THE MERIT of invention . . . Goethe enjoys in common with
many of his contemporaries. The distinguishing excellence of
this celebrated writer is the display of exquisite enthusiastic
passion. His pencil, dipped in the bow of heaven, sometimes
exhibits a strength and brilliancy of colouring that dazzles 'the
mind's eye'; and sometimes . . . displays the softest shade, the
most delicate and tender touches. . . .

Goethe is entitled to no vulgar merit for the judgment which
he displays in the choice of his subjects: aware that his powers
are most successfully applied when the softer sensibilities of our
nature are to be excited, when tenderness and pity are to be
called forth, he avoids all intricacy of plot, and generally selects
for the foundation of his drama some simple and affecting story
of domestic life, which may come home to the bosom of us all.

> (*Analytical Review*, August 1798, reviews of Goethe's *Stella* and *Cla-
> vigo* in English translation, signed L. L.—XXVIII, pp. 170, 175)

There is some evidence against these reviews being by Fuseli, as six
other reviews in the same volume signed L. L.—a signature appear-
ing now for the first time—none of them look like Fuseli's work and
some of them, e.g. *Proposals for Supplying London with Bread* and *Defence of Sunday Schools*, are quite certainly not by him. The style of the
first excerpt, however, very strongly recalls him, and the 'pencil
dipped in the rainbow' is one of his favourite phrases.

An eminent German contemporary—Goethe's friend, the Storm-and-Stress poet, Frederick Leopold Count Stolberg (1750–1819)

A MILD aristocrat in politics, but indebted for his rank to the feudal system, he is submissive to established forms; the baron frequently overreaches the man; the inconvenience or danger which might result from a rigid pursuit of truth checks the career of his philosophy, and futurity is sacrificed to the moment in his grasp. His poetry, often cold rapture, sparkles more in his prose than in his verse. . . . As an amateur of the fine arts it is enough to say that he too often follows and generally resembles his predecessors.[1]

(*Analytical Review*, December 1797, review of Stolberg's *Travels*, signed Z. Z.—XXVI, p. 545)

---

[1] Three years after the appearance of this review Stolberg went over to Catholicism. The account Fuseli here gives of him fails to do justice to the forcefulness of his personality. Stolberg is one of the very few personal links between the *Storm and Stress* of the early seventies and German Romanticism proper in the late nineties and after 1800.

LAVATER'S PASSIONATE FRIEND
—THE *COMPLAINTS*

Johann Kaspar Lavater (1741–1801), only a few months younger than Fuseli and like him a native of Zurich, had a great reputation throughout Western Europe during his lifetime for his pietistic mystical writings and for his work on physiognomy. He and Fuseli must early have become friends as fellow students under Bodmer. In autumn 1762, together with another student, Felix Hess, they successfully exposed and brought to justice the corrupt magistrate Grebel with their bold pamphlet *Der ungerechte Landvogt*. Their conduct was, however, condemned as incorrect by the civic authorities of Zurich and they were advised to absent themselves from the country for a time. Bodmer arranged for them to accompany Sulzer to Prussia in February 1763. Little over a year later Lavater and Hess went back to Zurich, while Fuseli travelled instead to London. He and Lavater did not meet again till October 1778, when Fuseli revisited his native town for the first and last time.

Separation from Lavater—Fuseli's 'Complaints'

Friend of my soul,

I am too weak and too timid to describe to you the fear of my soul, which has made the two days I have been separated from you the most terrible of my life, days full of unfeeling tearlessness. At the various posting-houses, and especially at Prenzlau, I hastily scribbled down what I had thought and sighed in hours of weeping and of more human sorrow, and this I will send you with a future letter. Of my little journey I will say no more to you than that Thursday night was, physically and spiritually, the most fearful I have ever been through—I could quite certainly not have endured another like it without taking serious harm. The north-east wind was raging, hail and rain strove with one another for the mastery, and three drunken students from Greifswald blasphemed at my side against God and all decorum and modesty. . . . Beloved of my soul, how I love you! How I kiss you! My God, my God! when shall I see you again, when shall I once more lay my hand in your hand, my breast against your breast, against that truest of all hearts, and be in bliss—a life such as you desire of me shall at least make me worthy of it, I cannot go on. . . . [erasures] . . . yet. . . .

(From a letter written towards the end of Fuseli's journey to Berlin, 16 October 1763)

Four weeks later—Berlin, 13 November 1763

I SUMMON you yourself to be the judge, whether your heart surges towards me as mine, God is my witness, does towards you —but that is my destiny, and my tears were not made to entice yours from your eyes. I lay down my pen for a moment to embrace your picture and kiss it through and through. . . . You ask for my 'Complaints'—I may not send them, for they are only for the Lavater with whom I slept, and I fear they might fall into the hands of him who wrote the two letters I am now answering. What does your sedateness want with words that burn? With a torrent that whirls all things before it? With periods that are naught but sighs? And with prophecies? It cannot be confined in metre, it could not even be confined in rhythmical prose[1]—and yet you shall have it. Then your first glance at it, one single line, will convince you that my reason for withholding it has not been that I am only now busy at it, with a pipe in my mouth and by the steady light of a lamp,

---

[1] The main body of the *Complaints* is in rhythmical prose, but two of the three sections conclude with a short passage of blank verse.

botching together 'Meditations during my Journey' . . . But my brain catches fire, I grow too excited, I must stop here—O you who sleep alone now—dream of me—O that my soul might meet with yours, as through the lattice the hand of the Shulamite met with her dew-drenched beloved.

Three weeks later—7 December 1763

. . . on Friday I shall be sending to you the *Complaints and Fantasies* of a soul in love, but not ignobly in love. . . .

(Muschg, pp. 70–1, 73, 75–6, 80, 88, German)

Passages from the 'Complaints'

Written 14–16 October 1763, on the journey to Berlin, after leaving Lavater at Barth, between Stralsund and Rostock, on the Baltic coast. The title, '*Klagen*', appears to have been suggested by the *Complaints* of Young's *Night Thoughts*.

I

O FATHERLAND! Arms outstretched in vain of him who begot me! O kisses and smiles of those who lay at one breast with me! O grave of her beneath whose heart I lay immortal, who clasped my hand last of the hands of her children, sighing 'My son, be virtuous!',[1] and pressing it against her dying eyes, sealed on them my bond to virtue! Scattered vaults of my brothers and sisters who fled from life when it had scarce begun to bud! O all you, whom my soul found like itself and loves! O mountains of freedom! valleys of peace! O sweet fountains of repose! Fatherland! What offence had you given, that my soul fled from you with but few tears, and now, dissolved in backward-lamenting grief, lavishes the hallowed sighs of homesickness, else awakened in the bosoms of your children by you alone, upon a chilly sky of

[1] Fuseli was eighteen years old when his mother died, 11 April 1759.

slavery, a land as comfortless as the waves that surround it,[1] as hazardous as the watery paths that fringe its coast!

Ah! when I left you, paternal land, he was at my side,[2] he in whom I found united all things I had lost in you! Through him this mournful northern sky was brightened to the serenity of your skies; through him the swampy land of serfdom became for me as the sunlit summit of your mountains, where never slave set foot, and around him were assembled for me the greatest sons, the guardian spirits of the fatherland. But now they, like you, are vanished—vanished for ever are for me those golden days of diligent content, of care-free peace! Banished am I, banished for ever from that cottage,[3] the chosen temple of purest friendship! Gone are they, gone for ever from me, those nights no mortal speech can shadow forth! Rent is that veil of hallowed feelings, that veil no imagination as yet could lift! Gone for ever are they—and I——

II

FRIEND of my soul! The vanished hours of that early life we spent hand in hand passed then as in a vision before my eyes, ushered by the guardian spirit. Those blessed hours of our growing friendship, when I was everything to you; when, in my lap, you unfolded your first great thoughts and were called my dove! The mighty hours, wherein I learnt at your side that virtue is not just an idea, that the bliss of drying the tears of the unfortunate is more than a poet's dream, that fatherland and freedom are not evanescent echoes! But alas! they also passed before my eyes, those hours which I slumbered away, unworthy

[1] *Barth*, where Fuseli had left Lavater, is situated on what might be regarded as a peninsula. The land Fuseli here speaks of is Prussia.

[2] Eight months previously, in February 1763, Fuseli and Lavater had left Zurich together, because of the disfavour they had involved themselves in with the authorities by their public attack on the corrupt magistrate Grebel.

[3] From about the beginning of May till the middle of October Fuseli and Lavater had been the guests of the liberal theologian Spalding in his cottage at Barth. This was perhaps the happiest period in Fuseli's life.

of you,[1] in the lap of those slothful pleasures fools call bliss; when I sought to satiate the ever-striving conscious mind in me with garbage! Yet were you then once more in my arms, my Lavater! Yet was it granted me, in those blessed days that made perfect your soul, to look upon your example and to remember that I, like you, am a necessary link in the chain of created beings, like you, immortal! O remembrance!—strife of despondency, of passions, of love, of hope, of shame! What determination, what resolutions assailed my soul at every gaze upon you! It was decided! *Then* I sank upon your countenance! *Then* I laid my hand upon your bared, softly-beating heart—and with uplifted, glistening eye swore upon that altar, by the tranquillity poured down upon you in each gentle breath, by the life you had led all those years without occasion for remorse, by all things still to come, that I would be like *you*!

III

LAVATER, you will die before your friend![2] that is why I have been torn away from you—it is better for *me* and for *you* that I should have been far away from you, when your eye grows dim and you become an angel.

O you, whom my soul loves, hear me—I will call up your life before your eyes. How swiftly the few days will fleet by that you have still to pass in Spalding's house[3]—days in which you think

---

[1] Up to this point Fuseli had encouraged Lavater to play the part of a great moral mentor to him, and Lavater to the last continued to try to play this part, thereby provoking the violent resentment of Fuseli, who had since become very much tougher and robuster.

[2] Actually Lavater died in 1801, as a result of a wound received in 1799 from the French soldiery, when he was ministering to the wounded, at the capture of Zurich. The following utterance of Fuseli's later years, recorded by Knowles, is of interest in connexion with this passage of the *Complaints:* 'You know I hate superstition. When I was in Switzerland (1778–9), talking with Lavater upon the appearance of the spirit after death, it was agreed between us, that if it were allowed by the Deity to visit earth, the first who died should appear to the other; my friend was the most scrupulous man in existence with regard to his word; he is dead, and I have not seen him' (Knowles, I, p. 379).

[3] Spalding's house: *see above*, p. 99, footnote 5.

the thoughts of years! Already you are in the arms of your parents, your sisters and brothers, already you have embraced your happy Hess![1] Your parents grow young again, your brothers and sisters and your friend are a blessing to the fatherland, an honour to their walk in life—you are the pillar of virtue and religion; young in years, aged in wisdom, with a body that is almost soul, a soul that sacrifices itself in every thought to God and its duties; in the arms of the highest conjugal and filial love; blessed by the old, called upon for council by the man of ripe years; listened to with emulous attention by the youth, welcomed with smiles by the child; extolled by the poor, whose sides you have warmed, and by the rich, whose hearts you have opened; recompensed with good deeds by the sick man whom you have restored to his home, thereby restoring both his home and him to the fatherland; silently feared by the free-thinker; looked upon as a rescuer by the honest doubter; rewarded by the dying man with his last smile—the champion of the cause of God and humanity from the height of the temple and from the seat of justice, you will begin to give back to the land of freedom her Golden Age.

But, when a few years have heaped these honours on your head—then think of him who, himself not destined to gaze upon such blessings, unknown and solitary, the tears for his Lavater yet undried upon his cheeks, wanders shade-like in a far-off land—and remember that nothing is permanent under the sun, not even virtue! Then in my fear-struck ears will resound the weeping and wailing of my fatherland! I shall have heard the immense sigh that you will heave for your Fuseli, a sigh that not even the untold sighs of those you love, not even those of Her, your chosen mate, will swallow up! Then may my life have been so spent that I may be worthy to follow the summons you will utter, telling me my vocation here below is at an end and that the moment you expire, I too must die! Perchance one single youth will walk behind my bier, shedding a tear for him who, alas! did but stumble before him along the path of virtue. Let

---

[1] Johann Jakob Hess (1741–1828), elder brother of the Felix Hess who had accompanied Fuseli and Lavater on their journeys and who was at this time still at Barth with Lavater (*see above*, p. 26).

all else in my life be forgotten for posterity, let it be extinguished like the dying tone of the unnoticed funeral knell, when dust is returned to dust! Let it fade like the rosemary strewn upon my bier!

REMEMBER, when in the fond innocent embraces of your betrothed you begin to be her highest bliss and she lives more in you than in herself; remember, some hallowed evening of love, when, her tender hand in your hand, her swelling bosom upon your breast, seated upon your lap, languid with kisses, leaning close against you, she loses herself in contemplation of her future life with you—O then, remember this paper, and him who once loved you, even as she does, your prophetic friend who was torn away from you—and lay it with a tear of love in Her hand! And you! loveliest among women! daughter of the gracious Heavens! Holy girl! read this paper, the record of the highest feelings of a mortal man! and consider, in your rapture, (the thought is harsh, indeed, yet compassionate) 'that this life is a river and its joy a dream! consider that he who loved your friend as you do was torn away from him! and keep guard over your soul, lest you lose it to him *utterly*! For he, whose days are as the years of other men, has not many years to live upon this earth, and him, who has traversed the arena of life from its starting-point to its goal, the grave, him neither the beseeching eyes of beauty nor the soft tear of love can withhold from out-soaring that goal!'

Lavater's betrothal—Fuseli introduces himself to the bride

Madam,

This is the hand of him who wrote the 'Complaints'; then it shook with affliction, now it trembles with joy. The heart that found you and preferred you testifies to your worth. There is perhaps no need for me to beg you to instruct him, or him to learn of you, that this is not yet the land of disembodied spirits and that there is a voluptuousness consonant with virtue. I enjoin you to kiss him twice each day *from me*. My soul will often hover about the lips of both—would it were granted to my hand to embrace both of you! I am with respect and pure friendship, Madam,

Your Fuseli.

(Enclosed with a letter to Lavater from Lyons, 10 May 1766—Muschg, pp. 133–4, German)

Two years later (6 May 1768) Fuseli concludes a letter to Lavater with the following Asclepiadean strophe, which has been picked out as one of the best specimens of his lyric:

> *Jeden glühenden Kuss auf angebeteter*
> *Lippen glühenden Kuss, auf die ersterbenden*
> *Rosenhügel der Lust einsam gesiegelt—gäb*
> *Ich für deine Umarmung hin!*

(Muschg, p. 145)

These verses can be roughly rendered in English thus:

> *Each tempestuous kiss printed on lips I adore,*
> *Flushed to kiss in response, printed on swooning sweet*
> *Rosy knolls of desire, secretly ravished—all*
> *Freely I'd part with for your embrace!*

SECTION THREE

FROM SWITZERLAND TO ENGLAND —EXPERIENCES AND IMPRESSIONS OF A SEMI-VOLUNTARY EXILE

Knowles, wishing possibly to pay Fuseli the handsomest compliment he can conceive of, says that he was 'in his notions and habits . . . completely an Englishman'. This is not corroborated by any other of Fuseli's English acquaintances. To them all he was always 'the wild little hectoring Swiss-man'; it is even recorded of him that he 'held the English as a nation in undisguised contempt, and openly declared that they were good for nothing but to use bad language and drink beer' (George Richmond in *The Richmond Papers*). In his own crusty way he must, however, have loved England and been proud of it as the land of his adoption. When he arrived in London in March 1764, he found something that he wanted and that neither Switzerland nor Germany had been able to supply—it was a kind of second birth to him; and although he was later to prolong the delicious Roman episode year after year, beyond all practical necessities, he never forgot that he belonged to England and was bound sooner or later to go back to London. Migration to England meant to him all along, however, something very different from being assimilated to and absorbed in a congenial element, abandoning himself to an elective affinity. He was as much of a square peg in a round hole, as much at daggers drawn with his whole environment in London as he ever had been or would have been in Zurich—only with the difference that in London he had all the excuses of the foreigner and the artist for his eccentricity; in London there was nobody who had known him as a child, trying to make him conform. Whenever he came in contact with his early associates, they promptly presumed on their old familiarity to bring disciplinary pressure to bear upon him; his letters to Lavater and what he says of his short return to Zurich in 1778–9 show how savagely he resented this, and how powerless he was to prevent it. The only course for him was to keep out of reach of his compatriots, and to retain for himself the licence of the sympathetically tolerated outsider, as it had been accorded to him in England, and as he would scarcely have found it in any other country. England gave him independence, freedom from supervision, a clean slate, a fresh start, a vast and infinitely varied field for observation and activity—all things he needed very much more than a home away from home. The first months were hard. Excellently though he had acquired the English language, he was soon to find out that his pronunciation of it was faulty—and faulty it remained to the last. 'In a gloomy state of mind he sallied forth', Knowles records of his first days in London, 'in search of a post-office. . . . Meeting with a vulgar fellow, he inquired his way to the post-office in a broad German pronunciation. This produced only a horse-laugh from the man. The forlorn situation in which he was placed burst on his mind—he stamped with his foot, while tears trickled down his cheeks.' But he soon found his feet. Sometimes, indeed, he confesses, 'a tremor of homesickness assails me; then an even gloomier sky and denser clouds cover Britannia' (Letter to Dalliker, November 1765). But on the whole he rejoices in his new independence and the self-confidence it gives him. He grows tougher and when next he is exposed to the pressure of Zurich standards, amongst the Swiss colony in Lyons, he keeps his end up by 'affecting the Englishman' (*see* letter to Lavater, 12 April 1766).

Switzerland judged by the principles of Rousseau

O ROUSSEAU, if a state as small and confined as my fatherland so loudly confirms the melancholy truth of your theories, what will the royal capitals of earth do? How my soul marvels at this man. . . .

> (Letter to Bodmer, Berlin, 2 February 1764—Muschg, p. 99, German)

SWITZERLAND IS a scarcely visible speck of earth; if one is to see it, it must shine like a diamond, and it is dirty, God knows. The Swiss and the canton to which I owe my birth have fallen, and —as I see it—fallen to the very lowest dregs. Honour has given way to interest, virtue to expediency, religion to charlatanism and craziness, and what is worst of all, to the meanest, most bourgeois and stinking varieties of all these pests. It is not for you to compete with the Britons or with France in sinfulness. A councillor and citizen who weeps or turns pale at the hanging or banishment of a murderer or thief, just because he himself wears a collar instead of a rope; a crew of citizens, shopkeepers and merchants preying on the state with unparalleled frenzy, gluttony, debauchery, *bourgeoisgentilhommie*, senselessness and tinsel; a gang of parsons and professors, doctors and bureaucrats, who have established a covenant of salt[1] for ever with ignorance, damning Jesus Christ and Rousseau to rave with Calvin, as their adversaries do with Loyola; who piss wine when they should see water; in whose eyes one reads '*Noli me tangere*'; and an etc. etc., which I cannot see to the tail-end of—that is all there is inhabiting my fatherland—I can write no more—damn the pen!

(Letter to Lavater, London, 6 December 1765—Muschg, p. 118, German)

Swiss shortcomings looked back upon thirty years later

HER FANCY, cradled by Ossian, had peopled the primaeval scenery of Alps and rocks and glaciers with a primitive race, if not of giants, at least of patriarchal form and manners; and she was offended at finding the vices and crimes, from which she had sought an asylum, though in diminished shapes, meet her again. The expectations of Romantic fancy, like those of ignorance, are indefinite; the fair author might have been taught by recollection that the virtue of Little Switzerland, no more than that of Greece, could have long continued pure amid the inroads of colossal neighbouring corruption, and the consequent shock of domestic interests. . . . Without attempting to deny constitutional defects, or to palliate acts of oppression in the governments of Switzerland over the mass of native peasantry or

[1] Cp. Numbers xviii. 19: 'It is a covenant of salt for ever, before the Lord, unto thee and to thy seed with thee.'

the inhabitants of conquered provinces, it may be asked whether the blessings they enjoyed in their former situation[1] did not overbalance the restraints they unjustly suffered, or even render them objects of envy to the neighbouring nations. None that during the former governments of France and Italy entered the Helvetic territory from Lombardy, Alsace or Swabia will be hardy or ignorant enough to deny this.

(*Analytical Review*, June 1798, review of Helen Maria Williams' *Tour in Switzerland*, signed R. R.—XXVII, pp. 561–2)

From Fuseli's first letter to Switzerland after he has been four months in London

Disturbed at not having heard from him, Lavater has written in the name of all his Zurich friends and tried to find out, amongst other things, whether Fuseli needs financial help. The first half of Fuseli's reply—30 July 1764—is written in English.

BEHOLD I know Your thoughts, for Ye say:
'The mountain falling comes to naught; are the consolations of God small with Thee? Where is the house of the Prince? Is there any secret thing with Thee?' I know You ask me, therefore my soul chooses silence and death rather than writing. Not that I fear your questions, for I am clean without transgression, I am innocent; neither is there any iniquity in me. But I am made to possess months of vanity and wearisome nights are appointed to me. My days are swifter than a weaver's shuttle, and are spent without hope. Surely there is a vein of silver and a gold-stream, I do not know whence! But did I ever say, Bring unto me? Or give me of your substance? I also could speak as You do, if your soul were in my soul's stead; I could heap up money against You as You do, were we changed place! But I would do more! I would strengthen You with my mouth and the moving of my lips should assuage your grief. But now You all hold each other's arm and kiss and say: He must write first, for he is alone, and we

---

[1] That is to say, before the French invasion.

are many—even the fat ones say thus,[1] they whom my soul weeps for every moment.[2]

(Federmann, p. 132)

One Year in London

FOR A MAN with a soul the theatre in London is alone worth the journey; and although there are immense numbers here who are blind with their eyes open, there are also persons one could not so easily come across anywhere else. German literature and I have so little to do with one another that I don't even know anything about Klopstock, and although I have not yet found any reason to think that there is a better poet now living, the blasphemous theology he has imbibed from Cramer[3] and the unnatural subtlety of the sentiments of his personages have made the greater part of his last six cantos[4] utterly unreadable for me.

(From a letter to Professor Sulzer, 17 April 1765—Federmann, p. 113, German)

[1] *thus*—conjectural emendation of the present editor for Federmann's reading 'even the fat ones say *they*'.

[2] This ingenious cento made up of some fourteen detached phrases from nine different chapters of the Book of Job—Authorised Version—contains comparatively few terms of Fuseli's actual devising, though the meaning is all his own. He has changed 'strangling and death' to 'silence and death', 'I could heap up words against you' to 'I could heap up money against you'. 'I know you ask me', 'not that I fear your questions', '*of* silver and a goldstream I do not know whence' and 'were we changed places' are of Fuseli's own devising, and so also is the end from 'But now You all . . .'

[3] *Andreas Cramer. See above*, p. 91.

[4] Cantos I–X of the *Messiah* had been in print since 1756 and no further instalment was to appear till 1769. The family of Orelli in Zurich recorded Fuseli as having declared: 'The first ten cantos of the *Messiah* are the singing of a swan, the last ten the croaking of a raven. But far superior to the *Messiah* is *Chriemhild's Revenge* (the *Nibelungen*), the greatest of all other German poems' (Federmann, p. 29). Ernst Beutler plausibly supposes that these words originally occurred in Fuseli's *History of German Poetry* of 1769 (*see above*, p. 19).

One and a half years in London—Fuseli as private tutor

> In after-life he used to remark jocosely to his friends, 'The noble family of Walde-grave took me for a bear-leader, but they found me the bear' (Knowles, p. 42)

I AM WRITING to *you*, when there are so many others I ought to write to, above all a father, whom my heart forever embraces with filial sentiments, a brother whom I love, and sisters who are my sisters. I am in luck's way, as much as I could wish to be at the noonday of my life, and *that* is the reason for a stubbornly maintained silence. Were I downcast and in trouble, I might perhaps have written, if not in prose, then in an elegy; but to be happily situated and yet not independent keeps my heart in a kind of uncertainty I do not care to communicate to anybody. Fluctuation is the essence of life, and although I am scolded and made fun of on this account by my other friends, the first for not writing, the second for regarding my situation as uncertain, and although I have made various efforts to gratify my friends, I nevertheless find that my heart was born to doubt and can never speak so positively here of the affairs of this life, at least of those which are in part subject to the sceptre of opinion, fashion and interest, as it will be able to do once the urn is filled and reality begins. . . .

I am so fortunate as to be highly loved by the family with whom I live. I am neither servile nor presumptuous, neither quick and dazzling nor slow and rusty, and I have learnt with Persius[1] to laugh at him who thinks his knowledge lost unless he can flaunt it under other people's noses. It is a bare statement of facts, when I say that I have sat at table with everyone eminent in England and have been and am more than tolerated; and this I tell you, not because it makes me proud, but in order to

---

[1] *See* Persius, Satire I, v. 26: '*O mores, usque adeone scire tuum nihil est, nisi te scire sciat alter?*' In G. G. Ramsay's Loeb version: 'Good heavens! Is all your knowledge to be so utterly for nothing unless other people know that you possess it?'

please my friends with a circumstantial account of things. When I came to an agreement with Lord Waldegrave, it was for six months. He assigned to me his own table, the services of the young lord's valet and fifty guineas with accommodation etc., and both parties were left at liberty to do as they chose at the end of that time. The result was that the young Baron having, on the advice of Mr. Woods and myself, been condemned to visit Anticyra[1] ... I was asked to go with him, to oblige a family I loved. And so in about a month's time Lord Chewton and I will leave for France and stay there at least a year. ...

Self-love, like all fools, is talkative. That is a further reason for my silence, otherwise I should not have waited till now to tell you that I have a better opinion of myself since I have had occasion to put my behaviour and feelings in ill and good fortune to the test; since I have found that obscurity, neglect and, if not extreme poverty, at least anything but superfluity have had no other influence on me than to make me *proud*. As soon as I decided to live with Lord Waldegrave, I decided also to be as independent as possible—that I refused money offered to me, and often spurned the fattening hand of wealth, has perhaps profited me more than ever it would have done to know by heart the great folio 'Moral Philosophy'[2] in Latin of Wolff.

(From a letter to Salomon Dälliker, 12–15 November 1765—Muschg, pp. 101–4, German)

English Taste and Character

Gessner apostrophised in a letter to Dälliker of November 1765:

THE ENGLISHMAN eats roastbeef and plumpudding, drinks port

---

[1] *Anticyra*—there were two Greek cities of this name, both famed for their hellebore. As hellebore was the chief remedy for madness, Anticyra is frequently referred to by Horace, Juvenal and other Roman poets as the place where, if anywhere, men might be cured of their folly. Fuseli uses 'to visit Anticyra' for to go on the grand tour, which, it is hoped, may cure young Lord Chewton of his folly.

[2] *Christian Wolff* (1679–1754), one of the chief philosophers of the German Enlightenment.

and claret; therefore, if you will be read by him,[1] you must open
the portals of Hell with the hand of Milton, convulse his ear or
his sides with Shakespeare's buskin or sock, raise him above the
stars with Dryden's Cecilia or sink him to the melancholy of the
grave with Gray. Intermediate tones, though they were as sweet
as honey, as lovely as the flush of dawn, send him to sleep; nor
can he persuade himself that metre is an empty dream.

(Muschg, p. 110, German)

English Literature in 1766

ENGLAND IS feeling the same shortage of original minds as the
rest of Europe. Her only poet is my friend Armstrong. Gray,
whose 'Elegy written in a Country Churchyard' you know, fell
off, when he tried writing odes . . . Akenside has buried himself
in the complexities of anatomy. Churchill, the butcher's dog, is
dead. Macpherson and Franklin are only translators. Have you
seen Percy's three volumes, 'The Reliques of Ancient English
Poetry'? If not, I will send them to the reviver of *Minnesang*.[2]
. . . Tragedy is at the last gasp; Murphy has gone awhoring after
the gods of Voltaire, and Dodsley has shed blood like water;
Colman is the only comic poet, but he has given up writing,
because Garrick is too rich to act, and has set himself the useless
task of translating Terence into blank verse.

(Letter of 7 February 1766 to Bodmer—Muschg, p. 125, German)

[1] The translator has here conjecturally emended the text to bring out
what is obviously intended. The original of the letter no longer exists.
Fuseli says that Gessner is the only one of his Zurich friends whom he finds
known as a writer in England, and goes on to insist that Gessner's Idylls,
gentle as they are, and written in rhythmical prose, can never be the right
thing for the robust taste of English readers. The reading in the copy of the
letter that survives is 'wenn du ihn daher *lesen* willst'—'therefore if you will
read him'. Cp. pp. 89–90.

[2] It had been one of Bodmer's chief achievements to rediscover Middle
High German poetry. He published versions both of the Nibelungen and
of mediaeval love-lyric (*Minnesang*).

A Character

On 6 May 1768 Fuseli wrote to Lavater: 'I am enclosing also two or three of the papers I have contributed to some of the London magazines; the little thing entitled *"Character"* is the real character of a dear friend of mine here, and has met with considerable success.' It has been possible to identify this essay and three or four other contributions of Fuseli's, beyond any reasonable doubt, in the *Universal Museum*, which towards the end of 1767 came into the hands of the bookseller Joseph Johnson, his lifelong friend, with whom he was at this time living. The 'dear friend' here portrayed under the name of Nicodemo Tardi is most probably the poet John Armstrong.

NICODEMO TARDI was a man on whom Nature seemed to have poured parts and virtues without design; a penetrating head without application; a spirit of enterprise without execution; a heart boiling with passions, wrapt up in phlegm, made to captivate and yet to live neglected; to mark the tide of fortune, and to let it pass by. Tardi, an easy adept of what is by the world called misfortunes, made two notions the standards of his conduct for life, derived each from the predominant ingredients of his constitution, blood and phlegm. The one, which he called *Humanity*, was in fact no more but a claim to every attribute of Mortality; the other, styled *Chance*, was such a reliance on accident as left it to the hour, the minute, the moment, to furnish him with action, appetite, subsistence.

Such being his wayward guide, the institutions and sanctions of society could have little influence on Tardi; they were ciphers: for him proper time and business, ease, wealth, prerogative were sounds devoid of sense—they, and whatever the fickle fashions of ages dictate, are in fact no more—words in sand; but let him who can despise such social nostrums first be wise enough not to hunt after the evils which beget them. Tardi should have lived among a race where interests, perfidy, ideal credit, appointments, engagements are unknown names; where a man is a man; where honesty only strikes the bargain; where friendship proves never a bawd; where Nature alone forms and supports connections etc.—marriage.

Tardi was trained up to disappointment: he despised it; if it attended his chair, it was in the habit of a servant. It was noble in Tardi: in ruling it, he did well; but why did he keep it, since he could not keep it for himself alone? It was well for Procrustes to be a tall man, and to lie in a large bed; but it was cruel to rack others to the same length upon it.

Tardi, accomplished, of superior sense and almost unlimited taste, was modest even to a fault. Let others boast that they never crowded the *levée* of genius, supplanted a rival or condemned him who presumed to dispute their excellence of maxims[1]—the kernel of virtues was never designed for them. Tardi, with more heroic patience, would listen to a fool he despised, thank him for a rag of observation or anecdote picked from the sweepings of his own study; would deliver with diffidence, and neither talk of himself, nor slander; would walk when he might have rode; sleep on deck, when he had a bed in the cabin;[2] excuse absent faults; plead for frailties, and even crimes—such was Tardi's modesty—yet what would have amazed you was, that satire never cut with keener edge than in his company; that whatever Tardi spoke has a prologue, an epilogue and five acts; that all your arguments never could make Tardi blot one line of what he had wrote; and that, amidst showers of complaisance, you found yourself obliged to wait Tardi's convenience, and to keep his hours or to abandon his company.

(Unsigned contribution to the *Universal Museum*, September 1767, pp. 445–6)

[1] The original reads here: 'or him who presumed to dispute their excellence of maxims, condemned'—possibly a misprint, more likely an inadvertent slip into German word-order.

[2] Fuseli met Armstrong in Germany early in 1764, on his way to England, and probably they were travelling companions. This phrase about 'sleeping on deck' may, therefore, contain an allusion to real circumstances, and not be merely figurative.

English Newspapers—the Liberty of the Press

ROUSSEAU . . . should have known that the public papers[1] are the hobby-horses of the nation—whilst at the same time they are the bog[2] of the public; hence he should have laughed at their contents, equally insensible of their encomiums and scandal. How could *he,* had it not been for his utter ignorance of English customs, how could *he* ever have ventured to build his fame and character on *corruption*? on a *cancer*?—for such newspapers might perhaps be demonstrated to be for England, together with all magazines;—if it is true, that the nations which are really free, those characters that are most virtuous, or of real literary merit, scorn to promulgate what they enjoy, leave licence to such as can *only cry* for liberty, and tattle to parrots encaged and cooped-up magpies.

(1767—*Remarks on Rousseau,* pp. 117–18)

The New Poetry in England up to 1775

THE ENGLISH don't boast that they have produced a poet yet in this century, unless it be Richardson. Thomson's tame catalogue, which has so often been translated to you, Young's pyramids of dough, Pope's metrical and rimed prose—they don't call *them* poetry by a long chalk, just as little as they would concede that title to the tearful prettinesses of Wieland or Gessner—and so God help you!

(Letter to Lavater of March 1775—Muschg, p. 174, German)

Fuseli on England in 1794

. . . a country dear to fame, whose race nearly peopled one

---

[1] Soon after his arrival in England Rousseau was much attacked, but also much defended, in the newspapers. The attacks he regarded as part and evidence of a vast organised conspiracy against him. The contributions in his defence he ignored.

[2] *Bog* presumably here for *bog-house,* privy.

hemisphere, balances the power of both, distributes the wealth of the globe, irradiates science, soars on the wing of fancy, the first in discovery and every useful art.

(*Analytical Review*, June 1794, review of History of the Thames, signed Z.Z.—XIX, p. 113)

SECTION FOUR

FUSELI
ON THE CULTURAL PRETENSIONS
OF GERMANY AND FRANCE

The countries which, after Switzerland itself, had far more obvious claims on Fuseli's allegiance than England are Germany and France. By them the culture of Zurich was, from reasons of language, geographical contiguity and the particular constellation of European culture in the mid-eighteenth century, largely dominated. Whatever claims those two lands seemed to lay upon him, however, he rejected with his characteristic violence. His quarrel with Germany was to begin with in the main political—he spurned it as the land of tyranny and serfdom embodied for him in the figure of Frederick the Great; his quarrel with France, on the other hand, amounted to an instinctive, almost physical dislike, the real object of which was less the national character of the French than the still powerful culture of the age of Louis XIV and the *éclaircissement*, symbolised for him particularly by the detested Voltaire. It is remarkable that in later years, when the course of events had brought about many alterations both in Germany and in France, and greatly modified much that he had criticised, he did not revise his old opinions. He continues to speak with little respect of France, and virtually ignores the immense efflorescence of German culture in the age of Goethe (*see* Introduction, pp. 17–22).

Frederick the Great—Fuseli and Kings

HOW MY soul tramples this king underfoot! I weep for anger, that he should so desecrate himself: he has given d'Alembert a pension of 8,000 dollars, on the sole condition that he should attend him four weeks a year in Berlin or at Potsdam. But in order that this pension may not be paid from his own purse, he has scraped it together out of the pay of the commanders of many small fortresses, eighty-year-old wounded officers with nothing else to live on, and those who had already received an instalment of their pension this year have had to refund it immediately. Earth's kings are the worms of earth, and I am what I am. . . .

(Letter to Lavater, 16 October 1763—Muschg, p. 72, German)

The Kings of Earth—to Bodmer

One of the very few original poems of Fuseli's in English known to survive—*see* Introduction, p. 28–29; sent with a letter to Bodmer from Tours on 9 September 1766, and written about that date.

God said to Fred'ric: 'Be the first of names—
  Let Fame thy feats in thunder tell the age,
  Posterity re-echo—for I add
  To laurels blood, and Voltaire to thy heart.'

He turn'd to Lewis:[1] from th'all-dazzling look
  The Mock-King shrunk: when Gaul's Sty-Daemon thus:
  'Thy Fate damns France, there let him rule and add
  A Bourbon-brain, Bigotry, Pompadour.'

The shrieks of mangled Colombona[2] have
  Their fill, shall be aveng'd—Let Lisbon howl,

[1] Having dismissed Frederick the Great, Fuseli deals with Louis XV of France.
[2] The cruelties of the Portuguese invaders and colonists of Ceylon from 1505 till the capture of Colombo by the Dutch in 1656 are here regarded

And mourning Joseph,[1] till Iberia ripens,
Share Earthquake, Daggers, Inquisition, Priests.

His nod call'd me. I trembled, lest a Throne
Should be my lot—but mildly smiling He:
'Take thou thy wish—the genial mind, the Tear,
Thy Friend be Bodmer and thy Mistress——?'[2]

German Nationalism

MY CONTEMPT for Klopstock's taste in painting . . . is conformable to the arrogance with which he puts the English in their place.[3] His ignorance of their poetry is absurd. *Citizen! Fatherland! Freedom!*—if he were at least a Swiss! But where is the fatherland of a German, a slave? Is it in Swabia, Brandenburg, Austria or Saxony? Is it in the swamps that swallowed up the Roman legions under Varus? Was Rome ever defeated, when it fought on an *honest* soil? Even a Frenchman—curses upon him! —has more right to call his country 'Fatherland' than a Quedlingburgian, Osnabruckian or any of the other puffed-up spawn of toads grovelling between Rügen and Ulm. What is there that a serf can take a pride in but the livery of his master? And of which master? The first, second or third? Freedom!—o my God! Freedom, from the flatterer of Christian![4]

(Letter to Lavater, March 1775—Muschg, p. 174, German)

as having called down divine retribution in the earthquake which ravaged Lisbon in 1755. Fuseli was specially interested in the earthquake of Lisbon and its bearing on the justice of God, because of the controversy between Voltaire and Rousseau on the question.

[1] Joseph I, King of Portugal 1750–77.

[2] In a German ode to *Pistorius*, written in May 1765, Fuseli indicates that he would wish the famous actress Mary Ann Yates (1728–87), whom he certainly knew, to be his mistress.

[3] See Klopstock's patriotic odes *passim*, especially *Mein Vaterland* and *Vaterlandslied*.

[4] Christian VII, King of Denmark (1766–1808), and his father, Frederick V, were patrons of Klopstock, who addressed various poems to them, especially to the father.

A typical German Dilettante

THAT SIMPLICITY of taste which appears to inspire our author
amid the scenes of nature forsakes him when haunting the
abodes of art. . . . Raphael is his idol, an endless hymn quivers
on his lips at the name of Raphael; but we cannot be at a loss
[*sic*] how to appreciate the justness of his admiration, when,
instead of his *propriety*, we find him perpetually chaunting his
grace. Boldly to kick aside the tripod from which Winckelmann,
Lessing and Mengs promulgated their false or frigid oracles
required, no doubt, a truer taste and less national deference
than a German dilettante can be supposed to possess. . . .

(*Analytical Review*, December 1797, review of Stolberg's *Travels*
signed Z. Z.—XXVI, p. 548)

Germany in 1770 (the year of Goethe's meeting with Herder in Strasbourg)

I AM SORRY that you see Bodmer so seldom, and still sorrier that
the craziest of all nations occupies his attention in his old age.
Except for Klopstock, Ernesti[1] and Michaelis,[2] there is not a
man of real genius in Germany.

(Letter to Lavater, 30 July 1770—Muschg, p. 159, German)

French claims to Cultural Hegemony

THIS *abbé*,[3] I say, thinks it very hard the French should be
denied a taste for music, when they are allowed to excel in all

---

[1] *Johann August Ernesti* (1707–81), Professor of Theology, one of the
pioneers of the Higher Criticism of the Bible. Fuseli met him personally
when he was in Leipzig in 1762.

[2] *Johann David Michaelis* (1717–91)—another pioneer of the Higher
Criticism whom Fuseli had met when he was in Germany.

[3] The *Abbé Laugier*, who had defended French music against Rousseau in
his anonymously published *Apologie de la musique française*, 1754.

119

the other arts. Might I ask him what arts he means? Is it painting? I believe it demonstrable that, from the days of Jean Cousin to ours, the bulk of the French have been absolute barbarians in painting. Take away Poussin, who could not live under the French sky and may be considered as an Italian with Le Sueur and Le Brun [1]—all the rest, their Vouets, Lemoines, Mignards, Jouvenets, Coypels, Bouchers, Vanloos, Pierres, Restouts in history, and their Rigauds, Largillières, Tocques in portrait-painting, have all held, and their disciples probably will hold, the eel of Science by the tail. Is it sculpture? If giving a radiant polish to marble, if to guide the chisel well, is sculpture, Puget, Pigalle, Adam and the 'Ons' [2] are great men. Is it poetry? Their language never knew nature, and their verse dies without rime. What is it then they excel in? Dancing, and the great end which all their arts aspire to—Trifling.

(1767—*Remarks on Rousseau*, pp. 92–3)

---

[1] Cp. Sir Joshua Reynolds: 'The best of the French school, Poussin Le Sueur and Le Brun . . . may be said, though Frenchmen, to be a colony from the Roman school' (IVth Discourse, December 1771).

[2] The French sculptors François Girardon (1628–1715), Edme Bouchardon (1698–1762), Claude Michel Clodion (1738–1814) and Jean-Antoine Houdon (1741–1828), also Jean Goujon (?1510–68).

FUSELI AND ROUSSEAU—THE *REMARKS*

The most important factor in Fuseli's early development is probably his admiration of Rousseau, whom he began to idolise at the age of eighteen and habitually compared with Socrates and Jesus Christ. This Rousseau-worship finds its record in the only original longer publication of his earlier years and the most striking of all his writings, the *Remarks on Rousseau* of 1767, provoked by the quarrel between Rousseau and Hume. That quarrel, however, lowered Rousseau in his eyes. As Fuseli saw it, Rousseau had, in coming to England as a foreign refugee, ineffectually succumbed to that very discomfiture arising from the peculiarities of English manners and customs which he himself had been in danger of succumbing to under similar circumstances only two years earlier, but which he had then triumphed over. This was one of the ways in which Rousseau had disappointed him. We have the word of Godwin and Knowles for it that he thought much less highly of Rousseau in his later years, and this is borne out by the fact that he very seldom refers to him after 1767, and then never again with the old enthusiasm. The opportunity to manhandle Voltaire was certainly one of the chief inducements for him to write on the Rousseau-Hume affair. He was always a magnificent, picturesque hater, and proud of it too.

Enlightened Religion—Rousseau and Jesus

OF ROUSSEAU, since his affair with the blackguards of Geneva and his *Lettres de la Montagne*, I have heard nothing except from time to time that he thinks of coming here, that he is living on an island in the lake of Bienne, and that he compares himself with a dog.[1] In my ravished eyes he gleams without a spot. If the goodness of an action or the promulgation of a truth is to be judged by the results, I agree with you that Rousseau would have done better to keep some of his tenets to himself, however clearly demonstrated they were. But then I also do not see why Jesus Christ sent forth the dogmatic and mystical part of his religion into the wide world, since—I appeal to his own judgment-seat—it has so far either proved and still proves to be the source of all the schisms, blasphemies, ravings, absurdities, bloodshed and atrocities of those signed with the cross, or else diminishes our devotion to his divine morality.

(Letter to Dälliker, November 1765—Muschg, p. 113, German)

Meeting with Rousseau—England and Revolution

SO FAR as Rousseau is concerned, I despise the behaviour of my compatriots—actual or associated[2]—too much to be surprised at any crazy accusation or morbid punishment they may pronounce against him. Lukewarmness is the typical quality of our times. The philosopher and the theologian alike, the merchant and the civic authorities are bound to hate him on principle. *Urit fulgore suo qui praegravat*[3]; I spent a few hours with him and was as happy as a man can be. I saw him in Paris with Hume,[4]

---

[1] At the time of this letter Rousseau had already been expelled from the island of St. Pierre and was in Strasbourg, still undecided whether to go to England, to Prussia or to Holland.

[2] Rousseau had been persecuted both by the Bernese, who were full members of the Swiss Confederacy, and by Geneva, which at this time was only an associated member. He was forced to leave Switzerland.

[3] Horace, *Epistles*, II, i, v. 13: 'For the radiancy of him who gives mediocre talents no chance to shine is a consuming fire.' Fuseli implies quite clearly that he feels himself Rousseau's peer.

[4] From 16 December 1765 to 4 January 1766 Rousseau was in Paris with Hume. In July 1766 he broke completely with Hume, accusing him of being in a conspiracy with all his old enemies to discredit him. This occasioned the writing of Fuseli's *Remarks on the Writings and Conduct of John James Rousseau*, published in April 1767, after his own venture in France with young

whom he has accompanied to England. In England he will be able to enjoy the tranquillity for which he yearns. For there he will not be able to take an active part in affairs, which would be his ruin, England being too far gone for any reform short of one brought about by a revolution, and that is in Rousseau's own opinion a recourse every bit as much to be feared as desired.

(Letter to Bodmer from Lyons, 7th Feb. 1766—Muschg, pp. 124–5, German)

The Preface to Fuseli's 'Remarks on Rousseau' (1767)

(Without the original footnotes)

READER, who by chance (for to his accidental majesty I consecrate this book) dost happen to light on these leaves, misconstrue not to pedagogic rage or lust of truth my motive for leading thee this ramble.

And first—because it has been decided by the voice of the world that 'Truth is not to be told'. Throw a glance on society, open the annals of time—truth has been, and is, the destroyer of peace and the parent of revolution.

And will be so—for this plain reason: because it is of epidemic nature; because a man cannot see, or fancy to see, its most transient spark, but with dog-star rage he will pursue it through thick and thin, sink the mob at his heels in the quagmires which the jack-a-lanthorn dances o'er, or at their head break through all the barricades of power, nets of politics and cobwebs of speculation, nay spare not even the silken ties of temper and affection to come at it.

Had it not—to give a few modern instances—had it not been for these paroxysms of his, could Luther have indulged himself quietly in the fat luxury of a convent, [then] Leo's[1] golden age

---

Lord Chewton had turned out disastrously through his boxing the young nobleman's ears. Fuseli returned to England about October or November 1766.

[1] The Medicean Pope Leo X, 1513–21, patron of Michelangelo and Raphael, during whose papacy the Reformation broke out.

of literature and taste had not been overrun by the armies of fanaticism; Charles, Philip and Alba had not turned their red-hot furies loose on Europe; Smithfield, Merindol, Cabrières and Toulouse[1] would not have blazed; the Henrys, the Louis', the ———[2] would not have been stabbed, abominated, expelled; no Holy Tribunal would smother the howlings of humanity, nor earthquakes shake a throne; Truth, the wretched victim itself, had not been torn to tatters under the hands of its defenders; the Father, Son and Holy Ghost, the Virgin and their host of black, white and grey[3] had not been darted upon Luther; Luther had not damned Zwingli; Calvin had not burnt Servetus[4]; a Bishop might have signified something above a paper mitre; no sneaking, praying, psalm-singing, scripture-expounding villain would have been called a Dissenter; the Moravians[5] would not have adored their ass in the dark; no spirit had whipped into a maid's head; the Quakers would not work their damnation with fear and trembling—in short, we might all be of one mind, jolly fellows, and peaceably enjoy each *our rib of the word made flesh*—as Boccaccio[6] says.

The horrid outline of so petty an article in the catalogue of truth as Luther, and its length of appendages, force me to skip the rest:—how it is owing to the same itch of propagating truth

---

[1] Merindol and Cabrieres, near Avignon, were in 1545 the scene of terrible massacres of Waldensians, as Toulouse was in 1562 and 1572 of Huguenots, and Smithfield from 1555–8 of English Protestants.

[2] The blank Fuseli leaves here is quite certainly meant for the Stuarts. When he came to London in 1764 the recollections of the 1745 Rebellion were still lively.

[3] Cp. *Paradise Lost*, III, 475: 'White, black and grey with all their trumpery . . .' for the Carmelites, Dominicans and Franciscans.

[4] The Socinian Michael Servetus (1511–53), burnt for heresy by Calvin at Geneva.

[5] The Moravians had settled in large numbers in England in the eighteenth century and were given official recognition by an Act of Parliament in 1749. There were many not always unfounded rumours in circulation about their supposed fanaticism and excesses.

[6] In the 10th story of the VIth day of the *Decameron* Fra Cipolla, in enumerating spurious relics, speaks of '*una delle coste del Verbum carofatti alle finestre*'. Fuseli was proud of this little blasphemy. *See* p. 135.

that America is made a slaughter-house and Africa a stable;[1] how, from the same pruriency of tongue to call each thing by its name, quarrels brutalise the mob, and duels mangle the breast of urbanity, whilst prying, hag-eyed Curiosity bids Infamy blow the trumpet of Fame, pierces the sanctuaries of power, drags their hobby-horses into light, and on your Grèves, Terreaux and Tyburns[2] racks, burns, hangs and smashes the bones of every government, society and police[3] under the moon.

If, from these remarks, it follows evidently that truth ought not to be told in *civil* matters, it may be presumed that it can be of little use in *speculation*—for such I take *now* to be what is commonly called *moral truth*. Dive from the turnkeys of state, the nobles[4] that demand what right God has to be God, the chaplains that anthem the 'Thing',[5] down to the mug-flushed crews of the news-flag,[6] or the frantic club of clerks and 'prentices destined for a fly-sh-t mouth[7] at Juliet's balcony—dive, and tell me, what are the ravings of nature to the politician? the virulence of morality to the herds of pleasure? what to the man of business the implacability of duty? Cursed mar-plots they are,

[1] The extermination of the ancient Mexicans and Peruvians and of the Red Indians. The capturing of negroes as slaves in Africa.

[2] The places of execution in Paris, Lyons and London.

[3] *Police* used in the now obsolete sense of 'civilised organisation', 'polity'.

[4] Whether Fuseli is referring to irreligion amongst the nobility in general, or has some individual (such as, for example, Bolingbroke) in mind, cannot be determined.

[5] The odious institution of the Royal Chaplains was part of the plot then going on to recapture control of Church and State for the Crown, that plot which Burke was to denounce three years later in his *Thoughts on the Present Discontents*. The poets Edward Young, William Dodd and Dr. John Brown (*see* p. 127) were all King's Chaplains. The obscure expression '*to anthem the "Thing"*', meaning evidently to flatter unlawful power, contains perhaps a reference to Chapters VI and VII of *Joshua*, where some of the children of Israel 'trespass in the accursed thing'. Other examples of the 'accursed thing' being spoken of with a contemporary political connotation could be cited. The *N.E.D.* does not indicate whether the colloquial use of 'The Thing' for 'the correct thing' became current early enough for Fuseli to be using it in 1767.

[6] *Mug-flushed crews of the news-flag*—the exact meaning of this phrase cannot be determined.

[7] *A fly-sh-t mouth*—possibly what is now known as giving the raspberry.

and long have been kicked out of all good company. Their ha-ha's[1] yawn so ghastly upon ye, they force upon your eye and mind perspectives, consequences, proportions so absurd, that nobody truly in love with himself ever wishes to see or compare them. You must, indeed, know very little of the *Pilatism*[2] of our days to usher them to the world! Enter any office, shop, stall, produce your scheme, drug, book, and provided it is not quackery, palliative, sophism, I'll be shot, if not all their *honest* owners with more or less contempt, just as you advance east or westward,[3] will with Clarence's murderer whisper ye: '*Truth! it beggars any man that keeps it; and if you mean to thrive well, endeavour to trust to yourself, and live without it.*'[4]

By this time—that is to say, if the preface, as it was written, is read last—the reader will do me the justice to believe me innocent of the following sheets of maxims, the antipodes of those which I have laid before him in this prefatory chapter. They are the effusions of a gentleman now on his travels, and were committed to my care as the editor only. It was neither in my power to refuse them, nor is it to give the reader a satisfactory reason for publishing what I think exceptionable. Let it suffice to say, that I made use of every dissuasive argument to my friend:— the dreadful consequences of indiscreet truth (supposing even the paradoxes of Rousseau to be such), their revolting air, the fate of the *author*, the surfeit of the public,[5] the ridicule of impotence exhibited to *review*, the odiousness of personal reflections. To all this I received the answer of an author: I was allowed to dissent, provided I would publish; and, to oblige my

---

[1] *Ha-ha*—a deep abrupt trench as barrier, known chiefly now from its employment in landscape-gardening. Pure and lofty ethics present to the worldling just such alarming, abyss-like barriers.

[2] Reference, of course, to Pilate's famous question: 'What is truth?'

[3] Whether you are from the City or from Westminster, i.e. whether you are of the nobility or a mere citizen.

[4] Adapted freely, with omissions, from *Richard III*, Act I, scene iv. It is not *truth*, but *conscience* that the Second Murderer is speaking of.

[5] Fuseli's *Remarks on Rousseau* were amongst the last of the innumerable publications evoked by the quarrel between Rousseau and Hume, and the reviewers both in Paris and in London had long since begun to protest that the world had heard more than enough of the affair.

friend, undertook to turn him upon the town, on condition, however, that the friend should not smother the impartial man, nor the *editor* bribe the judge; that I should be entitled to prefix to this ramble a kind of vindicatory preface, and the following fragment of a letter written to him in remonstrance against his enterprise:

'Why, my friend, would you tear the ties of observance to that state and church whose member you are? I am mistaken, if some right reverend prelate will not pronounce the publisher of religious doubts, and the author who, from the mountain,[1] was pulled down on miracles, a *Freethinker* and *Unbeliever*. I am wrong, if Dr. Brown[2] (who dared to oppose Mr. Hume, and died), should he return, or any political writer, 'yet lingering on the brink of hell',[3] would not start the poison of anarchy and high treason in the distinguisher of sovereign and government,[4] or that of punishable boldness in the derider of representative liberty; not to speak of those passages where he [Rousseau] denies the English their right to the title of a good-natured people, and even of man; damns their premiums and encouragements of agriculture; wantonly calls them children that frolic in the idea of eating a vast deal of sugar when men; reflects on the refinements of rank and the exalted elegance of thought of our nobility in the ravings of that phantastic Edward, whose primitive notions ought to be dated from the days when Jupiter was wrapt up in horse-dung.[5] What melancholy rancour could suggest to him the ill-natured remark, that England deserves to lose her liberty for the manner of her elections—as if an honest tar might not be allowed to boil his leg of mutton in red wine, or a deserving clergyman make use of his vote to fish for a living! May I admire that chaos of pickles, J. Mandeville,[6] or

---

[1] The attack on the belief in miracles in Rousseau's *Lettres de la montagne* (1765) was the principal occasion of his expulsion from Neuchâtel.

[2] *Dr. John Brown* (1715–66), Royal Chaplain (*see* p. 125) and man of letters, had attacked Hume in his *Estimate of the Manners and Principles of the Times* (1757). He committed suicide on 22 September 1766.

[3] Quotation from Armstrong's poem *On Taste*.

[4] *See* Rousseau's *Contrât social*.

[5] *See* Juvenal's sixth Satire, v. 15 and below, p. 130. (*Edward, see* p. 128, note 2.)   [6] Mandeville's *Fable of the Bees* (1714/1723).

those children of chance which, from a sudden shock of printing types, jumped into light, and were called *Memoirs*,[1] if there is one of all those subtle investigators of nature styled novelists who shall not start in his *Nouvelle Héloise* more childish, uncouth simplicity, more elvish-marked, absurd, eccentric characters, more chasms of subject, incident and plot, in half an hour, than the boars of any village in Provence can root up truffles in a day. Has he not disputed on self-murder? Has he not blasphemed man into being naturally good? Has he not, to the abhorrence of every good schoolmaster, affirmed that the idea of God can have no meaning for a boy of ten years; that to him Heaven is a basket of sweetmeats, and Hell a school? Does he care for original sin?—he, who despises the eternity of hell-pains, and though living upon the immortality of the soul, yet thinks it not geometrically demonstrable? If he seems to allow of a free determination of the will, he thinks of the interventions of private Providence as of the diseased patchwork of a Geneva watch.[2] And is a man guilty of this enormous lump of *errors*, or *worse*, to be defended, and his pernicious maxims to be scattered abroad by you, who imbibed religion and constitutional sentiments with your mother-milk?'

Divine Honours for Rousseau

HE HAD[3] a clearness and precision of ideas which furnished him with expressions of almost intuitive justness. He had not so

[1] Possibly an allusion to the *Memoirs of Europe* (1710) of the notorious Mrs. Manley.

[2] Fuseli gives in his footnotes the sources of most of the many utterances of Rousseau here cited or alluded to, and the rest can all be traced. 'That phantastic Edward' is *Mylord Eduard Bomston*, the noble English friend and champion of St. Preux in the *Nouvelle Hélosïe*.

[3] It is significant that this crowning eulogy at the turning-point in the *Remarks on Rousseau* stands throughout in the past, and not in the present tense. Fuseli distinguishes sharply between Rousseau as he had been before the trouble with Hume and as he was after it. Even so, Fuseli can no longer praise the Rousseau who had not yet disappointed him as unreservedly as he had done in his letters up to February 1766, where he is constantly likened to Socrates and Christ.

much read as meditated. His talent was to reduce a book to one idea, to encompass the sphere of possibilities, and to compare them with existence. Master of nature's boldest strokes and all its simplicity, he was luxuriant, yet modest, and true to virtue, though courted by the passions. His delicacy of mind was such that he would immediately discover the most remote or disguised resemblance or deviation of moral principles. Familiar with man in his different states, he knew his springs of activity, his rights, his strength, his foibles. He had, besides, the peculiar advantage over the rest of those who call themselves wise, that, free of systems, partisans and sects, he steered right onward, seized the good and the true with that strength and elegance of fancy, that effusion of sentiments, which first forced[1] him to write. Take all together, and you have an elegant and nervous writer, the purest moralist, the most penetrating politician—and a good man.

(1767—*Remarks on Rousseau*, pp. 93–5)

The finer Moral Sense of Rousseau

BESIDES, the great number,—the rabble, if you will,—cannot conceive reality beyond the gross outlines of conscience and honour. The refined tale of moral sense is nonsense in their ear; they, with Vespasian, enjoy the smell of chamber-pot taxes. Go and tell them you starve, because you scorn to intercept the purse destined for the palm of indigence;[2] because you despise to creep, only to trample on; because you are too human to beam in the hand of party rage or cabal—tell them so!—but thank your stars, if the grave and busy bring in their verdict 'lunacy' only; if the politician and philosopher content them-

[1] *See* Rousseau's own well-known account of how he first came to write, in the letter to Malesherbes of 12 January 1762, which, though at that time still unpublished, was somehow known to Fuseli, who briefly refers to it in a footnote.

[2] On 30 October 1762 Rousseau had refused a pension offered to him by Frederick the Great with the words: '*Vous voulez me donner du pain; n'y a-t-il aucun de vos sujets qui en manque?*' Great publicity had been given to this letter, and this phrase, in particular, had been much ridiculed. Fuseli certainly also has in mind the pension accepted by d'Alembert (*see above*, p. 117).

selves with damning you for a paradox-monger and sense-gelder; if the print-shops exhibit ye but for a savage[1]; and poets whisper you, that such fictions might have suited the days of beardless Jupiter,[2] but now . . .

Are somewhat late for being so primitive.[3]

(1767—*Remarks on Rousseau*, pp. 103–5)

The Temperaments of Rousseau and Hume

THAN THEM the elements never framed two more different characters. Their disparity is such that they could continue friends —from the poles only.

The one warm, of genial organs, but much too irritably strung; apt to receive and make sudden impressions—sentimental; with a fancy ever on the wing, and yet a head fitted to trace the flow of things to their source—hence melancholy; impatient of constraint—hence to indiscretion the slave of what truths he discovered; to excess fond of independence—hence incapable of affairs, with all the talents, and unfit for connexions, with all the qualities for them; a man in theory, a child in the practice of life.

The other c——.

(1767—*Remarks on Rousseau*, pp. 141–2)

The Gloom on Rousseau's spirit

PAIN WAS not the cloud which could cast a gloom over his spirit. It was benevolence disappointed that threw him into agonies. To be conscious that humanity was the constant spring

---

[1] On 30 January 1767 a satirical print *The Savage Man*, ridiculing Rousseau, had been published in London. Boswell was responsible for it.

[2] Cp. Juvenal's sixth Satire, vv. 14–16, '*et sub Jove, sed Jove nondum barbato*'.

[3] Adaptation of a line in Armstrong's *Benevolence*:

> But thriving malice tamely to forgive—
> 'Tis somewhat late to be so primitive.

Primitive here and on p. 127, line 23, refers to the primitive Christians, not to the man of nature.

of our actions; to support a life of distress for others, for religion and the rights of man; to despise all other views, refuse all other rewards, hope for no other success! And for this to be stigmatised, exiled, persecuted; for this to be ranked with impostors, public empoisoners, and all the abortions of crime! To see all those that meddle[1] with virtue in theory or practice united against you! Must not such a consequence show human nature to you in those abominable shades from which the best of all ages shrunk back? Yet are the complaints of Rousseau unsullied with clamorous abuse, revenge or hatred. They are the accents of pure woe, such as friendship utters over irreclaimable vice.

(1767—*Remarks on Rousseau*, pp. 114–15)

Disappointment in Rousseau—the fatal shortcoming

PERSUADED THAT his enemies would last with his life, and only change the weapons he had foiled for better ones; that those who could not level him to their talents would attempt to debase him to their principles, and that his name was *now* the only assailable thing about him, which he could not hope to see attacked by fair or discoverable means; he, exhausted and unequal to the visionary task, grew anxiously suspicious of the world around him, and suffering the prudence of virtue to be swallowed by pusillanimous scrupulosity, made it a duty to be for ever on the alarm, to lie on the torture of a restless fancy, to fear all, in order to ward all. Thus, creating monsters of his own, he sunk under his own blows and betrayed himself, to exchange for the *baseless fabric of a vision* the solid merit of generosity and gratitude.

(1767—*Remarks on Rousseau*, pp. 136–7)

The Trouncing of Voltaire

Fuseli here gives Voltaire the name *Pansophe*, because Voltaire had attacked Rousseau soon after his arrival in England in the scurrilous *Lettre au Docteur Pansophe*, the most notable passage in which, the

---

[1] Fuseli uses 'to meddle with' here and 'to tamper with' (*below*, p. 140) in the sense of 'to dabble in'.

harangue to the citizens of London, exhorting them to return to nature and eat grass in Hyde Park, is variously referred to and travestied in the present diatribe, as well as in the frontispiece Fuseli designed for his *Remarks*.

THERE IS one of the enemies of man, however, whom his hugeness distinguishes in the crowd: that threadworn, withered bastard of Fancy, that proud lesson of humility, *Pansophe!* Behold him, like some ecstatic Anabaptist, stark-naked in the streets of Leyden, rush in and cry: 'Brethren of London, Paris and Geneva! No four-legs! No acorns! No *sub dios!*[1] No female to be wrenched from the potent embraces of a son of earth! —Riches, society, rights! Religion to the great organ of life! Virtue, *virtù*! Stages, toilet, laws! Fiddles, agriculture! By Samonocodom and the Trinities beyond the Ganges! No acorns! No state of nature! No four-legs!' Why, Pansophe? A less cry than this had gathered a mob; nor did I ever dispute your jaws that power—but your eyes that of seeing. It is not fair to read yourself, when you take up a book. The misanthropic, inhuman principles of that Discourse[2] are—yours! And better had it been for us, for our hopeful posterity, and especially for you, had you, on four, been kicked to atoms by some splenetic son of Bileam, than to have raised yourself on two legs to dress the supper of Conculix; to paint the buttocks of Chandos's page; to erect the tremendous idol of Joan's Celestial lover; to act the upholsterer of Candide's bedchamber; or to find a maidenhood in Circassia, only to make its owner tell us in Norway, it was carried off by a tiger. As to your mob:—with hearts as wild as your own, they have had almost all, but rather all, the good luck of much weaker heads, or clumsier passions—pools of mischief and absurdity, but no breeze of their own to ruffle them into contagion and infamy.

(1767—*Remarks on Rousseau*, pp. 29–32)

[1] *Sub dio* or *sub divo*—in the open air; possibly an allusion to the phrase in Horace, *Odes*, III, ii: *Vitamque sub divo*, etc.

[2] I.e. of Rousseau's *Discours sur l'inégalité*, containing the doctrine of the state of nature. There are detailed allusions here to Voltaire's *Dictionnaire philosopique*, his *Pucelle* and to *Candide*, especially to the apocryphal second part of *Candide*, attributed now to Thorel de Champigneulies.

Voltaire's Universal Genius

BUT TO allow Arouet poetry alone is too haughty a homage done to that universal genius. To ingratiate yourself with *him*, you must as well dream of having encountered him on Newton's, Tacitus' and Plato's road, as of having seen him, deaddrunk from Hippocrene, jostle Sophocles and Shakespeare, Then, perhaps, he may now and then condescend to say something very pretty to ye, till you are rude enough to display superior parts, and to cut down a harvest which he meant for his own scythe.

(1767—*Remarks on Rousseau*, pp. 122-3)

Voltaire's claims to true Poetic Genius

YOU HAVE not only expected to become an universal genius, but you even seem to have persuaded yourself that the world would believe it on your bare word. My dear Sir, undeceive yourself. The world believes no such thing. . . . Nature, which gave you too much petulance, denied you that noble stretch of imagination, that poetic frenzy, that extensive greatness and facility of conception, which are ingredients of absolute necessity in the composition of the epick bard; in a word, you never had sufficient warmth of fancy or glow of genius to attain the heights of heroic poetry. . . .

(1768—Dedication of *La Philosophie du Sage*)

The *Universal Museum* for March and April 1768 contains under the heading *Literary Correspondence* the long bogus Dedication to Voltaire, 'obtained from the printer by a great favour', of a factitious satirical work entitled *La Philosophie du Sage* purported to be on the point of publication in Amsterdam. The imaginary correspondent signs himself X. Y. and dates his letter to the editor of the *Universal Museum*, 'Amsterdam, 17 March 1768'. The supposed dedication, an extremely insulting document, is given in two columns, in faulty French, which is intended to represent the original, and in English translation. All the circumstances point to Fuseli being the real author. Cunningham indicates that Fuseli was disappointed because Voltaire apparently never heard a word about the attacks on him in the *Remarks on Rousseau*, and it can well be assumed that he hit on the

133

idea of following up those attacks a year later with stinging invective addressed directly to his victim in his own language and published through such a medium that it could scarcely fail to come before his eyes. There is, however, no record of Voltaire ever having heard of this somewhat crude attack upon him. If he had done so, it would not have been in his nature to ignore it.

Self-portrait at the Age of Twenty-six

Fuseli's own anonymous review of his pamphlet on Rousseau, published in the *Critical Review*, May 1767.

THIS REMARKER upon the writings and conduct of Rousseau is one of those *rarae aves* whom it is difficult to define; of a character which it is difficult to fix.

He is evidently a gentleman, a scholar, a philosopher, a genius and a man of wit; though by some of his readers his pretensions to any of these titles[1] will be called in question; and by others his character in a summary way will be sunk into that of a downright sceptic (perhaps atheist) and libertine.

For, say the first, will a gentleman labour to disturb the public tranquillity? a scholar revile the schools? a philosopher damn all sects? a genius despise all restraints? and a man of wit blaspheme sacred things?—Nevertheless, he may be——

Here the candid and benevolent will pause a while; and regret that the gentleman in private life should affront the public in a body, whom as individuals he would be far from offending; that the scholar should depart from his first principles, and become ungrateful to his teachers; that the philosopher should only wear a gown to cover his lewdness; that true genius should *o'erstep the modesty of nature* and the decorum of habit; and that the sparkling wit, not contented with such flesh as the

---

[1] The original reads here: 'his pretensions to *either* will be called in question'. The use of 'either' for any one of several antecedents is recorded as obsolete in the *New English Dictionary*. Similar obsolete usages, which have been left unmodified in the present reprint, as they present no obstacles to the understanding of the meaning, are 'in one or two places *excepted*' (i.e. except in one or two places); a . . . *shrugging* figure; the real . . . *estimation* of the rider (i.e. value).

market affords in the public stews, should profane by wishing to wanton with *the Word made flesh*![1]—Nevertheless he may be——

What? cry the zealots! Can he be less a wretch than he appears to be? Can sophistry itself find any pretext in his behalf? Is he not a blasphemer of God and a reviler of men? Order with him is chaos, and chaos order!—Heaven! church! bishops! seminaries! sciences! All fall before him!—Confusion on his head! Away with him!—Pincers, fire and faggot were made for such miscreants!

But we cannot give him up so easily to the tormentors, since we profess candour and moderation; and having balanced his beauties against his blemishes, we find that the former greatly preponderate.

A staunch advocate for Rousseau must needs be displeasing to many sober-minded people, who conform to present modes and readily subscribe, without further inquiry, to adopted systems;—but the merit of the Remarker does not consist in being a mere epitomiser of his author; he has opinions of his own, so singular, so novel, and, like a true critic, so independent of his author, that we are sorry to quote a verse of severe condemnation against him:

How Van *wants grace, who never wanted wit.*[2]

The Remarker has been said to be a copy, in a great measure, of the inimitable Tristram;[3] tho' we must own, that in one or

[1] *To wanton with the Word made flesh*: reference to the profane tag from Boccaccio introduced by Fuseli on the (unnumbered) fourth page of the Preface to his Rousseau pamphlet (*see* p. 124).

[2] Pope on Vanbrugh, Imitation of first epistle of second book of Horace, v. 289. Fuseli again and again admitted that 'grace' was not amongst his qualities. He certainly has his own case in mind, when he speaks of Michelangelo's deficiency in grace, as nearly everything he says of Michelangelo applies also to himself.

[3] The *Remarks on Rousseau* are hardly ever referred to by any contemporaries without this attribution of them to Sterne being mentioned. And yet not one of those who mentions it believes in it. There is all the difference in the world between Sterne's airy graceful playfulness and the strained violence of Fuseli. It can be taken as fairly certain that the rumour of Sterne's authorship was systematically disseminated by Fuseli himself and those of his friends who were in the secret, to stimulate curiosity and divert attention from the real author. There is no record of Sterne having spoken of or even seen the book.

two places excepted, we cannot find out the resemblance. But that he is a great admirer of Shakespeare will be very evident to every critic in the works of that *child of nature*, whose phrase and language he introduces with a certain aptness, that we don't remember to have met elsewhere.

Upon the whole we recommend this little work to such only of our readers as are capable of separating the metal from the dross, and can discern the true orient, notwithstanding the foul incrustations which sully and deform it.—At the same time we beg leave to recommend more decency and propriety to the accomplished author in his next essay, as he values the general favour and the approbation of the public.

To this work is prefixed an ingenious, well-designed and satirical frontispiece, in which Voltaire is introduced, in a fine flowing peruke, with a pair of jackboots and spurs, and a whip in his hand, bestriding a monster which he has bridled, saddled and brought to the ground. Over his head, pendant by their necks upon a gibbet, are Justice and Liberty, upon the beam of which is seen all that remains of the temple of Liberty. On the right side of the piece, in front, upon a little eminence, stands an arch, shrugging figure, representing Rousseau, in a furred gown and cap, pointing with his right hand to the beast and his burthen, and with the plummet of Truth in his left, sounding, as we may suppose, the sincerity and real estimation of the rider.

We own that we are much affected at the awkward situation of our darling principles, Justice and Liberty; and are entirely ignorant of what they have done to deserve to be gibbeted.

If the little gentleman in fur, by virtue of his plummet and line, has found out, as he seems to insinuate, that Voltaire has been their executioner, we are of opinion that he ought to be hanged up in their stead.[1]

---

[1] This detailed interpretation of the intentionally cryptic and often misunderstood frontispiece to the Rousseau pamphlet would alone be sufficient, both by its fullness and by its style, to prove that nobody but Fuseli could have written the review. It is a piece of characteristic irony, that Fuseli omits to mention that the 'monster' on which Voltaire rides is Humanity itself.

SECTION SIX

FUSELI'S COLLABORATION IN
LAVATER'S *PHYSIOGNOMY*

The only writings of Fuseli's that have survived from his extremely important Roman years (1770–8) are a handful of not very valuable poems and a number of letters to Lavater. These letters, so far as they are not about money—'There is no getting him to write, unless he wants me to send him money,' says Lavater to Herder in 1774— are chiefly concerned with Lavater's immense work on Physiognomy, in which Fuseli took the greatest interest down to his death. When Henry Hunter's English translation of the *Essays on Physiognomy* from the French version was published (1789–1810), Fuseli acted as editor, carefully supervising both the text and the engraving of the innumerable plates, and also writing the *Advertisement*. When Thomas Holcroft published in 1789 his translation from an abridgment of the original German text, Fuseli violently attacked him in the *Analytical Review* (December 1789, April 1790). In 1788 Fuseli published with great success his own extremely free English rendering of the little companion work to the *Physiognomy*—Lavater's *Vermischte unphysiognomische Regeln*, under the title *Aphorisms on Man*. It was only natural that Lavater, when he began to collect material for his *Physiognomy*, about 1770, should have applied to Fuseli in particular for drawings of heads. Fuseli sent him many such drawings. He takes offence at almost everything the conciliatory Lavater writes to him, often less from real anger than because he relishes his own virtuosity in fierceness and abuse.

Lavater's Intractable Collaborator

THE GREATEST mistake you have made in all the subjects you have proposed, is that you will always masticate everything in advance for me. Realise that invention is the soul of the painter and that without it a painter might just as well belong to the cobblers' guild. Your imagination and mine may be the same; but if I am to execute the pictures of that imagination, they must flame up in my head, not in yours.

(Letter from Rome, May 1771—Muschg, p. 166, German)

Lavater dissatisfied with a head of Christ drawn for him by Fuseli

IT IS just as impossible to depict Jesus Christ for a Christian as it is to depict God for his worshipper; Raphael and Michelangelo performed both, and with human dignity too—but the view of the back-parts that Moses had was better still.

(As above)

Odious Comparisons—(1) Chodowiecki

I HAVE lost the desire and perhaps also the ability to squeeze great thoughts and noble lines into a space of three inches, so that even a bungling engraver must see the point of them. . . . I leave it to the 'most soulful' draughtsman of Europe[1] to draw the Iliad in a nutshell or the chariot and horses of Elijah on a gnat's wing. I need space, height, depth, length. Let those who will, raise a storm in a wine-glass or weep over a rose, I can't do

---

[1] Lavater had annoyed Fuseli by designating the popular artist Daniel Chodowiecki (1726–1801), who made many drawings for the *Physiognomy* as the 'most soulful draughtsman' of Europe.

it. . . . I will send you things, which perhaps have not yet
entered into the head of the 'most soulful' draughtsman of
Europe, and which your physiognomy will not fulminate
against.

> (Letters to Lavater from Rome, 2 November 1770 and 4 November
> 1773—Muschg, pp. 161, 167, German)

Odious Comparisons—(2) Benjamin West

The American-born Benjamin West—1738–1820—was Fuseli's *bête
noire*. The Royal Academy brought the two constantly into close contact with one another. In the *Lectures* Fuseli hints his contempt for
West; in the *Analytical Review* he gives it full rein. Lavater had compared West with Fuseli in his *Physiognomy*.

WHAT DO you mean by setting my name beside his? He has
great, very great advantages over me in technique and in
brush-work, and amongst the vast batches of figure-concoc-
tions that have come and still continue to come piping-hot
on to the market from his cook-shop there are two or three
good things, but he has scarcely ever thought, and he hasn't
any soul.

> (Letter to Lavater from Rome, 14 June 1777—Muschg, pp. 176–7,
> German)

Lavater's misinterpretation of Rembrandt's 'Ecce Homo' in the 'Physiognomy'

THE THINGS you have vaguely felt and written down about the
Christ before Pilate neither do justice to Rembrandt nor credit to
your own eye. You seem either not to have seen his engraving
yourself, or else—which strikes me as incomprehensible—not to
have understood it properly. The master of true composition
feels, and even a mere grouper of figures like West cannot help
realising, that it is the divinest composition ever to proceed
from a human heart, botched though it indeed is with a hanker-

ing after the secondhand shop, with nature at her frowsiest, and with the lowest dregs of passions:

> *Fiery their force and heavenly is the fount*
> *Engendering them—but in such measure dulled*
> *As bodies foul encumber, joints of clay*
> *And limbs a prey to death disfeature it.*[1]

Jesus Christ in the light above Jerusalem; the sea of the thronging multitude and the waves of the Pharisees etc., encroaching upon the shore—and then lo! Pilate hands them the rod of death,[2] that they may break it themselves—and you have taken Pilate for one of the Pharisees, and the rod of death for a stick, and have failed to hear the metallic clamour: 'His blood be on us.'

(Letter of 14 June 1777, as above, German)

In Defence of Lavater—Fuseli as Arbitrator between the Older Rationalism and the New Enthusiasm

OUR AUTHOR arraigns Mr. Lavater for 'extending to religion the same enthusiasm which he has *employed* in his researches on physiognomy etc.' In this expression there is not, perhaps, much propriety, if he means not to insinuate that Mr. Lavater is an artful man. If Mr. Lavater be weak enough to tamper with *animal magnetism*,[3] he is certainly too wise to mix it with his religious tenets; but a belief in the 'efficacy of absolute faith' is if we are not mistaken, a belief in the text of that gospel, whose

[1] Three lines from Vergil's *Aeneid*, VI, 730–2, '*Igneus est ollis . . .*', quoted by Fuseli in the original Latin.

[2] *The rod of death* (*der Blutstab*)—a ceremonial rod broken at the passing of the sentence of death in old German courts, corresponding therefore to the black cap of English judicial usage.

[3] Not only Lavater, but the whole of his own and the following generation of independent and poetic minds in German-speaking territories attached immense importance to animal magnetism or Mesmerism, often deducing very curious theories from these phenomena. Here Fuseli parts company with the tradition he originally grew up in. 'Tamper with' = to dabble in.

champion the *rector of Bemerton*[1] professes himself, and whose mysteries and miracles are surely not circumscribed by those narrow limits of self-conceited reason which he prescribes to a man whose faith is tempered by the most unremitting exertions of Christian duty, by melting charity and universal benevolence.

(*Analytical Review*, February 1790, review of Coxe's *Travels in Switzerland*, signed R. R.—VI, p. 157)

[1] W. Coxe, author of the book of travels here reviewed, was himself a clergyman and rector of Bemerton, as his title-page declares.

SECTION SEVEN

FUSELI ON WOMEN

<hr/>

'Raphael . . . fell, as the strong of all ages
fell, by women' (anonymously published
article in *Universal Museum*, February
1768)

'Fuseli was always very susceptible of the passion of love', writes
Knowles (p. 55). His drawings show that there was scarcely any way
of envisaging the erotic, from the most sentimental and idealised to
the most frankly obscene, that he did not whole-heartedly indulge in.
The same story is told by his writings and by all the biographical
records of him. When he was not reading Petrarch, he was reading
Aretino. When he is not shocking people with improper conversation, he is in his turn being shocked by the improper conversation of
others. When he met Sterne, he 'was miserably disappointed, as
nothing seemed to please him but talking obscenely' (Knowles,
p. 373). Leigh Hunt records of Fuseli that he was not 'always as
decorous as an old man ought to be. . . . The licenses he took were
coarse, and had not sufficient regard to his company' (*Lord Byron and
his Contemporaries*). That this is not simply a contradiction between
the younger and the older Fuseli, to be accounted for by the changes
passing time brings with it, is proved by his early letters and above
all by the *Remarks on Rousseau*. He seems even to have been given to
boasting of his profligacy. 'It was a story which he loved to repeat,
how he lay on his back day after day, and week succeeding week,
with upturned and wondering eyes, musing on the splendid ceiling
of the Sistine Chapel,' writes Cunningham. 'He sometimes, indeed,
added that such a posture of repose was necessary for *a body
fatigued like his with the pleasant gratifications of a luxurious city*.'
His obscenity was certainly that not of the naïve sensualist, but of

the disappointed sentimentalist. Professor Ganz accounts for Fuseli's obscene drawings (*see below*, p. 215) as expressing the contempt and moral indignation of the satirist.

Encounter of a Sentimental Traveller in Lyons

IT IS the custom here for ladies of the highest rank to go on foot through mire and rain and spouting gutters in certain quarters of the city, during Lent, to collect alms for the poor-house. These ladies called on Mylord and myself yesterday—ye ministers of grace, what a goddess one of them was! A cajoling eye, full of serene sky-blue, intimidated my eyes, a little lily-white hand emboldened my hand. Trembling I took her fingers in mine, bowing over them and saying: '*Madame, que les membres de l'église sont bien heureux de trouver une telle main pour éveiller la charité des hérétiques!*' With delighted surprise at the princely gift of a twenty guilder piece she curtsied, gave me a look, smiled and fluttered away again.

(Letter to Lavater, 19 February 1766—Muschg, p. 129, German)

The Moral Dangers of all Novels, and of the 'Nouvelle Héloïse' in particular

BUT IT were better, perhaps, *Héloïse* might be unintelligible to all. What, in the name of mutiny, what consequences will it have for wenches, to know that there are kisses, out of family, beyond the selfishness of parental pity or vanity, beyond the sober touch of brothers and sisters or the icicles on the lips of maiden friendship; kisses at once the flash of lightning and the morning's dew, joys the storm of pleasure and the balm of life? To know that the roseate bowers of their fathers' garden may, every leaf, every bud of them, be taught to breathe, to whisper bliss, to tell each its own tale of the mother of love? To know that stays paint to the eagle eye of love here their luxuriance of bosom and milky orbs of rapture, and there the slender waist and rising hips; that with the perfumes of their toilet contagion

143

spreads, that aprons will invite Hamlet to build tabernacles between Beauty's legs, and petticoats appear to Romeo the gates of Heaven——

What will be the consequence of all this?

They will open them[1]—yea, and dream at the same time that virginity may drop a maidenhead, and matrimony pick it up; that nature now and then lays a stumbling-block in Virtue's way to teach her to walk.

Your daughter may prove a harlot—very like—and may have read *Héloïse*, and mightily been pleased with it. But pray examine two things: how she came to read romances, and whether the dogs-ears go any farther than where Julia gives the *rendez-vous*.

(1767—*Remarks on Rousseau*, pp. 36*a*–39*a*)

Woman's Conscience

A MAN has a character, and dares to do no more than what becomes a man;[2] but women, they say, have none,[3] and therefore are never out of their sphere. Let temples, sacraments, parents, honour, nature, misery; let life stript of all feminine endearments, vanity, delicacy, pride; let mangled conscience and hag-ridden disease, let hatred, jealousy, revenge bar her gates, dispute her every inch of ground, fulminate her ear, assail her with torrents of tears, entangle her way with silken nets or strew it all with daggers; if a woman is bent on a purpose, swift as the thoughts of love, or lewdness, or fury, 'tis all one—she will throw herself headlong, and palpitate ecstasy on the bosom of perdition! She will break your heart or have hers broken.

---

[1] The Geneva and Edinburgh copies of the *Remarks* have, instead of the words 'open them', eight asterisks. The British Museum, Bodleian and Cambridge copies print the two words in full.

[2] Cp. *Macbeth*, I, vii: 'I dare do all that may become a man; Who dares do more is none.'

[3] Cp. Pope, *Moral Essays*, Epistle II: 'Most women have no characters at all.'

Meleager in the arms of his wife, refusing to fight in defence of Calydon

And could you really live with a wife which you had reason to suspect liked another better than yourself, and had made the comparison? You parasite of manhood! You blister of humanity! You unmeaning, poor, forked thing! A dog wears his own coat, but you are sunk almost as low as your footman.

(1767—*Remarks on Rousseau*, pp. 45*a*–47*a*)

The Virtue of Women

I RELUCTANTLY allow, that the article of believing in the virtue of women must, in common life, be confined to the catechism of charity only. But that the trumpeters of female excellence should think it impossible that a woman may conquer a passion from principles, should look upon Julia's agreeing to see her former lover in presence of a husband acquainted with both their hearts, and an impartial examiner, as on a sign of insincerity, or at best as on a wanton periclitation of pride, is, I think, making but a sorry compliment to the fair.

(1767—*Remarks on Rousseau*, p. 47*a*)

Women

SUCH IS the fugitive essence, such the intangible texture of female genius, that few combinations of circumstances ever seemed to favour its transmission to posterity.

IN AN age of luxury women have taste, decide and dictate; for in an age of luxury woman aspires to the functions of man, and man slides into the offices of woman. The epoch of eunuchs was ever the epoch of viragos.

FEMALE AFFECTION is ever in proportion to the impression of superiority in the object. Woman fondles, pities, despises and forgets what is below her; she values, bears and wrangles with her equal; she adores what is above her.

(1788–1818—*Aphorisms* 225–7)

M.H.F.   145   K

Amorous Curves

THE FORMS of virtue are erect, the forms of pleasure undulate: Minerva's drapery descends in long, uninterrupted lines; a thousand amorous curves embrace the limbs of Flora.

(1788–1818—Aphorism 194)

Woman and Asceticism

YOUR ACCOUNT of the Nunneries you have visited confirms Hamlet's verdict: 'Frailty, thy name is woman!' How self-contradictory, that the 'animal of beauty', as Dante calls woman, should exchange her claims to social admiration and pleasure, and the substantial charms of life, for the sterile embrace of a crucifix, or of some withered sister, by the dim glimmer of cloistered light,—lost to hope, and marked by oblivion for her own! Tyranny, deception and, most of all, that substitute for every other want, 'the undistinguished space of woman's will', can alone account for such phenomena.

(31 August 1809, letter to Knowles)

1789–92—'The Active Affections of Miss Wollstonecraft'

'The coquetting of a married man of fifty with a tender female philosopher of thirty-one can never be an agreeable subject of contemplation' (Cunningham)

In a letter of 28 September 1826 William Godwin, in a remarkable fit of very much belated delicacy, asks Knowles that Mary Wollstonecraft may be 'very slightly mentioned, or not at all' in the projected biography of Fuseli. He had himself published the fullest account of the relationship between Fuseli and Mary in 1798, in his *Memoirs of the Author of a Vindication of the Rights of Woman*, and there was little left for Knowles to add. Knowles very rightly ignored Godwin's unreasonable request. The relevant portions of Godwin's own narrative are here given in condensed form, supplemented with

146

two extracts from Knowles, which are distinguished by being enclosed in square brackets. Cunningham's ribald treatment of this episode is not only less reliable, but also less entertaining than Godwin's solemn endeavour to invest the circumstances with an aura of sanctity. On hearing of Godwin's marriage with Mary, Fuseli wrote to a friend 'that the assertrix of female rights has given her hand to the *balancier* of political justice'. Fuseli had little sympathy with feminism, and his generalisations on female genius, female affection and on woman aspiring to the functions of man, in Aphorisms 225–7 (see p. 145), can probably be regarded as a veiled commentary on Mary Wollstonecraft's character and mentality (cp. Browning's *Jocoseria*).

MARY . . . saw Mr. Fuseli frequently; he amused, delighted and instructed her. As a painter, it was impossible she should not wish to see his works, and consequently to visit his house. She visited him; her visits were returned. Notwithstanding the inequality of their years, Mary was not of a temper to live upon terms of so much intimacy with a man of merit and genius, without loving him. The delight she enjoyed in his society she transferred by association to his person. What she experienced in this respect was no doubt heightened by the state of celibacy and restraint in which she had hitherto lived, and to which the rules of polished society condemn an unmarried woman. She conceived a personal and ardent affection for him. Mr. Fuseli was a married man, and his wife was the acquaintance of Mary. She readily perceived the restrictions which this circumstance seemed to impose upon her; but she made light of any difficulty that might arise out of them . . . She conceived it both practicable and eligible to cultivate a distinguishing affection for him, and to foster it by the endearments of personal intercourse and a reciprocation of kindness, without departing in the smallest degree from the rules she prescribed to herself . . . ['She hoped,' she said, 'to unite herself to his mind.'] . . . She had, at first, considered it as reasonable and judicious to cultivate what I may be permitted to call a Platonic affection for him; but she did not, in the sequel, find all the satisfaction in this plan which she had originally expected from it. It was in vain that she enjoyed much pleasure in his society, and that she enjoyed it frequently. Her ardent imagination was continually conjuring up pictures of the happiness she should have found, if fortune had favoured their more intimate union. . . . General conversation and society could not satisfy her. . . . [At last Mrs. Wollstonecraft appears to have grown desperate, for she had the temerity to go to Mrs. Fuseli, and to tell her that she wished to become an inmate in her family; and she added, 'as I am above deceit, it is right to say that this proposal arises from the sincere affection which I have for your husband, for I find that I cannot live without the satisfaction of seeing and conversing with him daily'. This frank avowal immediately opened the eyes of Mrs. Fuseli, who . . . instantly forbade her the house. No resource was now left for Mrs. Wollstonecraft, but to fly from the object, which she regarded, . . . and on the 8th of December, 1792, (she) left London for France. . . . She died on the 10th September 1797, after having given birth to a female child. . . . Fuseli . . . barely noticed the catastrophe in the postscript of a letter to Mr. Roscoe, in these terms,—'Poor Mary!']

SECTION EIGHT

ANNA LANDOLT'S IMPETUOUS LOVER

October 1778 to March 1779, between leaving Rome and settling for good in England, Fuseli, then thirty-eight years old, spent six months in Zurich and there fell in love with a niece of Lavater's, Anna Landolt. This was the most serious passion of his life. He was eager to marry Anna, but she appears to have regarded him only with a mixture of alarm and lukewarm interest, and the doubtful reputation he still had in his native town, coupled with his still uncertain worldly position, gave him very little chance as a suitor. Shortly after his arrival in London he heard that Anna was about to contract a marriage of convenience with her wealthy cousin, the merchant Schinz. In a letter written to Northcote from Lugano on 29 September 1778 Fuseli says: 'At the sound of Rome, my heart swells, my eye kindles and frenzy seizes me.' Taken together with other evidence this suggests that he was at this time still convalescing from a stormy love affair in Rome, the object of which may have been the humbly born Nanina of the Bolognette Palace who becomes in Knowles' inexact reprint of the letter to Northcote 'Navina in the Bolognese Palace'. (*See* Stephen Gwynn, *Memorial of an 18th-Century Painter*, 1898, quoted by Federmann.) Fuseli had by now apparently almost given up writing verse, but the emotional stress of his disappointed love for Anna Landolt (whom he always refers to as *Nanna*) found an outlet in two poems, almost the last he wrote, so far as we know, and certainly the most valuable. In the second of these poems there appear to be oblique references to the Nanina, as well as to the Swiss Nanna, and also to some English girl about whom nothing is known. Fuseli's erotic entanglements at this time would seem to have been remarkably complex. It was at Baden, the Swiss spa near Zurich, that Fuseli must have taken leave of Anna in March 1779, before beginning his long-drawn-out journey to London via Mulhouse, Namur and Ostend.

An Nannas Lieblingsreh

Wie selig wärst du, Mündel der reinsten Hand,
des schönsten Auges Liebling, du hüpfendes
    Geschöpf der Einfalt, wenn in Nannas
        duftendem Schosse dein schüchtern Haupt ruht:

Verstündest du, was das ist, von Nannas Hand
gepflegt zu werden! Sögst du Gefühle ein!
    Empfingest du von ihres Busens
        schmachtender Sprödigkeit Sympathien!

Sie küsste dich—beim Himmel! Ihr Rosenmund
lippte dein Auge! Zephyre küssen nicht
    die neu entknospte Blume leiser,
        säuseln nicht über Violen schneller,

weht es im Lenze! Doch du empfandest nicht!
Raschgleitend flohst du von deiner Königin—
    und liessest mir die trübe Glosse,
        dass ich ein Sklave, du frei seist, über!

Baden, 1779

Alcaics—to Nanna's Pet Fawn

How blessèd were you, charge of the purest hand,
the fairest eye's sweet darling, you frolicsome
    and guileless fawn, your timid head in
        fragrance of Nanna's dear lap reposing—

an inkling if only you had, what heavenly hand
hers is, that tends you—sentient, athirst for her!
    if, languishing, her bosom's coyness
        wakened responsive emotions in you!

She kissed you—Heavens!—nuzzling with rosy mouth
your eyelids, lip to lid! Not a breeze there is
    so gently kisses budding flowers or
      over new violets swifter ripples,

when spring's astir. Rare favour to waste on you!
One twist, one bound—and off! you have fled from her!
    For me remains the glum reflection:
      you are the freeman and I the bondslave.

From a letter to Lavater, written at Namur, 16 April 1779

AH, LAVATER! The thoughts of this night benumb me! I am
in the dark, and the gloom of the future thickens around me,
the further I advance. Will *she* remember me? And if *she* remembered me, what good will it do? She must, she will belong
to another. O God, I could not stay, and ought not to have
gone. I must write to *her*, or *she* to me, circumspection and
ceremony are of no use here. She ought to have the better and
not the declining years of my life, and I scorn to become her
husband when my body shall no longer be a fit object for her
desires. What it is now, you, 'poor weakling', know, and one
of your acquaintances besides could inform her. . . . I know what
moral you will extract from this state of mind for me:

             Perseverance.
    Hard work.   Saving money.

And so be it, God helping—but fail not to contribute your
share. . . .

                     (Muschg, pp. 182–3, German)

From a letter written at Namur, 18 April 1779,
to Madame Orell

I AM sitting here, dear Orell, in a town full of soldiers, priests, colliers, lodging-house-keepers and shopgirls, my phiz[1] on both fists, my two eyes now swimming with tears, now roving hither and thither, and can hear a raven calling 'Peep-bo!' and 'Who's there?' beneath my window. Who's there? But none of those voices that my soul flies towards answers! My soul is nauseated by the polite attentions with which people overwhelm me. I sit at the table of my fellow-countrymen like one dead, and catch myself now at sea, now in the mountains that separate me from you and from——! My words flow like the last tired drops in the glass, and my eye takes flight into the dark. O darkness, my light! What would become of Fuseli now, if he had no nights! . . .

Have you been in Baden since we parted? Tell your friend there what I was unable to tell her, and what I can also scarcely put down on paper, for my soul is as proud as hers. But if her heart responds sympathetically to vibrations from afar, she must indeed know more about me than you can tell her. Each earthly night since I left her, I have lain in her bed—when she perceived me, a voice from her bed always asked me, 'How is Fr—— Schw——?'[2] O how I would answer that dainty-demure languishing of yours, if once you were in my arms! And for your sake, you slanting eye of love, you creature of roses, lilies and violets, you womanly virginity, you precious coaxer of tears, you who make me wring my hands so des-

---

[1] Fuseli uses a gross Swiss vulgarism for 'face'—the word *Grind*, which in standard German means *scurf* or *scab*.

[2] *Fr—— Schw——*: Presumably *Frau Schweizer* (1751–1814), misleadingly referred to in most publications on Fuseli by her maiden name *Magdalena Hess*, although she had been married to J. C. Schweizer since 1775, three or four years before Fuseli first made her acquaintance. This Magdalena Schweizer-Hess was notoriously frivolous and irresponsible. Schweizer had, according to his biographer David Hess, in 1801 still not forgotten the qualms of jealousy Fuseli had caused him twenty-two years earlier (*see below*, p. 155, footnote 2).

perately—for your sake Italy and my native land are become foreign countries for me and the spring sunshine darkness. But go and take another—for I have belonged to another, and perhaps I still do.

(Muschg, pp. 184–6, German)

Nannas Auge

Auge derer, die ich liebe,
meiner Seele Wallfahrt du,
Stern am Himmel meiner Triebe,
meiner müden Wünsche Ruh.
Auge, wie noch keines blickte,
das der Liebe Pfeile schoss,
das zum Engel mich entzückte,
weil es Schmerzen in mich goss.

Augen, wie sie Dichter malen,
sah ich, rang und überwand;
Farb gibt Herzen keine Qualen,
Dichterfarb ist Herzen Tand.
Blaues Schmachten, schwarzes Blitzen,
Britisches und Römerfeuer—
Mag ein schwarzes Aug' erhitzen
werde blauen Augen teuer.

Aug', in dir malt ohne Farbe
eine Seele sich, ein Herz;
du verwundest ohne Narbe
wie du heilest ohne Schmerz.
Schmeichelnder als Frühlingslüfte,
doch wie Lilienodem stark,
sanft wie junger Rosen Düfte
dringst du durch mein tiefstes Mark.

To Nanna's Eye

Eye of her I love! a palmer
is my soul, and you the shrine;
Star, my weary longings' calmer,
as in their clouded heav'n you shine.
Eye!—none other, arrows darting,
looks upon me as does yours,
when into my gashes smarting
angel-ravishment it pours.

Eyes I saw as poets paint them,
saw, and struggling overcame;
paint lures hearts, but can't attaint them,
for hearts all riming's but a game.
Black for flashing, blue to languish,
Roman ardour, British glow—
if the black bring burning anguish,
blue eyes soon assuage the throe.

Eye without garish hue depicting
faithfully a soul, a heart,
wounds with ne'er a scar inflicting,
as you heal with ne'er a smart!
Bland as sweet airs that spring discloses,
yet keen as lily perfume too,
mild as breath of budding roses,
you pierce my being through and through.

This poem is written on the back of a drawing of a girl's head which
bears beneath it the inscription, *M. H. Ostende.* This points to a date
late in April 1779, between Fuseli's leaving Namur and his arrival
in London. One is strongly inclined to assume that the girl's head of
the drawing must be that of Nanna, but the initials *M. H.* will only
admit of the conclusion that it must be either Magdalena or Martha
Hess. Comparisons with other portraits of these two sisters by Fuseli
show no striking resemblance to the present head. Muschg inter-
prets the poem as expressing renunciation.

From a letter written to Lavater from London on 16 June 1779

IS SHE in Zurich now? Last night I had her in bed with me—tossed my bedclothes hugger-mugger—wound my hot and tight-clasped hands about her—fused her body and her *soul* together with my own—poured into her my spirit, breath and strength. Anyone who touches her now commits adultery and incest! She is *mine*, and I am *hers*. And have her I will—I will toil and sweat for her, and lie alone, until I have won her. And woe to him, who dares to desire her; church and altar are but stone and wood——

Do your utmost to bring this about. I am as convinced as I am of my own existence, that nothing but the infernal Zurich family humbug and a handful of money stand between her and me. But whether you sacrifice her or not, because she is your niece—I will enforce my first right to her, or else die in the attempt—and perhaps kill somebody too. What God or nature hath joined, let no man—let no business-man[1] sunder.

(Muschg, pp. 191–2)

From a letter to Lavater from London, 13 August 1779

ANSWER ME at length, and immediately, that is to say, as soon as you have read this letter. Lots about Nanna and Maddy,[2]

---

[1] Fuseli first wrote '*der Mensch nicht*', then crossed it out and put instead '*kein Kaufmann*'. Schinz, who married Anna Landolt, was a merchant.

[2] *Nännen und Mäden—Nännen* must be Anna Landolt. *Mäden* is possibly Magdalena Hess, whose portrait Fuseli had painted when he was in Zurich, and who in 1775 married Johann Caspar Schweizer, a man of some importance in the history of the period. As Magdalena Schweizer she appears in Goethe's life; Goethe came into possession of Fuseli's portrait of her, which is still in Weimar. This Magdalena had a sister, Martha Hess, who seems to have died, probably of consumption, in December 1779. Fuseli made sketches of both sisters, and seems to have been somewhat in love with them as well as with Anna Landolt. It is strange that we have no drawing of

and so you will save me from Polly and Nancy and Peggy *Basciami.*

(Muschg, p. 194)

Anna Landolt from him. The present outline of this episode is based on the assumption that the Nanna Fuseli wanted to marry was, as Knowles states, Anna Landolt—this is the version of the facts accepted by Muschg in his edition of the letters. Paul Ganz, however, in the introduction to his *Hans Heinrich Füsslis Zeichnungen* (Bern-Olten, 1947), speaks only of Martha Hess as the true Nanna. There is still much to be straightened out here. *Polly, Nancy* and *Peggy* in the present letter are, of course, representative for the whole category of London courtesans.

PART TWO

FUSELI'S

PHILOSOPHY

OF LIFE

'He is evidently a gentleman, a scholar, a philosopher, a genius and a man of wit'
(Review of the *Remarks*)

For philosophy proper Fuseli would seem to have had little taste or aptitude, although it must have fallen within the sphere of his studies at Zurich. He seems to have disliked Plato, of whom he asserts at the age of nineteen that Socrates never communicated his deepest wisdom to him, and perhaps had good reasons for not doing so. This throws some light on his frequent later scornful application of the epithet 'Platonic' to the great German cultural revival and all its works. It is in keeping with this that, while scoffing at the German dogmatic rationalist Wolff, he declares his adherence to a sensualistic empiricism similar to that of Hobbes and Locke, insisting that 'our ideas are the offsprings of our senses' (*see below*, Part III, Section 1). The 'Ideal' of which he has so much to say in his aesthetic theories (*see* Part IV, Section 1) must therefore be interpreted in a relative or derivative sense, and not transcendentally. A hankering after the 'Infinite' he indeed sometimes has, but he seldom speaks of it without a certain irony—(*see below*, Part V, Section 5). The place of formal philosophy was, however, for him, largely occupied by theology, that is to say by an extremely modernistic and ultimately quite secularised theology. It was from this angle that he approached the thinker who interested and influenced him most, Rousseau. He has all Rousseau's disgust with civilised man, sharpened with a sardonic acerbity of his own, and this stays with him to the end. Such belief in the 'man of nature' as he imbibed from Rousseau in early years seems, however, very soon to vanish, and with it all confidence in the ultimate perfectibility of man on earth. It is to these questions that he again and again returns.

SECTION ONE

FUSELI AND CHRISTIANITY

Fuseli is nearly always found in the opposition. He is ready to disagree with everybody, before they have opened their mouths. Just as obscenity provokes him to prudishness and prudishness to obscenity (*see above*, Part I, Section 7), so also he tends to attack Christianity when others defend it, and to defend it when they attack it, especially in a numerous company. The American painter, Washington Allston, on his visit to London in 1801, found himself forced to avoid Fuseli, whom he greatly admired, 'because I could not stand his profanity' (Flegg's *Life and Letters of Washington Allston*, New York, 1892). Farington, a good churchman, also sometimes suffered under Fuseli's irreverence: 'Fuseli said he had on this visit (to Lord Rivers) a dispute with his Lordship upon religion and, as it appeared, Fuseli was not an advocate for public or perhaps for any worship, saying *everything had been given to us and we had nothing to ask for*. Such were the light and inconsiderate sentiments which he uttered' (*Farington Diary*, 12 January 1808). Cunningham, or his informant, received, however, a very different impression: 'The *ci-devant* friend of Miss Wollstonecraft was no scoffer at revelation,' he writes, 'nor would he suffer anyone in his presence to call it in question.' Few were those who were ever able, like Haydon on one solitary occasion, to find themselves in agreement with Fuseli on these, or, indeed, on any other questions: 'On Monday following, I spent the evening with Fuseli. . . . A long argument on Christianity: both agreed that its beautiful morality proved its divinity' (*Journals* for 1808). This is a theme on which Fuseli had dwelt forty years earlier in his *Remarks on Rousseau*. There is to the last something of the spoilt priest, or rather of the spoilt Zwinglian minister, about him. He was seldom a good prophet, but he certainly was one when, in the last year of his life, he pictured the art of the future finding itself reduced

159

to deploring the loss of the religion from which it had so resolutely emancipated itself. Knowles records Fuseli as having said: 'There are no real Christians, for the religion of Christ died with its great Author; for where do we witness in those who bear his name the self-abasement and charity of their master, which qualities he not only taught, but practised?' This is very much like the way in which many of the great men and also many of the nonentities of those and following generations have spoken of Christ; in particular it reminds one of a famous utterance of Goethe's to Chancellor von Müller: 'Who nowadays is a Christian as Christ wanted him to be?' But it is inconceivable that Fuseli would ever have spoken in the way in which Goethe did in the continuation of this conversation, when he breezily claimed that he alone came up to the demands of Christ. Fuseli feels to the last something unique and awe-inspiring about the person of Christ which renders it impossible for him to play fast and loose with him, to compare himself with him or to accommodate him arbitrarily to his own private imaginings, as Goethe does in his *Wandering Jew*, Blake in his *Everlasting Gospel*, D. H. Lawrence in his *Escaped Cock* and as many others have done in similar rhapsodies. What Fuseli felt about this question comes out most clearly in the words he wrote shortly before his death on Leonardo's Christ (*see below*, Part IV, Section 2). He is concerned with something more than the aesthetic evaluation of a work of art, when he speaks, in terms that preserve in attenuated form something of the orthodox tradition he despised, of 'divine, or what is the same, incomprehensible and infinite powers . . . embodied . . . in quiet and simple features of humanity' (Lecture XI, p. 10) as unique attributes of Christ.

Christianity

WE ARE more impressed by Gothic than by Greek mythology, because the bands are not yet rent which tie us to its magic; he has a powerful hold us on who holds us by our superstition or by a theory of honour.

(1788–1818—Aphorism 105)

Christ and the gods of ancient Greece

It was one of the favourite aspirations of the new pantheism which arose with Romanticism, to establish a synthesis between Christ and the old pagan divinities, and to do this in a very much more

and sense give graces to terror on one side, it agonises at every pore, nay shudders with inward horror, to see perfection insulted, unrewarded, punished, become the flaw of Providence and humanity.

But if ever an effect diametrically opposite to the cause has amazed observation, 'tis, that, as long as immortality was no more but a guess of conjecture, men hugged it with the most restless ardour: death was the victory of virtue, the most exalted reward of benevolence, a complete atonement for affliction—since Jesus Christ has brought it to light, we'd jump the life to come——

If it were not for so unaccountable a prejudice, where, pray, could Rousseau have torn the thread of Julia's life with more propriety, than where he tears it? He suffered the fruit to ripen into mellowness before he shook the branch, and you blame him for dishing it up before it was cancer-bit? What would Julia the granddam have done not yet done by Julia the wife and mother? . . . Why should she then be grudged to have obtained what the boding Moor, in his noon of bliss, begged in vain of his cruel stars:

> *If it were now to die,*[1]
> *'Twere now to be most happy; for I fear*
> *My soul has her content so absolute,*
> *That not another comfort like to this*
> *Succeeds in unknown fate!*

Oh! you of Heloisa's mourners, who roamed over the wilds of sympathetic joys and visionary bliss, tell me, did ever the idol of your soul appear to your ecstatic eye in the pallid robe of Life's autumnal dress? Wouldst thou, O Petrarch,[2] have remembered 'the ringlets waving pure with radiant gold, and the lightnings of Laura's angel-face', on the bald head of a matron,

[1] Fuseli quotes this line from *Othello*, II, i, in the form: 'If I were now to die . . .' This is an emendation introduced by Rowe in his second edition in 1714 and running through all editions down to and including Dr. Johnson's in 1765.

[2] Petrarch, Sonnet CCLI:

> *Le crespe chiome d' or puro lucente*
> *E'l lampeggiar dell'angelico riso . . .*

in the blunt eye of marriage? The grave alone could give immortality to thy love.

(1767—*Remarks on Rousseau*, pp. 50a–71)

Death, Immortality and Poetic Justice

THERE (i.e. in ancient Greece and Rome) amidst the acclama-
tions of religion, the prophetic mother[1] pours on her knees
adoration for the great reward of obedience,—Cleobis and Biton
dead at her feet. There Socrates and Cato, with a last sigh o'er
the carrions of Athens and Rome, snatch eternity and die.
There Arria presents the reeking dagger to her pallid husband:
—'Paetus! it smarts not.'[2]

These were the public sentiments; and *here*, when one exhibits the spectacle which Seneca, rotten as he was, pronounced
a god-like one, throws all his readers at the feet of wronged
Clarissa, and rewards the well-fought battle with death—immortality—'tis against poetical justice!

When Shakespeare, to lesson mankind, afflicts innocence and
virtue, nor, in the latitude of the ravings, crimes, follies he ex-
poses, can find any reward this side the grave for them; when, to
warn fathers against the dotage of predilection, the fury of prejudice and the destructive consequences of flattery, he destroys
the family of Lear, and wraps Cordelia in the storm, one gentle
feeler[3] changes her dagger to a husband, and adulterates the
simplicity of filial piety with love, and another[4] could not for all
the world read the play a second time, till he turned commentator. When the same poet, to stamp on power the mark of
private virtue, and to consecrate wedlock, thunders law and
nature to ambition, tears the womb of incest, and dashes all
its horrors into light, they mince passion to a tear for pretty,

[1] The priestess Cydippe, whose sons Cleobis and Biton died in their sleep
in answer to her prayer that they might be granted what was best for mortals.

[2] Paetus hesitating to perform the command of Claudius that he should
kill himself, his wife Arria stabbed herself to show him the way.

[3] Nahum Tate was responsible for the altered version of *King Lear*, which
ends with Edgar marrying Cordelia.

[4] Dr. Johnson, 1765, in his preface to *King Lear*.

harmless, blasted Ophelia, and arraign the great instructor of mankind at the bar of Drury Lane. But could you expect worse from those who, with the gravity of a Welsh goat, discuss whether Lear's madness was owing to his abdication of power or the ingratitude of his daughters?[1]

The truth is, there are few who do not grind their taste for beauty on gross appetite, and fewer still who build virtue on conscience. We all practise or love it, as the divines say, *sub intuitu boni*. And if it is certain that a child prefers a bit of sugar in the hand to a shop of sweetmeats to-morrow, we are likelier to do what is right for fortune in this life than for happiness in the next. Let a miser, meeting misery from church, imagine howling or Hallelujah as long as you please,—the halfpenny lies snug; let him remember the next lottery, 'twill perhaps be given. Go on from these dregs of human nature to its most generous juices, and you'll find that we all hate to serve God for nothing, or worse than nothing,—death,—immortality.

(1767—*Remarks on Rousseau*, footnote on pp. 67–9)

[1] Fuseli repeatedly expresses his scorn of Arthur Murphy for talking in this manner of Lear in 1754 in the *Gray's-Inn Journal*. Dr. Johnson follows the theme up.

CHILDHOOD AND THE NAÏVE

The aspect of Rousseau's belief in the Man of Nature which most deeply and permanently appealed to Fuseli was his apotheosis of the child. Even on this theme Fuseli cannot, however, often speak without something of his characteristic ferocity, which is here directed against parents and schoolmasters. In this connexion the following passage from Farington's diary is of interest: 'Fuseli gave us an account of his infancy. He said that at eight years of age he was so passionately fond of drawing that, it being the custom to send him to bed early, he used to steal bits of candles, and when the family had retired to bed he contrived to get a light and sit up all night drawing. . . . *Letters* were *beat into him*. His father, as was the usage in Zurich, determined what his children should be without consulting their inclinations. He resolved that Fuseli should be a scholar and that his brother should be a painter, whereas it should have been reversed. He passed those early days in drawing and crying; every day floods of tears at being forced to read, which were relieved by stolen hours for his favourite amusement. . . . It was in Italy that he applied to *literature* (i.e. learning) *with inclination.* . . . The basis on which his after acquisitions in this way were raised had been flogged into him' (*Farington Diary*, 1 October 1802).

The method of Rousseau's 'Emile'

SUCH IS the method of Emile: insinuating virtue, without giving one single precept; at the first of precepts the book ends. Now that's what of all things they can bear least: not one precept of virtue! And there is not one schoolmaster in the kingdom, but what would heartily throw the book, and all its nonsense, in the Thames, or —— —— —— —— ——, could he but afford it.

(1767—*Remarks on Rousseau*, pp. 35–6)

Parents and children in the Middle Ages and now

IN THE fogs of popery, whether the tyranny of parents rung the alarum bell of filial rights, or the baggage of daughters hung so heavy on the neck of pedigrees, that by its own weight it dropped into the kennel; whether Kitty slept on the balcony to catch the nightingale, or Agatha threw off her veil to make mouths in a glass, and swallowed paternosters till they burst her belly[1]—whatever boy or girl proved haggard, 'twas a changeling, an abortion, substituted by an incubus; and sometimes a tender religious mother would carry her offspring to the next bridge, to know whether it was a goblin she was going to suckle, or her own child. In the first case, the little monster, whistled at by the legion in the water, would jump out of the basket and plunge to join his brethren; in the other, the child would cross himself. It may, and with charity too, be presumed that the number of devil-brats somewhat exceeded that of babies.

In our clear days of reformation and sense, the devil has obtained his absolution. Let a daughter refuse to suckle fools and chronicle small-beer, to call a money-bag vigour, or vigour a heart; let her scorn to counterpoise a bladder of a husband by the carats pendant in her ear, and, mindless of rank, stoop to read some Othello's face in his heart,[2] and dare to loose[3] a

[1] Extreme example of the obscurity of the younger Fuseli's Swiss-English allusive style. The meaning appears to be: 'Whether parents drove their children to revolt by harshness or let them drift into evil courses by neglect, whether daughters went wrong through too little restraint (sleeping on the balcony) or too much (by being forced to become nuns) . . .'

[2] 'I saw Othello's visage in his mind'—*Othello*, I, iii.

[3] This 'loose' is possibly a misprint for 'lose'. Or perhaps Fuseli intends some such meaning as 'to free herself from the encumbering shackles of a father's control'.

173

father with him; let Concealment feed on her damask cheek—
or turn her loose, down from the waist a centaur[1]: 'tis all one,
'tis reading, 'tis playhouse, 'tis sentiment, 'tis those damned
romances that have turned her head——

And will for ever, I am afraid,—till fathers and mothers
learn to be something more than the parents of their own
passions.

(1767—*Remarks on Rousseau*, pp. 40*a*–42*a*)

The Picturesqueness of Infancy as opposed to that of Decrepitude

IF THE picturesque be founded on ideas of age and decay, in
contradistinction to those of youth and freshness, it may be
asked what are the principles from which the forms and actions
of children derive their power of pleasing. It cannot be simply
from beauty, if proportion and symmetry be as essential to that
quality as softness and a smooth surface. Their parts melt not
into each other by imperceptible undulation, but, when ex-
erted, are marked by indents, folds and cuts, smooth indeed, but
sudden, and thus relieve that uninterrupted breadth of masses,
which in repose approach nearer to ugliness than beauty. The
head, belly and knees of children preponderate over the neck,
hips and legs. The young fauns, satyrs and centaurs of ancient,
and the pucks, fairies and goblins of modern mythology are
hairy and rough; but crispness and sprouting curls are a characteristic of all infants. Their action, sudden in its onset, rapid in
its transitions, and unrestrained by reflection, surprises whilst it
delights. Their expression, 'naïve', arch and equally contrasted
by imbecility and appetite, now mimics the man, now shrinks
back into the child, but never admits of languor. The same may
be said of all young animals in general; they surprise and please
from a principle directly opposite to decay: the colt, kid and
young ass, the kitten and the whelp, the lioncel and the cub of

[1] Cp. *King Lear*, IV, vi: 'Down to the waist they are centaurs, Though
women all above.' There is a characteristic anacoluthon in Fuseli's sentence
construction here.

every carnivorous beast, from their disproportion of limbs, the unexpected variety of their motions, starts and gambols, the sprouting and more curled inequalities of their surface, appear to us to excel the full-grown or decaying animal in the powers of exciting surprise, and keeping attention on the wing.

Perhaps the same reason which makes sketches more picturesque than finished pictures may be given for the superior picturesqueness of children and the young of all the creation: the elements of motion, form and growth exist, but the transitions from part to part are either not delineated, or abruptly marked. And for similar reasons the lyric may be considered the most picturesque of poetic compositions.

(*Analytical Review*, November 1794, review of Uvedale Price's *Essay on the Picturesque*, signed R. R.—XX, pp. 264–5)

Children

ALL ACTIONS and attitudes of children are graceful, because they are the luxuriant and immediate offspring of the moment —divested of affectation, and free from all pretence.

(1788–1817—Aphorism 45).

SECTION FOUR

THE ELUSIVENESS
OF ALL ABSOLUTE STANDARDS,
AND THE SENSE OF EVIL

One of the qualities that most clearly separates Fuseli from the dominant cultural tendencies of his age, and perhaps also largely accounts for the much greater appeal he makes to us, is that he has no conviction, either instinctive or theoretical, that there is an immanent harmony or movement towards harmony in all things, and that he consequently cannot calm himself with cheerful optimistic views of human nature and destiny. His temperament and work are essentially harsh and inharmonious, and therein the very reverse of those of the man who most completely embodied the spiritual aspirations of the age—Goethe. Thence, perhaps, Fuseli's distrust of the 'Platonic'. The sense of evil, which most of his distinguished contemporaries were engaged in exorcising, often with considerable success, is immensely strong in him. Whether he believed in God or not, he cannot get on without belief in the Devil. He was proud of his nickname *'Painter in ordinary to the Devil'* and said of it once: 'Aye! he has sat to me many times' (Cunningham). When somebody asked him, on seeing his painting of *Oedipus and his Daughters*, what the old man was afraid of, he answered: 'Afraid, Sir, why, of going to Hell!' (Cunningham). He is strong on sin, to the point of being the most enthusiastic apologist that Milton's allegory of Sin and Death has ever found, and frequently treats that allegory pictorially, not only in his Milton Gallery.

A Blackguard and a Genteel Virtue

VIRTUE, indeed, is independent of modes and whims, illocal, simple, unalterable; but not so those who call themselves its votaries; if not the slaves, at least influenced by temper, education, prejudices, talents, life. Some feel it, some deduct[1] it from reason. Of some it accompanies, of others it guides the life. Some want it in full dress, some plain. Aristippus admires it at Alexander's table, Archimedes runs naked after it through the streets. Socrates practises, Plato teaches it. Some clothe it with mortality; others, with Ulysses, find its phantom only, among the Cimmerians. It floats on motives, interests, circumstances, characters, errors. Misconstrued, misapplied, it often founders on chance, trifles, whims, fashions. There is a blackguard, and there is a genteel virtue. Some can have its dignity, others its honesty only; most cannot have it at all. What wonder, if, in that eternal rotation of accidents, its effects are at best but desultory, and its real presence often escapes your eyes?

(1767—*Remarks on Rousseau*, pp. 140–1)

Discrepancies between the Good, the Beautiful and the True

SOME OF the most genuine effusions of genius in art, some of the most estimable qualities in society, may be beholden for our homage to very disputable principles. The admission of a master's humanity to his slave supposes the validity of an execrable right; and the courage shown in a duel cannot be applauded without submitting to the dictates of feudal barbarity. Had the poet's conception prepared us for the rashness of Lear, the ambition of Macbeth's wife, and the villany of Iago by the usual gradations of nature, he could not have rushed on our heart with the irresistibility that now subdues it. Had the line

---

[1] *Deduct* in the sense of *deduce* has, according to the *New English Dictionary*, been obsolete since 1600. Fuseli has probably here simply made the typical foreigner's blunder of mixing up two words of closely similar form.

of Correggio floated in a less expanse, he would have lost the spell of light and shade which has enthralled all eyes; and Rubens, had he not invigorated bodies to hills of flesh, and tinged his pencil in the rainbow, would not have been the painter of magnificence.

(1788–1818—Aphorism 27 and Corollary)

Ambiguity in the Relationship between Author and Reader

MISAPPLICATION is inseparable from writing. A statesman of determined character may find instructions of tyranny in the subtle systems of Augustus and Tiberius, so admirably developed in the *Annals,* and shut his eyes against the rest: Machiavelli's *Prince* has been refuted by the pen which adopted its spirit[1]; the author of *Pamela* has been said to have perverted more females than he ever instructed; and Rousseau declared her a *fille perdue* who read his *Héloïse*; so much for Boccalini. . . .

(*Analytical Review,* November 1793, review of Murphy's *Tacitus,* signed Z. Z.—XVII, p. 245)

The Sense of Evil

HE WHO means to remain ignorant of the enormities of human debasement must remain ignorant of literature, history and poetry; the images of Ezekiel[2] are as bold as those of Juvenal —to point out these excrescences is to mark the rocks and whirlpools that endanger life. . . .

(*Analytical Review,* September 1789, review of Madan's translation of Juvenal, signed R. R.—V, p. 29)

[1] Frederick the Great.
[2] Cp. 'Is not every Vice possible to Man described in the Bible openly?' (Blake's *Laocoon*).

SECTION FIVE

DEPRAVITY AND CIVILISATION—
FUSELI THE 'CYNIC'

Writing in 1798 in his indiscreet *Memoirs of Mary Wollstonecraft* Godwin says of Fuseli: 'Smitten with Rousseau's conception of the perfection of the savage state and the essential abortiveness of all
civilisation, Mr. Fuseli looks at all our little attempts at improvement with a spirit that borders perhaps too much upon contempt
and indifference. . . . I believe Mary came something more of a
cynic out of the school of Mr. Fuseli than she went into it.' Godwin
is not the only contemporary of Fuseli's to accuse him of cynicism.
Farington attributes to Fuseli in his diary (29 July 1815) a 'cynical
feeling' which frequently led him to say 'that which He did not
believe'. Nearly all along the line Fuseli is in conflict with the cherished beliefs, hopes and ideals prevailing among the advanced minds
of his day. He not only fails to share their optimistic faith in civilisation and its future; he does not even *want* to share it. Before he
weighs the conformity of that faith with facts, likelihood and feasi-
bility, he has already impatiently spurned it as implying too poor and
inadequate an ideal. This is so unintelligible, so outrageous to his
contemporaries, that they can only cast doubts on his ingenuousness,
suspect him of saying what he does not really believe, or dismiss
him as a 'cynic'. For Godwin, to whom progress and human perfectibility are sacrosanct dogmas, Fuseli's attitude towards civilisation is necessarily an object of moral disapprobation. Actually
Godwin's personal acquaintance with Fuseli was slight, as he himself stated in a letter to Knowles of 28 September 1826. Most of
what he knew about him he learnt from Mary Wollstonecraft, and
what he gives us in his brief sentence is not only an account of
Fuseli's views, but also his own attempt to refute those views by
tracing them back to suspect foundations and sources. Fuseli had

never submissively abandoned his own mental independence, even in the days when his devotion to Rousseau was at its height.[1] He did, indeed, consider all civilisation abortive—there Godwin is quite reliable—but it was only in his very early years, even if then, that this belief of his was based on enthusiasm for the supposed 'perfection of the savage state', and in his maturer period it was certainly based on something very different. There was something in Fuseli— possibly a mere last theological residue still uneliminated from his spiritual organism, more likely a temperamental preference for the tragic vision of mankind—that forced him to see civilisation as necessarily conditioned and accompanied by depravity. It is remarkable to find him at the age of twenty-two saying that he has 'pondered much on the limits beyond which a nation cannot be improved' and thinks of publishing something on the theme (letter to Lavater, 13 November 1763). For purposes of aesthetic contemplation, symbolisation and configuration, indeed, perfection and the ideal can, should and must, according to him, be conceived of only in terms of the human spirit and still more of the human body: 'Man exclusively possesses the most perfect form,' he says in his first lecture; and in the Aphorisms: 'Ideal is properly the representation of pure human essence.' But for all other purposes any ideal would lose its attractions for him, if it were conceivable that it could ever become the possession or attribute of such a creature as actual, living man—either of the human race as a whole, or of the individual, even of the most gifted individual, the man of supreme genius. He lived in an age which made man the legitimate claimant to all the highest ideal qualities and conditions, and he protested against this tendency, not out of cynicism, if a cynic be one to whom the ideal means nothing or too little, but just because the ideal meant too much to him. Others aimed at solving this problem on a lofty metaphysical plane—Goethe's *Faust* is a grandiose attempt at such a solution—but Fuseli did not want it to be solved at all. He was content that the absolute, ineradicable, tragic imperfection of all things human should bear eternal witness to the splendour of the perfect as an unattainable ideal. His utterances on the depravity of all civilisation should be seen in close connexion with his declarations that universality is the prerogative of Nature (not of man), creation the prerogative of Omnipotence (not of man).

[1] Fuseli insists on this in his own review of the *Remarks on Rousseau*: 'He has opinions of his own, so singular, so novel, and, like a true critic, *so independent of his author*' (*see above*, p. 135).

The State of Nature—'of all hypotheses the most proper to explain the contradictions of the human heart'

ROUSSEAU . . . traced man to the nipple of nature; found him wrapped up in instinct, taught his lore by appetite and fear, harmless because content, content because void of comparative ideas, solitary because without wants, snatching the moment on the wing from the past and future ones. Yet even in this wilderness of nature he stamps him with the sovereignty of vegetation and instinct: behold him, free, improvable, compassionate!

(1767—Remarks on Rousseau, p. 25)

Civilisation and Degeneracy—Council for Dictators

THERE IS a point from which no nation, if once arrived at, ever retrogrades (i.e. returns). Where laws are only the curb of the public, the attempt of transfusing them into manners is folly; and where force is the only check upon the conflict of social interests, the most subtle impostor is the best politician. Then you must change virtue to appearances, and give the pension of honesty to talent; then you must apply emollients, palliatives, call in arts, luxury, commerce, and the phantom of private and national honour. By their glittering advantages and insidious charms you must bribe or soothe to slavery those you dread, dismember the rabble and, seizing every opportunity, throw out tubs to let their rage evaporate in harmless play.

(1767—Remarks on Rousseau, pp. 81–2)

Modern Dress in Great Art—West's Innovation

THE OBJECTION against the imitation of modern dress is an objection of taste: because it is scarcely a human dress. The ancient statues were once modern, and Marius (in the Villa

Negroni) is as senatorially dressed as Beckford or Chatham. A man dressed, is as serious an idea as a man formed in stone or engraved on a gem. But if Chatham wore a dress which, a thousand years hence, may make it doubtful whether the human species could ever have been dressed so, it is proper for the sculptor to steer clear of the masquerade.

(*Analytical Review*, November 1791, review of Raspe's *Catalogue of Tassie's Gems*, signed R. R.—XI, pp. 260–1)

SECTION SIX

PASSING HOPES
FOR THE MODERN WORLD
AND THE FUTURE OF CIVILISATION

Fuseli's early adopted harsh and sceptical estimate of the modern
world gives way for a brief space, under the influence of the French
Revolution, to hopeful enthusiasm. He, who had always contrived to
formulate even his devotion to his greatest heroes, Michelangelo and
Shakespeare, in such a way as still to maintain the absolute superiority of the Ancients to the Moderns, is for a moment prepared to side
with the Moderns in this old dispute. But at the very beginning of
the Reign of Terror he is thoroughly disillusioned again, and reverts
to his old 'cynicism'. The French subjugation of Switzerland, which
was to bring with it the slaughter of his great friend Lavater, confirms all his apprehensions.

A few months after the fall of the Bastille

POSTERITY WILL learn with equal indignation and astonishment that the philosopher suffered his mind to evaporate with
the steams, and to subside with the dregs of a crucible; and that
the traveller, heedless of his equals, roamed either hemisphere
in quest of shores and views, or animals and plants, in an age
pregnant with the most gigantic efforts of character, shaken
with the convulsions of old, and the emersion of new empires:
whilst an unexampled vigour seemed to vibrate from pole to

183

pole through the human mind, and to challenge the general sympathy.

> (*Analytical Review*, December 1789, review of Coxe's *Travels in Switzerland*, signed R. R.—V, pp. 463–4)

The Ancients and the Moderns

IF, AS as been said, he who writes in a modern language writes on sand, he who writes in Latin or Greek copies only what has been already written; he is in a state of servitude, and the day of servitude, says Homer, takes away man's better half. . . . New thoughts, if they come, can seldom be admitted, for new thoughts cannot be expressed by prescription, and combinations not sanctioned by the Augustan oracles may be barbarisms. . . . Meanness of occupation confounds powers: Latin Milton is the fellow-drudge of Cowley, perhaps with less dexterity; and Dante would have been a clown at the side of either Scaliger.

> (*Analytical Review*, July 1790, review of John Jortin's *Tracts, Philological, Critical and Miscellaneous*, signed Y. Y.—VII, p. 242)

The Flame of Liberty in 1793

HE WHO reads the works of Tacitus according to the arrangement with which they have been transmitted to us by all the editors, will find that they inculcate the important and terrible maxim, that anarchy is the legitimate offspring of despotism, and that the tools of oppression end in becoming the engines of revolution. If the people be such as Tacitus describes, the dregs of a nation brought up by liberty, perverted by conquest, and, overwhelmed by its own weight, sinking into despotism, the anarchies that ensue will be little more than the temporary contests for rule of factions equally criminal; and the vital sparks of public virtue being in such a nation entirely extinguished, and that of private energy reduced to a tame remembrance of antiquated heroism, the bulk will subside again under the tyrant of the ruling party, and in degenerate silence subscribe to the law of force. The decision of force alone gave a sanction to the contests . . . and he who had strength enough to rule longer than a moment was the legitimate god of Rome. Neither that 'holy flame of liberty' which the dedicator ascribes to Agricola, nor the indignation of Tacitus himself, would have prevented the one, had Otho or Vitellius been victorious, from becoming the tool of either in making proselytes of slavery by war, or the other from holding the chain and conducting to the jaws of a prison the victims of that virtue he professed to adore. Had such been the 'flame of liberty' which animated Hampden, Sydney, Russell and all the boasted worthies of our glorious revolution, Mr. M(urphy) would not now probably have had an opportunity of pronouncing his panegyric on its blessings.[1]

(*Analytical Review*, November 1793, review of Murphy's *Tacitus*, signed
Z. Z.—XVII, pp. 242–3)

The Subjugation of Switzerland by the French Directory

THESE LETTERS, composed before the last expiring gasp of Helvetic independence, affect us with the sympathies of a traveller, who once more casts a farewell glance on the beauties of the Romantic landscape he traversed, yet illumined by the last rays of a sun setting amid the flashes and thunderclouds of a storm rising to involve hill, dale and cottage in undistinguished

[1] Throughout this passage, written presumably soon after the September Massacres, Fuseli is unmistakably alluding to developments in revolutionary France. It is interesting to see that at this comparatively early date he had definitely abandoned all those over-sanguine republican expectations with regard to the French Revolution which his collaborators in the *Analytical Review* maintained years later. In this same review he alludes approvingly to Burke. His dislike of the French as a nation, testified to nearly thirty years before in his pamphlet on Rousseau, had no doubt a considerable share in his sceptical view of the French Revolution. The phrase 'perverted by conquest' can only mean 'perverted by conquering other nations', not 'by being conquered'. Fuseli's cult of condensation frequently leads him to such misleading or ambiguous formulations.

ruins. If the Roman Tacitus . . . could not forbear . . . strewing the fragments of Jerusalem with flowers, what must we feel at the dissolution of a friendly nation, once the cradle, domain and barrier of liberty, endeared to us by political alliance, religious and moral analogy and long continued social intercourse?

(*Analytical Review*, June 1798, review of Helen Maria Williams's *Tour in Switzerland*, signed R. R.—XXVII, p. 561)

Fuseli on the Napoleonic Wars

FUSELI CONSIDERS Buonaparte a man buoyed up with pride and presumption and of unrestrained passion; and that he must suffer much in the opinion of the world, by his conduct and deportment.—He thinks the War will be short.

(*Farington Diary*, 28 May 1803)

FUSELI SAID Buonaparte had courage but not comprehension, and did not know how to estimate things.

(*Farington Diary*, 26 February 1804)

FUSELI, WHILE looking at Mr. Pitt's bust, said: 'It would have been well for this country if he had not been born in it. He brought us into the state we are now in. Had he left the French to themselves in all the matters of their Revolution, England would now have given law to the world. He should have done as other powers did during our Civil Wars, who, when they saw a king beheaded and Cromwell rise, still did not interfere.'

(*Farington Diary*, 20 July 1807)

FUSELI AND NORTHCOTE this evening to me execrated the conduct of Buonaparte towards Spain.—Fuseli said it was 'The brutality of domestic selfishness'.

(*Farington Diary*, 21 July 1808)

FUSELI ADMITTED that it would be well for England to have the Bourbons restored, as it was best for this country to have *weak princes* on the throne of France.

(*Farington Diary*, 29 March 1814)

GREAT ART
AND THE DEPRAVITY
OF ALL CULTURE

'—whatever a sinner like Warburton may snivel, it is neither from Homer, Virgil nor Milton that we have to learn morality, politics and religion . . .' (Fuseli in a letter of November 1765)

As early as 1767, in a footnote 'for painters only' to his *Remarks on Rousseau*, Fuseli discusses the question which was bound to be of central importance for him, whether art at its highest is independent of the necessary depravity of all civilisation, or can at least contrive to transcend that depravity. He does not see how Raphael, Correggio and Titian can be acquitted of having debased themselves to become the 'tools of flattery, superstition, of pleasure or coarse imitation'. One great painter only stands perhaps apart as an honourable exception: 'You may cry out here that I forget Michelangelo!—I did not forget him.' To the last Fuseli as a rule distinguishes Michelangelo from all other artists in this way. But not even the case of Michelangelo, about whom he also occasionally has his doubts, can shake Fuseli in his early adopted and stubbornly maintained conviction that the arts, even at their highest, are still always the products of cultured depravity and can never transcend the flaws of their origins. Herein again Fuseli pits himself against the dominant progressive tendencies of his age, whose great representative figures unanimously proclaimed that art was in every respect a perfect substitute for religion, and that poets are the unacknowledged legislators of mankind. All such assertions exasperate Fuseli. He has also just as little use for the notion which played so important a part in the thought of his age, that great art is, or could be, the product of a comparatively primitive, not yet depraved stage of civilisation. He insists that real art can never 'appear during the rudeness of infant societies' (Lecture XII). He has nothing but contempt for primitive art as such, or for any art he estimates as primitive, and that includes the whole of mediaeval art down to the end of the fifteenth century. His astonishing consistency on this point sometimes leads him to deny that the Greeks, when once they had begun to produce great art, were any whit more primitive or less depraved than his own contemporaries; and when he idealises them most extravagantly, in the variously recorded words 'The Greeks were Gods, the Greeks were gods!', what he is attributing to them is quite unmistakably something very different from that perfect humanity, that yet unshattered innocence and harmony so dear to the typical Graecophil theory of his day. His view of the individual artist tallies here exactly with his historical outlook on art as a whole. He splutters with contempt whenever he encounters the current assumptions of the age, that the man of genius is by nature necessarily virtuous, or that there is any need for him, *qua* artist to be so. What lies at the back of all this is not indifference to morality, but a kind of inverted, ineradicable Puritanism. That 'virtue' which he was so much concerned about in his early years has to the last an importance for him which it has for very few of his memorable contemporaries—it remains in his eyes something distinctive and definite that cannot just be used as a name for something else. Without the old austere, intransigent but now, for him, completely acidulated idea of virtue to serve as vinegar, existence and art would both be too insipid for Fuseli's perverse palate. A certain rottenness in all things, repeatedly ascertained and demonstrated by appeal to the elusive ideal of virtue, alone gives them the required piquancy and *haut-goût*.

The Arts and Sciences as rosy harlots

ROUSSEAU . . . drew the pedigree of the sciences and arts, showed them grafted on luxury and leisure, those on riches, and wealth on inequality; and from all this he concluded that every society supported by their fickle props resembles a palace founded on the Roman order[1]—castles in the air; that, having

[1] The fifth and last of the ancient architectural orders, known as Composite from the formation of its capital, and as Roman or Italic from its having originated in Italy.

weakened the spirit of nations, enervated genius, drawn humanity from its real object, substituted visionary bliss to real happiness, fettered the mind to unnatural wants, and adulterated the manners, all the merit they [i.e. the arts and sciences] can be allowed is that of being, like water for the dropsy, palliatives for the diseases they engender; or, if you want a prettier simile, that of resembling rosy harlots, who, by coaxing and magic embraces, give momentary springs and elasticity to those limbs which their abyss of pleasures sucked into languishment and impotence.

(1767—*Remarks on Rousseau*, pp. 9–10)

The Arts and Civilisation

WHATEVER IS commodious, amene or useful, depends in a great measure on the Arts: dress, furniture and habitation owe to their breath what they can boast of grace, propriety or shape: they teach Elegance to finish what Necessity invented, and make us enamoured of our wants.

(1825—Lecture XII, p. 42)

Art and Morals: Michelangelo's Dream

MICHELANGELO WAS less ambitious to express the nature of a dream, or to bespeak our attention to its picturesque effect and powerful contrasts, than to impress us with the lesson, that all is vanity and life a farce, unless engaged by virtue and the pursuits of mind.

(1805—Lecture IV, footnote on p. 197)

Naïveté and Sophistication in Art

> 'The Art forms a part of social education, nor can it appear during the rudeness of infant societies . . .' (Fuseli's XIIth Lecture—1825)

. . . the axiom, that the less the traces appear of the means by which a work has been produced, the more it resembles the operations of nature,[1] is not an axiom likely to spring from the infancy of art.

(1805—Lecture VI, p. 300)

The Stage a School of Morals?

I REASON here on the principles of those who consider the stage as a school of morals. There is, in tragedy chiefly, such a disparity between the spectator's and the hero's circumstances, that it requires the most painful abstraction to snatch one useful lesson from all the flatulency of his passion. The truth is, the most striking play may be written without any good tendency at all. Hold the mirror up to life, give action, draw characters, and your play is good. *Amyclas, dum tacerent, perdidit silentium*[2] is all you can learn from Monimia[3]; and who weeps not with Monimia? The moral of *Venice Preserved* is a jumble of contradictions; but Jaffier and Belvidera are the idols of our hearts. Your best comedies are the worst on the side of morals. Congreve is as plain [i.e. shameless] as Petronius; nay, he has a profligacy

---

[1] Reynolds develops at length in his IVth Discourse the thought of the Latin proverb: *Ars est celare artem*. 'An inferior artist', he writes, 'takes as much pains to discover as the greater artist to conceal the marks of his subordinate activity.' Fuseli dwells on the idea when defining 'Grace' in his first Lecture.

[2] 'The men of Amyclae preserving silence, their silence proved their destruction.' After many false alarms they are said to have forbidden any citizen to speak of the enemy and thus to have fallen an easy prey to the Lacedaemonians when they really did advance against them.

[3] Monimia is the heroine of Otway's *Orphan*.

of his own, and there is in all his women something most execrably rank; but who relishes not Congreve's salt? There are, besides, frailties, passions which will bribe the heart in spite of their appendage of evils; where the blood judges, pain, horror, death will vanish in the dazzling light of pleasure: Lothario's description of his night with Calista destroys all other impressions of the *Fair Penitent*.[1] The poet writes to please all; hence he will be cautious of applying caustics to the darling vices of the public; and from that his productions can never be of direct use. Slave trade is legal, for we must have sugar. To this principle Southerne sacrificed the laws of nature, conscience and the truth he had set out with; nay, to authorise inhumanity, lodged in the very sufferer's mouth a sentence which, but for its absurdity, must have branded our religion with the abhorrence of reason. 'I must blush', says Oronooko,

> *a whitely shame,*
> *To think I could design to make those free*
> *Who were by nature slaves; wretches designed*
> *To be their masters' dogs——*

To please, the poet must be extravagant, lest an individual should find himself stung and kick. He must give an Englishman 'his whore and ease, beef and a sea-coal fire'[2]; his miser and his prodigal, his *beau* and *belle*, his Frenchman, Sawney or Irish tool, must be excrescences of nature; he must agree with you that a grain of salt atones for a shore[3] of folly, and make a pin's head of honesty wide enough for a camel loaded with vice. In short, he must humour you.

[1] In the original the name of Rowe's tragedy is given as *The Fair Impenitent*, presumably only by inadvertency.

[2] From Otway's *Venice Preserved*.

[3] A *shore* of folly: presumably the common shore or sewer. The grain of salt appears not to be the proverbial *cum grano salis*, but rather an allusion to that salt which the Christian is urged in the New Testament to have in himself (Mark ix. 50). Fuseli is thinking of the favourite hero of English literature, the dissolute young good-for-nothing with a heart of gold, found in Restoration comedy and in the novels of Fielding and Smollett. The grain of good nature compensates in this type for all the immorality he is guilty of.

What folly is it then to demand virtue of an entertainment which would be ruined by giving it?

The benefit of the playhouse is wholly negative.[1] 'Tis a harmless entertainment in comparison with those which the greatest number might pursue during the hours of a play. 'Tis better to see *Sir John Brute*[2] than to act him in the streets; 'tis pleasure, instead of debauchery.

(1767—*Remarks on Rousseau*, footnote on pp. 74-7)

Genius and Morality—and Benjamin West

'Virtue, always indispensable, is of the first consequence in the life of the elegant artist; whose contemplations are, or should be, always sedate, and whose mind should be always tranquil and at home. But that is impossible on the supposition that his life is not the regular life of virtue. History will constantly show us in all the brightest characters of the world the most conspicuous virtues' (Benjamin West's Presidential Discourse to the Royal Academy, December 1792)

HOW FAR the mode of life and the pursuits of an artist emasculate the mind or furnish incentives to virtue, is not the question: the advice is certainly wholesome. The flaw we find is, that it is scanty, and propped with more than questionable assertions, for Caesar and Bacon were not virtuous. Virtue is purity of mind combined with energy of action. The passage before us recommends virtue because it produces decorum and sedateness; but these are so far from being incompatible with, that they generally serve as a cloak for the sneaking vices of artists, for dissimulation, conceit, envy, detraction, cabal, servility, flattery, meanness and craft; prompted, exasperated, or checked by the tide and ebb of success, or the malignant suggestions of

[1] Fuseli here and always uses *negative* where we should nowadays employ the word *neutral*. This usage is normal in the eighteenth century, both in English and in German.

[2] *Sir John Brute*—the dissolute husband of Vanbrugh's *Provoked Wife*.

rivalship. To say that a mean or vicious character cannot arrive at eminence in art, is to say that a villain cannot possess exquisite organs. . . . 'Meretricious patronage', or that 'which makes the arts the pander to a corrupt and slavish gratification', occupies all the annals of ancient and modern history, from Pericles and Phidias to Alexander and Apelles, from him to the imperial era, down to the restoration of art by the Julios, Leos, Cosimos, on to our own days, in which, indeed, panders of another species bid fair to supplant it.

(*Analytical Review*, May 1793, review of West's Presidential Discourse, signed R. R.—XVI, pp. 51–2)

Art and Morality

SURELY NONE will deny that the activity of the mind is best employed when directed to the benefit of society; but to assert that the ancients thought so in the choice of subjects for painting and sculpture, is either not to know, or to pervert facts: for of all the relics we yet possess of the performances enumerated in the catalogues of Pliny, recorded by Pausanias, and remembered or imagined by Philostratus, what proportion bear those which impress our mind with a moral to those that merely aim at affecting our senses with delight or admiration by the power of execution? . . . What were the subjects, or the greatest number of subjects, perpetuated by their genius? Images of superstition; gods and demi-gods of that ferocious age to which our author has refused the very knowledge of the word virtue; monuments of national pride; tyrants deified for trampling on humanity; incentives to refinement in vice, or dignified trifles. . . . It is ludicrous to give a consequence to the arts which they can never possess. Their moral usefulness is at best accidental and negative. It is their greatest praise to furnish the most innocent amusement for those nations to whom luxury is become as necessary as existence, and amongst whom alone they can rear themselves to any degree of eminence.

(*Analytical Review*, July 1793, review of Bromley's *Philosophical and Critical History of the Fine Arts* . . ., signed Z. Z.—XVI, pp. 242–3)

SECTION EIGHT

CULTURE AND THE MASSES

Rejecting as he so uncompromisingly did the redemptive and religious evaluation of art and culture, Fuseli was bound also to reject all liberal aspirations towards equality of opportunity and the democratisation of higher education. The learned professions and the arts, he maintained, should be accessible only to a small self-appointed élite, and nobody else should have any say in them. This was the axiom he appealed to in his own justification when, as often happened, he was charged with writing so obscurely that few could understand him. It is possible for him to persist in stout republicanism in politics, while remaining a fierce oligarch or dictator in culture, because for him culture and politics are two separate spheres that scarcely touch one another. He is suspicious of all schemes to bring them closer together. He can, indeed, a year before his death, begin a paragraph with the surprising admission that 'the artist and the public are ever in strict reciprocity'; but this paragraph concludes: 'To prosper, the Art not only must feel itself free, it ought to reign' (Lecture XII). His tone towards the common run of humanity, at best never gracious, becomes a screech of contempt, when he sees them laying their hands on art. 'He asserted in conversation, if not in lectures, that the Royal Academy robbed the plough and the shoemaker's stall of very meritorious persons, and that many came to the sculptor's chisel and the painter's pencil, who might have handled the joiner's plane or the tailor's scissors with greater advantage to the public and profit to themselves' (Cunningham).

Higher Education for Everybody—Genius and the Mob

THE ONLY effectual means, in my opinion, for preserving its dignity and usefulness to Learning, were to make it the privilege of Genius. The rudiments of science should never have been levelled with those whom nature made to crawl; their ruggedness, a kind of subsultory method, even a conciseness bordering upon obscurity, presupposing much, implying much, might have been the test of real genius. The gravitation of minds varies to infinity, and providence has probably in most of her subjects combined inclinations and capacities—their united endeavours may be supposed equal to the opposition they meet with in their objects. There is a kind of intuition in genius— 'twas Raphael's, 'twas Pascal's. With this fence round the temple of Science, you would have saved it from the profanations of parental pride and pert pretence; from the itch of mere curiosity and the waste of leisure; from the skimming of fashion and the brazen memory of dunces; and the more useful departments of life would not be continually emptying to recruit the armies of *pen-chewers*. . . . There is but one tolerable objection to such a reformation, which is, that true genius will go on with more rapidity in its course of science, if the time of its apprenticeship is shortened by rudiments made easy. There may be some truth in this. But as you have to choose between two evils only, it is much more essential to keep the mob off, than to save a step or two to a man of parts; the advantages on either side admit of no comparison. What if even Newton or Leibniz had been later acquainted with some of their sublimest mathematic and metaphysic truths, or had even not had time to come up with them at all? Would you affect to think it as deplorable a misfortune to society, as that myriads of blockheads will, for a jingle of sophistry and false mathematics, lay the loom waste, and devour the fields they deserted?

(1767—*Remarks on Rousseau*, pp. 11–17)

Should history be intelligible to all?—Fuseli defends a style similar to his own

IF IT be true that history is the common property of all, at least of all whom education and the gentler ways of life enable to look beyond the immediate track of necessary business before them, its first property is to be intelligible to all who claim that prerogative ... [But] if history, like the science of politics, have its recesses, . . . if it recount actions only to trace their springs, and by delineating the past, to direct the future, content to instruct a superior class of readers, and confident to be understood, it wraps itself up in hints, crowds into one sentence a period, and for a tale often substitutes an image. . . . Must brevity necessarily be uncouth, or conciseness turgid . . . ?

(*Analytical Review*, February 1794, review of Murphy's *Tacitus*, concluded, here without signature—XVIII, p. 121)

The Pros and Cons of popular anecdotal works

NONE, we hope, will suspect us of an attempt to discourage serious studies, or to plead in favour of that deluge of superficial information which, by pretending to facilitate the access of knowledge to all, aims at nothing less than a general levelling of all ranks and orders in science and in arts, and finishes a flimsy education by arming ignorance, petulance and impertinence against the modesty of solid knowledge. What we set out with, we repeat—that those writers who, with intelligence, disinterestedness and taste, select the anecdotes of genius, the features of extraordinary men in their deshabille, on the spur of a great moment or when indulging in the genuine effusions of an unguarded hour, contribute, perhaps, more to a real knowledge of men and manners, open a clearer insight into the head and heart of others, than he who professedly sets out with a series of events to instruct, and who too often, with his formal lesson, is dismissed by a fit of yawning:

Tolle tuum, precor, Hannibalem victumque Syphacem
In castris, et cum tota Carthagine migra.[1]

(*Analytical Review*, May 1795, unsigned review of Seward's *Anecdotes
of Some Distinguished Persons*—XXI, p. 525)

Mediocrity in Art

NEITHER POETRY nor Painting spring from the necessities of
society, or furnish necessaries to life; offsprings of fancy, leisure
and lofty contemplation, organs of religion and government,
ornaments of society, and too often mere charms of the senses
and instruments of luxury, they derive their excellence from
novelty, degree and polish. What none indispensably want, all
may wish for, but few only are able to procure, acquires its
value from some exclusive quality, founded on intrinsic, or
some conventional merit, and that, or an equal substitute mediocrity cannot reach: hence, by suffering it to invade the province
of genius and talent, we rob the plough, the shop, the loom, the
school, perhaps the desk and pulpit, of a thousand useful hands.
A good mechanic, a trusty labourer, an honest tradesman, are
beings more important, of greater use to society, and better sup-
porters of the state, than an artist or a poet of mediocrity. When
I therefore say that it is the duty of the Academy to deter rather
than to delude, I am not afraid of having advanced a paradox
hostile to the progress of real Art. The capacities that time will
disclose, genius and talents, cannot be deterred by the exposition of difficulties, and it is the interest of society that all else
should.

(1825—Lecture X, pp. 390–1)

---

[1] 'Be off, pray, with your Hannibal, with your Syphax defeated in his
encampment and with your Carthage, lock, stock and barrel.' Verses 170–1
of Juvenal's sixth Satire (a favourite of Fuseli's), ingeniously quoted here
with a very different connotation from that they have in their original
context.

PART THREE

FUSELI'S

THEORY OF ART

SOME

FUNDAMENTAL

PRINCIPLES

Fuseli's approach to the plastic arts is to the last essentially that literary approach which the nineteenth century was to repudiate and which still appears to have not the slightest chance of being rehabilitated. His great demand is that 'each work of art should fully and essentially tell its own tale' (Lecture IV), that is to say, also, that it should have a tale to tell; and a painting or sculpture which has no tale to tell ceases for him, simply through that circumstance, to be a true work of art at all; it must be relegated to the 'inferior branches', where art has debased itself to something less than what it might be and ought to be. In these views Fuseli is to a considerable degree just a child of his age and an inheritor of the ideas of earlier generations. But more personal elements enter also into his views, making him a special case. He is not only on the surface, but through and through a painter-poet, for whom painting is a kind of poetry. One feels this in all his work. The 'literary', now for most serious purposes quite obsolete, distinction between 'conception' and 'execution' is furthermore of the most intimate private importance to him, because he feels himself handicapped by technical shortcomings. The many passages in which he abstractly exalts 'conception' above mere 'execution' should be read in the light of his frequent private lamentations over his own inability to execute as well as he can conceive. His innate sensitiveness, coupled with his lively personal concern in these problems, drives him to recognise, isolate and give an account of just what we nowadays so highly value as 'pure painting'; he does this with a clearness and deliberateness found amongst few of his contemporaries, but he does it only in order to be able to dismiss what we should call 'pure painting' with a grudging and qualified tribute as inferior to 'conception', 'mind' and 'idea'. This set of circumstances distinguishes even his most literary utterances on the plastic arts from those commonly found during his period, and makes them very much more interesting.

SECTION ONE

CREATION OR INVENTION?

Is art Creation?

OUR IDEAS are the offspring of our senses; we are not more able to create the form of a being we have not seen, without retrospect to one we know, than we are able to create a new sense. He whose fancy has conceived an idea of the most beautiful form must have composed it from actual existence. . . .

(1801—Lecture I, p. 38)

'Creation gives, Invention finds existence' (Aphorism 47)

THE MOST eminent of these technic powers, by the explicit acknowledgment of all ages, and the silent testimony of every breast, is *invention.* . . . The term *invention* never ought to be so far misconstrued as to be confounded with that of *creation*, incompatible with our notions of limited being, an idea of pure astonishment, and admissible only when we mention Omnipotence: to *invent* is to find: to find something, presupposes its existence somewhere, implicitly or explicitly, scattered or in a mass: nor should I have presumed to say so much on a word of a meaning so plain, had it not been, and were it not daily confounded, and by fashionable authorities too, with the term creation.

Form in its widest meaning, the visible universe that envelops our senses, and its counterpart, the invisible one that agitates our mind with visions bred on sense by fancy, are the element and the realm of invention; it discovers, selects, combines the *possible*, the *probable*, the *known*, in a mode that strikes with an air of truth and novelty, at once.

(1801—Lecture III, pp. 136–7)

Fuseli's objections to the idea of art as creation—an idea usually traced back to Shaftesbury's famous words: 'Such a poet is, indeed, a second maker: a just Prometheus under Jove' (*Advice to an Author*, 1710)—first emerge in his review of R. Payne Knight's *Landscape* in the *Analytical Review* for June 1794, Vol. XIX, p. 179 (*see* p. 254).

SECTION TWO

THE LIMITS OF PAINTING
AND POETRY—
THE *LAOCOON* PROBLEM

In summer 1766 Lavater wrote to Fuseli, asking him to review Lessing's newly published *Laocoon* in the *Lindauer Nachrichten*. Fuseli answered that he did not know the book and would not review it if he did. At this time he still mistakenly regarded Lessing, who had not spared Bodmer and Klopstock with his pungent criticism, as one of the worst enemies of the new literary movement (*see* letter to Bodmer of 22 December 1763). As late as 1788 he had still evidently not looked at the *Laocoon*, for, writing that year in the *Analytical Review*, he naïvely repeats all those old phrases about the identity of poetry and painting which Lessing had so searchingly criticised. Two or three years later he must have read the *Laocoon* at last and been very much impressed and disturbed by it. It seemed to cut from under his feet just that ground which he, as a poet-painter, specially needed. His derivation of the whole of Greek painting and sculpture from a phrase in Homer (*see below*, p. 224) and his classification of great painting as epic, dramatic or historic were certainly already embodied in the original, still unpublished manuscript of his *Aphorisms* of 1788—they were conceptions he could not get on without. He was never happy with a picture or statue until he had translated it into words—his virtuosity in such descriptions must have been assiduously cultivated and is obviously something he was very proud of. Ancient Greek paintings of which nothing is known except through the descriptions of Pliny and other writers were as real to him as pictures he had actually seen, and so it was also with Correggio's *Notte*, which he knew only from the description of Mengs, and the colouring of which he frequently speaks of in detail. This was all too much a part of his nature for him really to be able to give it up. But in some way he had to fit Lessing into his system. He did not simply reject or ignore him, as the German Romantics were to do. He charged him with 'tameness' and 'frigidity', but ultimately took over in theory most of his main contentions with no more than comparatively slight modifications and amplifications. It appears likely, however, that Lessing may have been responsible for Fuseli having no more to say in the last half of his life about the all-importance of poetic imagery, a fruitful topic on which he had formerly written so magnificently, especially in the letter to Lavater of March 1775 (*see above*, Part I, Section 1).

The Relationship between Poetry and Painting

THE ANALOGY between poetry and painting has been admitted in earliest times.

> *Painting is silent poetry*
> *And Poetry is a speaking picture*
>
> (Simonides)

Men of superior minds see nature through the medium of a fine imagination, so that, however different the machinery of their art and the quality of their materials, they will have a general resemblance in the ideal, and make very similar impressions. The painter's language is his colours, the poet's colours are his diction. The excellence of pictures or of language consists in raising clear, complete and circumstantial images and turning readers into spectators. A style in painting is the same as in writing; be it words or colours, they convey sentiments. Every epithet used by a good writer paints its object and paints it distinctly. . . . An historical picture well delineated, or a dramatic poem with a moral tendency embody truth by uniting it with pleasure, and improve the understanding at the same time that they gratify the fancy.

(*Analytical Review*, June 1788, unsigned article on *The Arts*—I, p. 216)

'Action and Time, the two great mediums of poetry'

POETIC IMITATION, we repeat it, is progressive, and less occupied with the *surface* of the object than its *action*. Hence all comparisons between the poet's and the painter's manners ought to be made with an eye to the respective end and limits of either art. Nor can these observations be deemed superfluous, except by those who are most in want of them, the descriptive tribe, who imagine they paint what they only perplex, and fondly dream of enriching the realms of fancy by silly excursions into the province of the florist, chemist or painter of still life.

> (*Analytical Review*, January 1793, review of Cowper's *Homer*, signed Z. Z.—XV, p. 5. Knowles, I, p. 89)

Poetry and the Plastic Arts

> 'The painter seizes merely the external form, and that only in a given attitude. The poet surrounds his object, pierces it, and discloses its most hidden qualities' (Roscoe)

MR. ROSCOE with great propriety places the essence of poetic diction (not of poetry itself, for that consists in invention), in representing its object in motion, to impress us with its variety of action and attitudes, in short, in following *time*, avoiding a minute anatomy of motionless surfaces, to which words, its vehicle, are totally inadequate. Surface can only be distinctly discriminated by line and colour. Hence it is evident that poetry cannot in this respect be either put in comparison with or be elevated above painting. The province of their expression and effect must be forever separate, though they perfectly coincide in their aim, which is to charm and convince the senses. Thus, when poetry attempts to describe an object, it must confine itself to one or a very few words in whatever merely relates to the shape or surface of that object, and its more profuse description is *only then* in its place, when that object begins to move. Such is the rule of nature and of Homer, from which no ancient or modern poet has deviated with impunity; and Ariosto, who has described the shape, figure and colour of Alcina in five stanzas, has laboured as much in vain to acquaint us with the ingredients of his witch-beauty as Constantius Manasses to give us a clear idea of Helen by his agglomeration of epithets, or as Haller of the gentiana by a description of nineteen lines. . . . Not the most expressive words of the most expressive language ever given to man, arranged by Homer or Milton or a power still superior to theirs, could produce a sensation equal to that which is instantaneously received by one glance on the face of the Venus de' Medici, or on that of the Apollo in Belvedere; and if the spark which Phidias caught from the Zeus of Homer were shot by his *waving* locks and the *nod* of his brow,[1] will it be denied that Ctesilas in his expiring warrior, from whose expression might be collected how much remained of life, or Aristides in the wounded mother who, in the pangs of death, struggled to remove her child from her palsied nipple, 'surrounded, pierced and disclosed the most hidden qualities of their objects'?

(*Analytical Review*, April 1796, review of Roscoe's *Lorenzo de' Medici*, signed Z. Z.—XXIII, pp. 348–9. Knowles, I, pp. 132–3)

The Limits of Poetry and the Plastic Arts

FROM LONG bigotted deference to the old maxim that poetry is painting in speech, and painting dumb poetry,[2] the two sisters, marked with features so different by nature, and the great masters of compositon, her oracles, have been constantly confounded with each other by the herds of mediocrity and thoughtless imitation. Hence that deluge of descriptive stuff, which

[1] I.e. even though Phidias may have been inspired to his head of Zeus by Homer just at that point where Homer, by displaying motion, demonstrated that poetry can do some things that painting cannot do, Ctesilas and Aristides redress the claims of painting (*see below*, p. 224).

[2] A statement attributed to Simonides (*see above*, p. 204). Lessing quotes it as a 'dazzling antithesis' at the very beginning of his *Laocoon*. The opening sentences of Fuseli's third Lecture are an almost literal translation of this passage in Lessing, who is then referred to in a footnote.

overwhelms by a rhapsody of successive sounds what can only be represented by figure, and the less frequent, but equally absurd attempt of combining moments and subdividing expression. Homer describes generally in one word, where action is not concerned; and the triple expression of a Paris by Euphranor belongs probably only to the writer[1] who, in talking of the Laocoon, expresses his astonishment at the windings of the serpents, and at the rope, when he mentions the group of Dirce. The futility of such mutual inroads of poetry and painting on each other has been shown by a late German writer[2] of great acuteness and some taste, though on a tame principle, and without drawing the inferences that obviously derive from his rules.

(*Analytical Review*, November 1794, review of Uvedale Price's *Essay on the Picturesque*, signed R. R.—XX, p. 259)

The Description of Nature

WE FORBEAR any of her elegant rhapsodies on the scenery of Switzerland. Torrents, Alps, lakes have roared, towered, spread, forests have waved and landscapes frowned or smiled in sudden alternatives of spring and winter in many a page before those of H. W., to little better purpose than to weary the reader and leave him in a chaos of undiscriminated imagery. It is not sufficient that an object has been immediately copied from nature, to interest us in its description; and it ought to be considered, whether the impression nature made can be conveyed in words. The interval that separates the moment of seeing and the hour of writing is generally big with languor. . . . Homer is understood, not because he describes objects, but because he shows them.

(*Analytical Review*, June 1798, review of Helen Maria Williams's *Tour in Switzerland*, signed R. R.—XXVII, pp. 565–6)

[1] Pliny. The passages in question are all discussed in greater detail in Fuseli's first Lecture and in the 1820 prefatory essay to the first six lectures.

[2] G. E. Lessing, in a treatise entitled 'Laocoon, or on the limits of poetry and painting' (Fuseli's own footnote).

SECTION THREE

SIMPLE AND MIXED
EXPRESSION

The theme of mixed and simple expression is one that belongs to Fuseli's period and no longer much appeals to us. Reynolds writes in his fifteenth Discourse (December 1790): 'An Artist . . . is not likely to be forever teasing the poor student with the beauties of *mixed passions*, or to perplex him with an imaginary union of excellencies incompatible with one another.' Fuseli, in writing on this theme, is chiefly concerned to differentiate himself as much as possible from the German school. Similarly he condemns Klopstock's 'subtilisation of sentiments'.

Mixed and Simple Expression

IT IS said that too much sentiment, too complex an expression of passions, is incompatible with sculpture: this, neither the dilettante, who has been instructed to look only for *inward* expression in the antique, nor he who delights in its *external* energy, will readily understand. The fact is, that *mixed* expression is equally unfit for the sculptor, engraver or painter; a *little* of many things is in art the destruction of the *whole*. Tydeus, Philoctetes, Ajax, Laocoon, intrepidity, indignation, defiance, pain, personified, can each have only one great feature on canvas, in marble, in metal and on gems.

(*Analytical Review*, November 1791, review of Raspe's *Catalogue of Tassie's Gems*, signed R. R.—XI, p. 262)

" Or in the emptier waste, resembling Air,
Weighs his spread wings . . ." (*Paradise Lost* II)

? Satan taking his flight from Chaos

Classical precedents for some measure of blended emotional themes

BUT MAY not dignity, elegance, and valour, or any other not irreconcilable qualities, be visible at once in a figure without destroying the primary feature of its character, or impairing its expression? Let us appeal to the Apollo. Is he not a figure of character and expression, and does he not possess all three in a supreme degree? Will it imply mediocrity of conception or confusion of character, if we were to say that his countenance, attitude, and form combines divine majesty, enchanting grace, and lofty indignation? Yet not all three, one ideal whole irradiated the mind of the artist who conceived the divine semblance.

(1801—Lecture I, p. 69)

The over-subtlety of German criticism

. . . all such mixtures impair the simplicity and clearness of expression: in the group of the Laocoon, the frigid ecstasies of German criticism[1] have discovered pity like a vapour swimming on the father's eyes; he is seen to suppress in the groan for his children the shriek for himself,—his nostrils are drawn upward to express indignation at unworthy sufferings, whilst he is said at the same time to implore celestial help. To these are added the winged effects of the serpent-poison, the writhings of the body, the spasms of the extremities: to the miraculous organisation of such expression, Agesander, the sculptor of the Laocoon, was too wise to lay claim. His figure is a class, it characterizes every beauty of virility verging on age; the prince, the priest, the father are visible, but, absorbed in the man, serve only to dignify the victim of *one* great expression; though poised by the artist, for us to apply the compass to the face of the Laocoon is to measure the wave fluctuating in the storm: this tempestuous front, this contracted nose, the immersion of these eyes

---

[1] Winckelmann in his *History of the Art of the Ancients*, 1764, Part I.

and, above all, that long-drawn mouth,[1] are separate and united seats of convulsion, features of nature struggling within the jaws of death.

(1801—Lecture I, pp. 71–2)

[1] This is directed against Lessing, who asserts that the sculptor has 'softened the cry to a sigh', because the opening of the mouth to cry aloud is ugly and it is the highest law of great art to sacrifice expression to beauty —a notion Fuseli particularly hated and repeatedly attacks. *See below,* Part V, Section 1.

SECTION FOUR

SUBJECT AND CONCEPTION

versus

MEDIUM AND EXECUTION

'Though all Nature seem to teem with objects of imitation, the "Choice" of subjects is a point of great importance to the Artist' (Fuseli, Lecture IV, p. 189)

Mere technique

NO EXCELLENCE of execution can atone for meanness of conception.[1]

(1788–1818—Aphorism 75)

WHENEVER THE medium of any work, whether lines, colour, grouping, diction, becomes so predominant as to absorb the

---

[1] Fuseli again and again treats 'execution' as something secondary, extrinsic and detachable from the essence of artistic power; herein he appears to us representative of an outlook on art that is now permanently superseded. On this theme, as on many others, Blake shows a bolder and more modern mind. 'He who admires Raphael must admire Raphael's execution. He who does not admire Raphael's execution cannot admire Raphael . . . does not even see Raphael', writes Blake variously in the margins of Reynolds' *Discourses*.

subject in its splendour, the work is degraded to an inferior order.

(1788–1818—Aphorism 53)

Mind and mere technique—Imitation and Copying

ADMITTING THAT, without acquiring the means of execution, it is impossible to give birth and consequence to thought—is it fair to conclude that power of execution can ever impart mind? It is a mind similar to Michelangelo alone, that ever can make use of him: but he who can imitate him will hardly condescend to copy.

(*Analytical Review*, May 1791, review of Reynolds's last Discourse, signed R. R.—X, p. 4)

Style and Manner

THERE ARE two ways of composing in poetry and painting: the one finds materials for a subject, the other finds a subject for materials; the one is the method of him who is said to write or work with *style*; the second that of those who indulge in what is called *manner*.

(*Analytical Review*, July 1789, unsigned account of Macklin's Gallery —IV, p. 370. Fuseli is here attacking Stothard)

SECTION FIVE

TRUE COMPOSITION
AND MERE GROUPING

Apposition and Composition—Primitive and Advanced Art

APPOSITION, or an assemblage of figures, numerically put together, without central masses and collateral gradation, without approximation or distance, and a want of perspective, have always marked the infancy of painting. Composition, or the formation of a striking centre into subordinate rays, belongs to painting in its vigour, when enumeration is no longer mistaken for order. In that infant state, individual lines, colour and expression are the only means by which one artist can assert his superiority over another.

(*Analytical Review*, October 1792, review of Hickey's *History of Painting and Sculpture*, signed R. R.—XIV, p. 164)

THE TECHNIC part of Composition alone, though carried to the highest pitch of perfection, if its ostentation absorb the subject, stamps inferiority on the master.

(1805—Lecture V, p. 243)

Composition and Grouping[1]

> 'So characteristically separate from real composition are the most splendid assemblages, the most happy combinations of figures . . .' (Fuseli, Corollary 65)

THE ASSERTION that grouping may not be composing, has been said to make a distinction without a difference: as if there had not been, still are, and always will be squadrons of artists, whose skill in grouping can no more be denied, than their claim to invention, and consequently to composition, admitted, if invention means the true conception of a subject and composition the best mode of representing it. After the demise of Leonardo and Michelangelo, their successors, however discordant else, uniformly agreed to lose the subject in the medium.

(1788–1818—Corollary to Aphorism 65)

---

[1] On 29 December 1815 the following conversation took place between Canova and Haydon: ' "How do you like West?" said I. *"Comme ça." "Au moins,"* said I *"il compose bien." "Non, Monsieur,"* said Canova, *"il met des figures en groupes."* ' This distinction between composition and grouping may have been just a commonplace of the times, but it is possible that here Canova was echoing remarks from his conversations with Fuseli, whom he had been seeing much of during the preceding weeks. It is always West whom Fuseli has particularly in mind when he thus distinguishes composition from grouping. *See above,* p. 139.

SECTION SIX

TERROR AND GRANDEUR

versus

HORROR AND DISGUST

Knowles, whose syntax was not his strongest point, writes of Fuseli: 'In carrying the terrible to its utmost limits, I know of no subject from his pencil calculated to create horror or disgust' (*Biography*, p. 405). This proves at most that Knowles may not have known anything like all there was to be known, not so much, for instance, as Flaxman, Haydon and Cunningham. On 13 July 1826 Flaxman, in speaking to Haydon of Fuseli's death, said: ' "He has left, I understand, behind him some drawings, shockingly indelicate." "Has he, sir?" asked Haydon. "Yes, Mr. Haydon. Poor wretch!" said Flaxman, looking ineffably modest' (Haydon's diary). Cunningham, writing in 1829, also mentions these shockingly indelicate drawings, and says of them: 'Fire, however, fell amongst most of these, when he died—nor do I blame the hand of his widow who kindled it.' Mr. Sacheverell Sitwell, who contributes some of the most picturesque touches to our new mythical envisagement of Fuseli, estimates that several hundreds of these exceptionable drawings may have escaped Mrs. Fuseli's kitchen-range, and it is on them that his researches have been concentrated. Nearly all of them, he tells us, are too obscene ever to be published,[1] even in our emancipated days, but what emerges from a careful study of them is that Fuseli was above all a 'master of static horror', and the same conclusion will be borne in upon us also by his less esoteric pictures, if only we properly

---

[1] Mr. Ruthven Todd has done what he can to meet this difficulty with reproductions of details from such obscene drawings in his *Tracks in the Snow* (London, 1947).

scrutinise them for 'abnormal points' (Sacheverell Sitwell, *Splendours and Miseries*, 1943). It is of interest in this connexion to note that, whatever Fuseli may in practice have been and done, officially and on principle he utterly disapproved of 'horror' in art, was always outraged when he encountered it in the work of others, and never wrote about it, except to condemn it. The horrible, in the sense in which Fuseli disapproves of it, is, indeed, perhaps not quite identical with the horrible in the sense in which Mr. Sitwell relishes it. Be that as it may, it was 'terror' as distinguished from 'horror' that Fuseli consciously and programmatically cultivated, and he has left us various precepts for obtaining it, the principal among them being the foreshortening of figures from ground-level, or from what is called in German 'the frog's perspective'. This is one of Fuseli's own favourite devices.

Horror and Terror in Painting and in Poetry

. . . he expatiates on the boundless licence granted to poetry, and the very narrow limits prescribed to painting with regard to the choice of objects: a notion, which owes its origins to the German critics. The truth is, that horror and loathsomeness in all its branches are equally banished from the painter's and the poet's province. Terror, as the chief ingredient of the sublime, composes in all instances, and in the utmost extent of the word, fit material for both. . . . Laocoon, with his sons, will always remain a sufficient answer to all that has been retailed in our days on the limits of the art by tame antiquarians from tamer painters.[1]

(*Analytical Review*, October 1792, review of Hickey's *History of Painting and Sculpture*, signed R. R.—XIV, p. 165)

'The insensibility, perhaps brutality of Artists'

LET HORROR and loathsomeness be banished from the instru-

[1] *Tame antiquarians* appears to be directed against both Winckelmann and Lessing; the reference is mainly to Lessing's *Laocoon*, which is in part a further development of certain ideas expressed by Winckelmann, in part a severe criticism of him. The *tame painter* alluded to by Fuseli is certainly Mengs.

ments of art, and the martyrdom of Stephen or Sebastian, Agnes or John becomes as admissible as that of Marsyas or Palamedes, Virginia or Regulus. It is the artist's fault, if the right moment be missed. If you see only blood-tipped arrows, brain-dashed stones, excoriating knives, the artist, not the subject is detestable; *this* furnished heroism, celestial resignation, the features of calm fortitude and beauty helpless but undismayed; the clown or brute alone, who handled it, pushed you down among the assassins from the hero's side.

(*Analytical Review*, December 1796, review of Roscoe's *Lorenzo de' Medici*, signed Z. Z.—XXIV, p. 566. Knowles, I, pp. 148–9)

Pity is akin to Hate

'—suffering deformity mingles disgust with pity' (Lecture IV, p. 194)

. . . sympathy and disgust are the irreconcilable parallels that must for ever separate legitimate terror and pity from horror and aversion. We cannot sympathise with what we detest or despise, nor fully pity what we shudder at or loathe . . . mangling is contagious, and spreads aversion from the slaughterman to the victim.

(1805—Lecture V, pp. 262–3)

The Disgusting in Art

THE LOATHSOME is abominable, and no engine of expression. When Spenser[1] dragged into light the entrails of the serpent slain by the Red Knight, he dreamt a butcher's dream and not a poet's . . .

(1788–1818—Aphorism 86 with part of Corollary)

---

[1] *Faerie Queene*, Book I, Canto 1.

Drawing the line in the cult of Horror—Aristides' *'Slain Mother'*

TIMANTHES HAD marked the limits that discriminate terror from the excess of horror; Aristides drew the line that separates it from disgust. His subject is one of those that touch the ambiguous line of a squeamish sense.

(1801—Lecture I, p. 65)

Recipes for Terror and Grandeur

ALL APPARATUS destroys grandeur: the minute catalogue of the cauldron's ingredients in Macbeth destroys the terror attendant on mysterious darkness; and the seraglio-trappings of Rubens annihilate his heroes.

(1788–1818—Aphorism 58)

The True Recipe for Terror

IT IS not by the accumulation of infernal or magic machinery, distinctly seen, by the introduction of Hecate and a chorus of female demons and witches, by surrounding him with successive apparitions at once, and a range of shadows moving above or before him, that Macbeth can be made an object of terror,— to render him so you must place him on a ridge, his down-dashed eye absorbed by the murky abyss; surround the horrid vision with darkness, exclude its limits, and shear its light to glimpses.

(1805—Lecture IV, pp. 225–6)

Recipe for Grandeur—foreshortening from ground level

IT DOES not appear that the great masters of legitimate composition in the sixteenth century attended to or understood the

218

advantages which elevation of site and a low horizon are capable of giving a subject. They place us in the gallery to behold their scenes; . . . the more remote groups do not approach, but fall or stand upon the foremost actors. As this impedes the principles of unity and grandeur in numerous compositions, so it impairs each individual form; which, to be grand, ought to rise upward in moderate foreshortening, command the horizon, or be in contact with the sky.

(1805—Lecture V, pp. 253–4)

THIS ART of giving to the principal figure the command of the horizon, is perhaps the only principle by which modern art might have gained an advantage over that of the ancients. . . .

(1805—Lecture IV, p. 226)

PART FOUR

FUSELI

ON THE HISTORY OF ART

—THE STUBBORNLY MAINTAINED

CLASSICAL HUSK

In opening his series of lectures in 1801 Fuseli says that his 'historic sketch of the origin and progress of our art . . . naturally divides itself into two parts, the art of the ancients, and its restoration among the moderns' (first edition of *Lectures*, 1803, p. 3). So far as art is concerned, the entire period between the breaking-up of ancient civilisation and the Renaissance (reckoned as not beginning till after 1500) was in Fuseli's eyes of no importance or interest whatsoever. *Gothic* still meant for him nothing but *barbarous*, and never was to mean anything else for him. He seems to have been remarkably insensitive to architecture—his paintings owe much of their peculiar character to the architectural and also the landscape factors in them being attenuated to a minimum—and there is no parallel in his evolution to the new stirrings in Goethe's heart at the sight of Strasbourg Minster in 1770, to Blake's entranced hours in Westminster Abbey, to Wordsworth's in King's College Chapel, or to Keats's in Winchester Cathedral. He hardly ever mentions architecture in any of his writings, but where he does so, he shows that none of the many fine Gothic buildings he must have seen had ever left him anything but antagonistic or at best indifferent: 'Disproportion is the element of hugeness,—proportion of grandeur; all Oriental, all Gothic styles of Architecture are huge; the Grecian alone is grand' (Aphorism 107). In literature, indeed, his taste was less exclusively anti-Gothic—two mediaeval works at least, the *Nibelungen* and Dante's *Divine Comedy*, were immensely important to him. But neither this nor any other similar circumstance restrains him from proclaiming in and out of season a peculiarly extravagant and aggressive, indeed most unclassically violent variant of the classical creed. 'Where is the great name among the moderns that ever could reach the line and proportions of the ancients?' he demands in his seventh Lecture. 'To attain the height of the Ancient was impossible for Modern Art,' he asserts in his twelfth. He had worshipped Winckelmann in earlier years, he turned fiercely and irreconcilably against him on going to Rome, but to the last he operates very largely with the principles of Winckelmann's or even of a still earlier classicism. He maintained that painting as a truly valid and pure art should concern itself exclusively with heroically idealised human figures, constructed according to the classical 'canon of proportion', for preference nude or Grecianly draped, engaged in some striking action which 'tells a story' and bodies forth an idea, set against a background with very little detail indicated, and hardly anything about it to suggest a particular locality or a particular historical period. That Fuseli in thus adopting the classical theories of his age also adapted them to his own very exceptional case and to what he considered his own peculiar powers and limitations, infusing into them a spirit that was by no means classical, is what anyone at all familiar with his work would expect, and his writings fulfil these expectations at every turn.

SECTION ONE

THE ABSOLUTE PRE-EMINENCE
OF GREEK ART

One of the most interesting points that arises in connexion with Fuseli's exposition of Greek art is the rough shock that was given to some of his cherished convictions during the last twenty years of his life by the Elgin Marbles, a shock comparable to those he received in his early years from Rousseau's loss of countenance, and in his middle years from the reading of Lessing's *Laocoon*. What was involved was the central dogma of eighteenth-century classicism, that great art should never be concerned with the individual, but only with the general and typical. 'The whole beauty and grandeur of the art consists, in my opinion, in being able to get above all singular forms, local customs, particularities and details of every kind,' writes Reynolds in his third Discourse (1770), and again: 'The painter . . . must disregard all local and temporary ornaments, and look only on those general habits which are everywhere and always the same.' Blake's comment on these passages was: 'A Folly! Singular and Particular Detail is the Foundation of the Sublime.' 'Generalizing in Every thing, the Man would soon be a Fool, but a Cunning Fool.' When Reynolds speaks of the 'disposition to abstractions, to generalising and classification' as 'the great glory of the human mind', Blake protests: 'To Generalise is to be an Idiot. To Particularise is the Alone Distinction of Merit. General Knowledges are those Knowledges that Idiots possess.' Here, and indeed all along the line, with two important exceptions to be considered later (*see* Part V, Section 1), Fuseli is on the side of Reynolds against Blake. The recognition forced upon him by the Parthenon marbles, that Phidias, of all artists, may after all have been concerned with individuals and with the particular, thoroughly disconcerts him.

Egyptian monstrousness and Greek perfection

'... the Greeks carried the art to a height
which no subsequent time or race has been
able to rival or even to approach' (Fuseli's
Ist Lecture, p. 25)

... we now approach that happy coast, where, from an arbitrary
hieroglyph, the palliative of ignorance, from a tool of despotism,
or a ponderous monument of eternal sleep, art emerged into
life, motion, and liberty; where situation, climate, national
character, religion, manners and government conspired to raise
it on that permanent basis which, after the ruins of the fabric
itself, still subsists and bids defiance to the ravages of time. As
uniform in the principle as various in its applications, the art
of the Greeks possessed in itself and propagated, like its chief
object Man, the germs of immortality.

(1801—Lecture I, pp. 23–4)

The Classical Canon of Proportion

ZEUXIS ... gave to the divine and heroic character in painting,
what Polycletus had given to the human in sculpture, ... a
canon of proportion. Phidias had discovered in the nod of the
Homeric Jupiter the characteristic of majesty, *inclination of the
head*.[1] ... From the head conclude to the proportions of the
neck, the limbs, the extremities; from the father to the race of
gods; all the sons of one, Zeus; derived from one source of tradition, Homer; formed by one artist, Phidias; on him measured

[1] According to an anecdote recorded by Strabo and Valerius Maximus
Phidias himself declared that his Olympian Zeus was inspired by the following lines in the first Iliad:

So spoke Cronion promising, and bowed his sable brows,
While down from that immortal head the Lord's ambrosial locks
Swung forward slowly with the words, and high Olympus quaked.

(Translation of W. H. D. Rouse)

It is interesting that Fuseli should have attached such importance as he
did to this anecdote.

" Through the ambrosial night . . ."

? Sarpedon borne off the battlefield by Sleep and Death

and decided by Parrhasius. In the simplicity of this principle, adhered to by the succeeding periods, lies the uninterrupted progress and the unattainable superiority of Grecian art.

(1801—Lecture I, pp. 40–1)

Classical Idealism—a Standard of Form

WHAT WAS it that the Academy intended by making the Antique the basis of your studies? What, but to lead you to the sources of Form; to initiate you in the true elements of human essence; to enable you to judge at your transition from the marble to life what was substance and possession to the individual, and what excrescence and want, what homogeneous, what discordant, what deformity, what beauty. It intended, by making you acquainted with a variety of figures, to qualify you for classing them according to character and function; ... in short, to supply by its stores, as far as time and circumstances permitted, what the *public* granted to the artists of Greece;[1] what Zeuxis demanded and obtained from the people of Croton;[2] what Eupompus pointed out to Lysippus;[3] what Raphael,[4] with better will than success, searched in his own mind; and what Andrea Mantegna, however unqualified to find himself, desired to impress on the mind of Albrecht Dürer—a standard of FORM.

(1810—Lecture VII, pp. 317–18)

The Benefits of Drawing from the Life

TO ME, after considering carefully what has been advanced on either side, it appears demonstrated, that the student is admitted

---

[1] Ample opportunities to see the human body nude on athletic and similar occasions—a point much insisted on by Winckelmann.

[2] The anecdote of Zeuxis selecting five naked virgins as models for his picture of Helen is variously located in Croton and in Agrigentum.

[3] Eupompus and Lysippus: *see* pp. 308–10.

[4] Fuseli frequently refers to the letter in which Raphael writes to C. B. Castiglione: 'Since there are so few beautiful women ... I make use of a certain idea in my own imagination.'

to the life to avail himself of the knowledge he acquired from the previous study of classic forms.

(1810—Lecture VII, p. 320)

Fuseli and the Elgin Marbles—Drawing from Life

In October 1790 Fuseli reviewed at length in the *Analytical Review* the second volume—published 1787—of James Stuart's and Nicholas Revett's still immensely valuable *Antiquities of Athens*. This is the volume dedicated to the Parthenon marbles. It appeared a good fifteen years before anybody thought of transferring these marbles to England. Fuseli, who insists very much on the inferiority of the drawings, is not more than moderately impressed by the sculptures. He writes:

ALL THESE, though many of them are little more than wrecks of forms, still more disfigured in the copies, claim the uniform praise due to every work of ancient Greece—of propriety and dignity, considered as ornaments, of correctness and style, examined as works of art. But still they have another claim to superiority over modern art: the general composition, notwithstanding a sufficient variety of contrast and action, possesses that simplicity, that parallelism or continuity of attitude and gesture, which produces energy of impression and through the eye forces itself on the memory of the beholder. One great sentiment predominates over the motions and expressions of the actors, and allows only as much variety of both as individuals claim. It is by this uninterrupted series of attitudes nearly similar, where horse joins man, and man joins horse, and all seem bent on the same object only, that the artist, who could abstract the general from the local and saw into futurity, contrives to impress us with awe, to interest us for ceremonies scarcely remembered.

(Analytical Review, VIII, p. 124)

Six years later, in reviewing Stuart and Revett's third volume, which deals with the so-called *Theseum*, Fuseli generates a very much greater enthusiasm for the comparatively inferior sculptures of that temple than he had been able to for those of the Parthenon, and lashes himself into a characteristic paroxysm of fury (it is hard to make out with whom), because there are no casts of them in London. (Lord Elgin's casts from the East Frieze of the *Theseum* are now in the British Museum, together with the Parthenon originals, in the Elgin Room, as No. 404.) Of the *Theseum* sculptures Fuseli writes in June 1796:

OF THESE it is perhaps unnecessary to say more than that they are the produce of the age of Phidias, and in that heroic style which, even in these feeble prints,[1] reminds us of the Castor and Pollux on the Quirinal.[2] He who can spare a tear from the griefs of the present moment may humanely drop it on these precious remains of human grandeur and human genius in ruins. . . .

(*Analytical Review*, XXIII, p. 562)

In 1808, shortly after the jealous and impudent bluff of the collector Richard Payne Knight with his 'You have lost your labour, my Lord, your marbles are overrated, they are not Greek, they are Roman of the time of Hadrian!' had condemned the Parthenon marbles to their long banishment in Lord Elgin's damp shed in Park Lane, Fuseli was one of the first to take a look at them. It was his twenty-two-year-old pupil, Benjamin Haydon, who dragged him off to see them. After one first flash of enthusiasm Fuseli wavered in his judgment, going over to the party of Payne Knight, for whose scholarship he had considerable deference. Haydon gives two accounts of his attempts to convert Fuseli to his own faith in the marbles. The following is a combination of these two passages:

I DROVE off to Fuseli, and fired him to such a degree that he ran upstairs, put on his coat, and away we sallied. I remember that first a coal-cart with eight horses stopped us, as it struggled up one of the lanes of the Strand. Then a flock of sheep blocked us

---

[1] Some of these 'feeble prints' were engraved by Blake. The draughtsman was William Pars (1742–82), brother of Blake's first drawing-master.

[2] *Castor and Pollux on the Quirinal*—the colossal statues of Monte Cavallo, which bear inscriptions (certainly spurious) attributing them to Phidias and Praxiteles. There are some very interesting sketches of them, with violent foreshortenings from ground-level, in Fuseli's Roman sketch-book. It is because he takes the ascription to Phidias as genuine that Fuseli, in his last years, relegates them from the highest to the lowest class of Greek sculpture, when Phidias has been so badly compromised in his eyes by the Parthenon marbles. See Plate 3, facing p. 168.

up; Fuseli, in a fury of haste and rage, burst into the middle of them, and they got between his little legs and jostled him so much that I screamed with laughter, in spite of my excitement. He swore all along the Strand like a little fury. At last we came to Park Lane. Never shall I forget his uncompromising enthusiasm. Thrown off his guard by their beauty, he strode about the collection in his fierce way, saying: 'De Greeks were godes! De Greeks were godes!' We went back to his house, where I dined with him, and we passed the evening looking over Quintillian and Pliny, and every other Greek author who alluded to the Parthenon and the Greek artists. Immortal period of my sanguine life! Had Fuseli always acted about the marbles as honestly as he did then, it would have been well for his reputation. A day or two afterwards, reflecting what he had written about the Apollo, etc.,[1] he tried to *unsay*, but it would not do. . . . He flew into a passion, and we were never cordial after. I regretted it, for no man owed more to Fuseli than I did.

(*Life of Benjamin Robert Haydon*, compiled by Tom Taylor, 1852, Vol. I, p. 86, and Vol. II, p. 92)

Haydon sets out vividly the point at issue in his dispute with Fuseli over the Elgin Marbles. He had felt himself emancipated by the marbles from the central dogma which Fuseli had inherited from eighteenth-century classicism and remorselessly drilled into all his pupils, that no absolutely great artist ever works direct from the life, except possibly by way of practice or in minor productions, but is guided instead by a generalised, abstract idea or 'canon'—thence the definition 'Nature is a collective idea' (*see below*, p. 232). Haydon writes:

IF I COPIED what I saw in life, Fuseli said, 'This is too much like life!' If I copied the marble, Wilkie said, 'That looks as if you had painted from stone!' . . . That combination of nature and idea which I had felt so much wanting in high art was here (in the Parthenon marbles) displayed to mid-day conviction. My heart beat! If I had seen nothing else, I had beheld sufficient to keep me to nature for the rest of my life. . . . I saw, in fact, the

---

[1] Vague recollections of the passage in Fuseli's first Lecture on the Greek 'canon of proportion'—*see* p. 224.

most heroic style of art, combined with all the essential detail of actual life, the thing was done for ever.

(Vol. I, pp. 82–4)

This was much more than a merely theoretical or academic controversy for Fuseli, whose extremely sensitive confidence in his own powers and uneasiness about his own limitations turned largely on his being able to appeal to the loftiest precedents (above all, the ancient Greeks and Michelangelo) for his own readily and even defiantly admitted insufficiency in drawing from the life. Incessantly the words must have been on his lips: 'Nature puts me out!'[1] If one knew nothing else about Fuseli, one knew that he had said that. None of his utterances has been so frequently recorded—it occurs not only in Knowles, but also repeatedly in the writings of Hazlitt and Haydon and, of course, in the biography of Cunningham, who gives it the ampler and probably enough authentic form: 'Damn Nature!—she always puts me out.' Fuseli did not go far wrong, if he suspected that his self-assertive young pupil Haydon, in forcing the Elgin Marbles down his throat, was at the same time launching a masked attack on one of the most vulnerable points in his own art. This comes out clearly enough in an entry in Haydon's diary for 15 December 1808, only three months after the eventful excursion to Park Lane:

WHAT ARE those painters doing, who, neglecting Nature, degenerate into manner, and then say that 'Nature puts them out,' still imitating her to the best of their recollections? Why does she put them out? . . . A real man of genius will not suffer Nature to put him out.

(Vol. I, p. 106)

Haydon seems to have remained unaware of how great a shock he had given Fuseli by his eloquent and cogent demonstration that the Parthenon sculptors must have worked direct from living models. Whether or not he was right, he certainly did convince Fuseli on this point, though he was not given the satisfaction of a point-blank admission. When Haydon at last won the battle for Lord Elgin and the marbles were given their due, in 1816, Fuseli remained silent. But in 1825, in one of his last lectures, he ventured on the treacherous ground again, and it is no mean triumph for Haydon that the

---

[1] Cp. Blake: 'Natural objects *always did and do* weaken, deaden and obliterate imagination in me' (1826—manuscript note on Wordsworth's *Ode on Immortality*).

grudging concession here made to him forces Fuseli to modify materially, within a few months of his death, his account of Greek art. He admits that there is a level—the lowest and least mature level, however—at which the Greeks actually did occasionally 'transcribe' nature, instead of 'imitating' her. To this lowest level of Greek art the Parthenon marbles are assigned. He sees himself, however, forced, at the same time, to degrade to this lowest level the two colossal statues on Monte Cavallo which he had hitherto put in the highest rank, very much overrating their genuineness and intrinsic value, according to accepted authoritative opinion, and introducing them again and again in his own work. He divides the 'sculptured works left by the ancients' into three classes:

1st. Imitations, not seldom transcripts of *Essential Nature*.

2nd. Homogeneous delineations of *Character*: and

3rd. The highest and last—*Ideal* figures.

The first shows to advantage what exists or existed; the second collects in one individual what is scattered in his class; the third subordinates existence and character to beauty and sublimity.

The astonishing remains of gods, demigods and heroes treasured in the Museum from the Parthenon and the Temple of Phigalia[1] constitute the first epoch. They establish the elements of proportion, they show what is essential in the composition and construction of the human frame. The artist's principle remained, however, negative (i.e. neutral); he understood the best he saw, but did not attempt to add, or conclude from what was to what might be. These works are commonly considered as the produce of the school of Phidias, and the substantiation of his principles; if they are, and there can be little doubt but they are, it must be owned that the eulogies lately lavished on them,[2] as presenting, even in their mutilated and

[1] The Temple of Phigalia—the friezes from the Temple of Apollo Epicurios acquired by the British Museum in 1814 and upheld by the anti-Elgin faction as infinitely superior to the Parthenon marbles.

[2] Fuseli is here certainly referring above all to Haydon's article *On the Judgment of Connoisseurs being preferred to that of Professional Men—The Elgin Marbles*, printed in the *Examiner* and *Champion* in 1816, and reprinted in Haydon's biography. 'It is this union of nature with ideal beauty,—the probabilities and accidents of bone, flesh and tendon etc. . . . that rank the Elgin Marbles above all other works of art in the world,' writes Haydon. 'The Elgin Marbles will as completely overthrow the old antique as ever one

battered surfaces, more of the real texture of the human frame, a better discrimination of bone, muscle and tendon than most of the works ascribed to more advanced periods, little agree with the verdict of the ancients, as pronounced by Pliny, on the real character of Phidias, the architect of gods, fitter to frame divinities than men, and leave him little more share in the formation of our figures than the conception. In beholding them we say, such is man, real unsophisticated man, man warm from the hand of nature, but not yet distinguished by her endless variety and difference of character. The Dioscuri of the Quirinal,[1] the Lapithae in conflict with the Centaurs from the Parthenon, and the heroes from the fabric of Ictinus[2] are brothers, and only differ in size and finish; whilst the Panathenaic processions offer the unvaried transcript of Athenian youth.

(1825—Lecture X, pp. 382–3)

Thus it was that Fuseli reacted to the most momentous development of his day in the field of Greek art, which he was so deeply interested in. He squared it as best he could, and at all costs, with his preconceived notions. His 'highest and last' class of 'ideal figures' is represented by the *Apollo Belvedere* and the *Venus dei Medici*. It should be noted, however, that he had all along been ready to concede that there had been a certain measure of not altogether reprehensible realism in the *latest* stages of Greek art (*see below*, p. 308—Lysippus and the school of nature). It was the possibility of its having been there as a determining principle from the earlier stages that upset all Fuseli's calculations.

Nature, a collective Idea

. . . by *nature* I understand the general and permanent principles of visible objects, not disfigured by accident, or distempered

system of philosophy overthrew another more enlightened.' Goethe, who was tarred with the same brush as Fuseli in these matters, dismisses Haydon's article impatiently in his *Vergleichung zweier antiken Pferdeköpfe* in *Ueber Kunst und Altertum* (1820). Haydon is immensely proud of having been mentioned at all by the 'great Goethe', even uncomplimentarily.

[1] *The Dioscuri of the Quirinal*—see above, p. 227, note 2.

[2] *The fabric of Ictinus*—Fuseli means here the Temple of Phigalia. The designation is not felicitous, as the Parthenon was also built by Ictinus.

by disease, not modified by fashion or local habits. Nature is a collective idea, and, though its essence exist in each individual of the species, can never in its perfection inhabit a single object.

(1801—Lecture I, p. 21)

Idealisation and Real Life in Poetry

HOMER INVESTED his heroes with ideal powers, but copied nature in delineating their moral character. Achilles, the irresistible in arms, clad in celestial armour, is a splendid being, created by himself; Achilles the fool of passions, is the real man delivered to him by tradition.

(1788–1818—Corollary to Aphorism 93)

Achilles—the Ideal Hero

> 'Ideal is properly the representation of pure
> human essence' (footnote to Corollary 151
> of the *Aphorisms*)

THE HEIGHT, the strength, the giant-stride and supercilious air of Ajax; the courage, the impetuosity, the never-failing aim, the never-bloodless stroke of Diomedes; the presence of mind, the powerful agility of Ulysses; the velocity of the lesser Ajax; Agamemnon's sense of prerogative and domineering spirit,— assign to each his separate class of heroism, yet lessen not their shades of imperfection. Ajax appears the warrior rather than the leader; Ulysses is too prudent to be more than brave; the hawk more than the eagle predominates in the son of Oileus; Agamemnon has the prerogative of power, but not of heroism; Diomedes alone might appear to have been raised too high, had he been endowed with an assuming spirit. So far the poet found, ennobled, classified; but all these he sums up, and creates an ideal form from their assemblage, in Achilles:—he is the grandson of Jupiter, the son of a goddess, the favourite of Heaven. . . . Before the pursuer of Hector vanishes the velocity of Ajax; from destroying Agamemnon he is prevented by Minerva; he gives

232

his armour to the son of Menoetius, and disperses all but the gods; his spear none can throw, and none can tear from the ground when thrown; a miracle alone can save those that oppose him singly; when else he fights, 'tis not to gain a battle, but to subvert Troy.

What Achilles is to his confederates, the Apollo, the Torso, the statues of the Quirinal, are to all other known figures of gods, of demigods, and heroes.

(1788–1818—Corollary to Aphorism 102)

Great Art is never concerned with the Individual

IT MUST however be owned, that he would commit a more venial error, and come nearer to the form we require in the Achilles of Homer, who should substitute the form of the Apollo or Hercules with the motion of the Gladiator to the real form, than he who should copy him from the best individual he could meet with: the reason is clear; there is a greater analogy between their form and action and that of Achilles, than between him and the best model we know alive.

(1810—Lecture VII, p. 324)

The Dignity of Historic Painting

... nothing trivial, nothing grovelling or mean should be suffered to approach it.

(1805—Lecture IV, p. 195)

The Common-place

COMMON-PLACE figures are as inadmissible in the grand style of painting as common-place characters or sentiments in poetry.

(1788–1818—Aphorism 55)

233

Dignity

DIGNITY IS the salt of art. . . . Dignity gives probability to the impossible: we listen to the monstrous tale of Ulysses with all the devotion due to a creed. By dignity, even deformity becomes an instrument of art; Vulcan limps like a god at the hand of Homer; the hump and withered arm of Richard are engines of terror or persuasion in Shakespeare; the crook-back[1] of Michelangelo strikes with awe.

(1788–1818—Aphorisms 167 and 168)

The Scale of 'Advantageous Subjects' for the Painter

TO BEGIN with advantageous subjects, (immediately above the scenes of vulgar life, of animals, and common landscape), the simple representation of actions purely human appears to be as nearly related to the art as to ourselves; their effect is immediate; they want no explanation; from them, therefore, we begin our scale. The next step leads us to pure historic subjects, singly or in a series; beyond these the delineation of character, or, properly speaking, the drama, invites; immediately above this we place the epic with its mythologic, allegoric and symbolic branches.

(1805—Lecture IV, pp. 192–3)

Actions purely Human

(That 'essential Nature' beneath which true Art cannot descend without forfeiting her dignity and betraying her vocation.)

THE SIMPLE representation of actions purely human, which . . . may be said to draw its substance immediately from the lap of

---

[1] In his spectacular dithyrambic passage on Michelangelo (*see* page 248) Fuseli also speaks of the 'humpback of Michelangelo's dwarf'. There is no figure in the works now attributed to Michelangelo to which these words can be made to apply.

Nature, to be as elemental as her emotions and the passions by which she sways us, finds its echo in all hearts, and imparts its charm to every eye; from the mutual caresses of maternal affection and infant simplicity, the whispers of love or eruptions of jealousy and revenge, to the terrors of life, struggling with danger, or grappling with death.

(1805—Lecture IV, p. 193)

How Art's legitimate pre-occupation with the 'Pure Emanations' of 'Essential Nature' can degenerate into the trivialities of mere local colour

NOR SHALL I follow it in its more contaminated descent, to those representations of local manners and national modifications of society, whose characteristic discrimination and humorous exuberance, for instance, we admire in Hogarth, but which, like the fleeting passions of the day, every hour contributes something to obliterate, which soon become unintelligible by time, or degenerate into caricature, the chronicle of scandal, the history-book of the vulgar.

(1801—Lecture III, p. 156)

SECTION TWO

THE REVIVAL OF ART
IN THE SIXTEENTH CENTURY

Two painters, and two only, fulfil or almost fulfil the ideal demands Fuseli makes upon the art: the 'epic' painter Michelangelo, and the 'dramatic' painter Raphael. Before and after them all is darkness or error—for Greek painting itself, which he conceives of as even higher, remains an unknown quantity, without which, indeed, he cannot operate, and by means of which he can put everything else, if it comes to the point Michelangelo and Raphael themselves, in the wrong, but still an unknown quantity, a figment of his own imagination. Mediaeval art and also the entire art of the early Renaissance in Italy, he knew surprisingly well, but mentions only to condemn it without mercy, the only real exception he makes being in favour of Jan van Eyck. Of the state of art in England under Henry VIII he writes: 'The monasteries and churches ... were the only secure repositories of the few ill-told pictures and awkward statues which were then in the kingdom. . . . The people struggled to emerge from that state of barbarism in which they had experienced such accumulated misery . . . The rays of science extended from Italy to England. Henry invited Michelangelo and Raphael to visit this country, but unfortunately for the arts, could not induce those two great men to quit the more genial soil of Italy. . . . Except Holbein, there was no painter, and the taste of the day confined him principally to portraits' (*Analytical Review*, June 1788). Blake, who in 1799, like Fuseli, and quite certainly under Fuseli's influence, had said of himself that the only thing he lived for was 'to renew the lost art of the Greeks' (to Trusler, 16 August 1799), and who a year later was to exult over 'the immense flood of Grecian light and glory which is coming on Europe' (to Cumberland, 2 July 1800), was some time after 1815 to

cry out: 'Grecian is Mathematic Form: Gothic is Living Form. . . .
The Classics! It is the Classics, and not Goths nor Monks that Deso-
late Europe with Wars' (*On Homer and Virgil*). In all probability it
was the sight of certain Dürers and similar non-classical paintings
that evoked from Blake in 1804 the memorable words: 'Suddenly, on
the day after visiting the Truchsessian Gallery of pictures, I was
again enlightened with the light I enjoyed in my youth, and which
has for exactly twenty years been closed from me . . .' (to Hayley,
23 October 1804). Wackenroder and Tieck had gone through a
similar experience on visiting Nuremberg in 1793, Keats was to go
through it too in 1818, when Haydon showed him a book of prints
comprising 'Specimens of the first and second age of Art in Italy'—
a book which, as Colvin points out, can only have been Lasinio's
Campo santo di Pisa (1814), the begetter, thirty years later, of that
mixed blessing, the Pre-Raphaelite Movement. 'I do not think I ever
had a greater treat out of Shakespeare,' Keats writes; 'full of
romance and the most tender feeling. . . . But Grotesque to a curious pitch—yet still making up a fine whole—even finer to me than
more accomplished works—as there was left so much room for
Imagination' (*Journal-letter* to George and Georgiana Keats, winter 1819–20). Fuseli, who knew so many of the works involved in
these sudden enlightenments, who knew them well and often not
only from reproductions, but also in the original, remains to the end
in this connexion a last-ditcher of eighteenth-century classicism.
The furthest back he will go is to Leonardo da Vinci. But when he
comes to speak of Michelangelo he is in his element—very often it is
then really himself that he is talking about, for he had come largely
to identify himself with Michelangelo, even to the point of reproducing in his own treatment of his Academy pupils one of Vasari's anecdotes about his hero. His interpretation of Michelangelo involves
him again and again in curiously contradictory assertions about
allegory, from which one can deduce that he was really groping for
what his German contemporaries had already found, namely some
such term as 'symbolism' to differentiate intense imaginative vision
from bald schematic allegory. It was not till he came to Rome, and
saw the Sistine Chapel with his own eyes, that he definitely decided
to give his allegiance to Michelangelo. Before that, almost certainly
under the influence of Mengs's *Reflections on Beauty and Taste in Painting*, he had been inclined to give the preference to Raphael, and
shortly before his death he startles one by turning on Michelangelo
with very sharp and fierce strictures. With, or even before, the death
of Michelangelo the brief 'period of genius' (Lecture XII) was,
according to Fuseli, over. The only thing that still really matters or
ever will matter in painting is the heritage of Michelangelo and
Raphael, the ideal of the *Grand Style*.

Painting before Michelangelo

... Vasari, after the long enumeration of painters and works antecedent to Michelangelo, and much futile praise bestowed on them ... is at last obliged to own that the date of real painting begins with that great name.

> (*Analytical Review*, October 1792, review of Hickey's *History of Painting and Sculpture*, signed R. R.—XIV, p. 163)

Italian Painting before Raphael

DURING THE fourteenth, and still more in the course of the fifteenth century, so much activity, so general a predilection for Art spread themselves over the greater part of Italy, that we are astonished at the farrago of various imagery produced at those periods.

> (1825—Lecture XII, p. 45)

Mediaeval Painting—the shockingness of Raphael's predecessors

GLARE IS always the first feature of a savage or an infant taste. The timid or barbarous beginner, afraid of impairing the splendour by diminishing the mass, exults in the Egyptian glare which he spreads over a surface unbroken by tint and not relieved by shade. Such are in general the flaming remnants of feudal decoration. This is the stage of missal painting; what Dante called *alluminar*, the art of Cimabue; its taste continued, though in degrees less shocking, to the time of Michelangelo and Raphael.

> (1810—Lecture VIII, pp. 338–9)

Fra Angelico of the 'missal-taste' and his pupil Gozzoli

... without embarrassing ourselves with the angelic prettinesses of Fra Giovanni da Fiesole, a name dearer to sanctity
than to art, and whom both his age and his missal-taste prove
the nursling of another school, we pass to Benozzo Gozzoli, his
pupil, who strove to forget his puny lessons in the bolder dictates of Masaccio. That he could not soon do it, is evident from
the profusion of ornamental glitter and tinsel colouring on the
frescoes of the Chapel Riccardi. He succeeded better at Pisa. ...

(1808—*History of Art*, p. 179)

Botticelli and his Contemporaries

MEDIOCRITY, tinsel ostentation and tasteless diligence mark the
greater number of that society of craftsmen whom Sixtus IV
conscribed ... to decorate or rather to disfigure the panels of
the grand Chapel which took its name from him. ... The super-
intendence of the whole the Pope, with the usual vanity and
ignorance of princes, gave to Sandro (Botticelli), the least qualified of the group, whose barbarous taste and dry minuteness
palsied, or assimilated to his own, the powers of his associates,
and rendered the whole a monument of puerile ostentation, and
conceits unworthy of its place.

(1808—*History of Art*, pp. 182–3)

Leonardo da Vinci—the true Inventor of Modern Art

SUCH WAS the dawn of modern art, when Leonardo da Vinci
broke forth with a splendour which distanced former excellence:
made up of all the elements that constitute the essence of genius,
favoured by education and circumstances, all ear, all eye, all
grasp; painter, poet, sculptor, anatomist, architect, engineer,
chemist, machinist, musician, man of science, and sometimes
empiric, he laid hold of every beauty in the enchanted circle,

239

but without exclusive attachment to one, dismissed in her turn each. Fitter to scatter hints than to teach by example, he wasted life, insatiate, in experiment. To a capacity which at once penetrated the principle and real aim of the art, he joined an inequality of fancy that at one moment lent him wings for the pursuit of beauty, and the next, flung him on the ground to crawl after deformity: we owe him chiaroscuro with all its magic, we owe him caricature with all its incongruities. His notions of the most elaborate finish and his want of perseverance were at least equal . . . Rubens, who was Leonardo's great admirer, . . . has said much to impress us with the beauties of his Last Supper in the refectory of the Dominicans at Milan, which he abandoned likewise without finishing the head of Christ,[1] exhausted by a wild chase after models for the heads and hands of the Apostles: had he been able to conceive the centre, the radii must have followed of course.

> (1801—Lecture II, pp. 81–2, with the original conclusion of the first edition)

Revised Judgment on Leonardo's Christ

THOSE WHO have asserted that Leonardo, in finishing the Last Supper, was so exhausted by his exertions to trace the characters and emotions of the disciples that, unable to fix the physiognomy of Christ, he found himself reduced to the necessity of leaving that head unfinished, either never saw it, or, if they did, were too low to reach the height, and too shallow to fathom the depth of the conception.[2]

> (1788–1818—Corollary to Aphorism 83)

[1] On 23 December 1795 Fuseli, in conversation, described Leonardo's Christ as 'a commonplace conception of the character' (*Farington Diary*).

[2] It is characteristic that Fuseli in thus aggressively swinging round from one dogmatic assertion on this point to its opposite had himself no opportunity to see the original fresco again. His later judgment is based on the crayon sketch of the head of Christ in the British Gallery (hardly an original) and still more on the copy of the whole picture by Marco Ugione, which was exhibited in London in 1817. This circumstance points to the present corollary not having been added to the manuscript of the *Aphorisms* until the final collation in September 1818.

'The Last Supper' of Leonardo da Vinci

THE FACE of the Saviour is an abyss of thought, and broods over the immense revolution in the economy of mankind, which throngs inwardly on his absorbed eye—as the spirit creative in the beginning over the water's darksome wave—undisturbed and quiet. . . . St. John and the two James's . . . neither are nor ought to be ideal, and had they been so, they could neither compete nor interfere with the sublimity that crowns the Saviour's brow, and stamps his countenance with the God.

(1825—Lecture XI, pp. 9–14)

Fuseli's reaction to Leonardo's Gioconda and her sisters

CHIAROSCURO'S MAGIC lent the charm by which his females allure to forms neither ideal nor much varied; sisters of one family, they attract by the light in which they radiate, by the shade that veils them—for the features of Giotto's or Memmi's Madonnas or virgin-saints floating in the same medium, would require little more to be their equals.

(1805—Lecture VI, p. 281)

Leonardo da Vinci's females once more

THE STRENGTH of his execution lay in the delineation of male heads; those of his females owe nearly all their charms to chiaroscuro, of which he is the supposed inventor: they are seldom more discriminated than the children they fondle; they are sisters of one family.

(1825—Lecture XI, p. 17)

Epic invention in Literature and Painting

THE EPIC plan . . . is the sublime allegory of a maxim. Here Invention arranges a plan by general ideas, the selection of the most prominent features of Nature, or favourable modes of society, visibly to substantiate some great maxim. . . . At this elevation heaven and earth mingle their boundaries, men are raised to demigods, and gods descend. This is the sphere of Homer, Phidias, and Michelangelo.

(1805—Lecture IV, pp. 196–7)

The Praise of Allegory

. . . general as the elements, universal and permanent as the affections of human nature, allegory breaks the fetters of time, it unites with boundless sway mythologic, feudal, local incongruities, fleeting modes of society and fugitive fashions. . . .

(1805—Lecture IV, footnote, p. 197)

Legitimate use of the Supernatural in Greek and Modern Poetry

. . . their Scylla and [Milton's] Portress of Hell, their daemons and our spectres, the shade of Patroclus and the ghost of Hamlet, their naiads, nymphs, and oreads, and our sylphs, gnomes, and fairies, their furies and our witches, differ less in essence, than in local, temporary, social modifications: their common origin was fancy, operating on the materials of nature, assisted by legendary tradition and the curiosity implanted in us of diving into the invisible. . . . Pindar praises Homer . . . for the power by which he contrived to connect his imaginary creation with the realities of nature and human passions; without this the fiction of the poet and the painter will leave us stupefied rather by its insolence, than impressed by its power; it will be considered only as a superior kind of legerdemain, an exertion of ingenuity to no adequate end.

(1801—Lecture III, pp. 140–1)

Moral Allegory and Imaginative Vividness

THAT GREAT principle, the necessity of a moral tendency or of some doctrine useful to mankind in the *whole* of an epic performance, admitted, are we therefore to sacrifice the uniformity of its parts, and thus to lose that credibility which *alone* can impress us with the importance of the maxim that dictated to the poet narration and to the artist imagery? Are the agents sometimes to be real beings, and sometimes abstract ideas? Is the Zeus of Homer, . . . by the purblind acuteness of a commentator, to be turned into aether; . . .? When Minerva, by her weight, makes the chariot of Diomedes groan, and Mars wounded, roars with the voice of ten thousand, are they nothing but the symbol of military discipline, and the sound of the battle's roar? Or Ate, seized by her hair, and by Zeus dashed from the battlements of heaven, is she only a metaphysic idea? Forbid it, Sense! As well might we say, that Milton, when he called the porteress of hell, Satan's daughter, *Sin*, and his son and dread antagonist, *Death*, meant only to impress us with ideas of privation and nonentity, and sacrificed the real agents of his poem to an unskilful choice of names! . . . What becomes of the interest the poet and the artist mean to excite in us, if, in the moment of reading or contemplating, we do not believe what the one tells and the other shows? It is that magic which places on the same basis of existence, and amalgamates the mythic or superhuman, and the human parts of the Ilias, of Paradise Lost, and of the Sistine Chapel, that enraptures, agitates, and whirls us along as readers or spectators.

(1805—Lecture IV, pp. 198–200)

The Superiority of the Ancients to the Moderns in Poetic Personification—Milton's Sin and Death

WHAT WERE the divinities that filled their temples but images of things, personifications of the powers of nature? And were not these the auxiliaries of their poets? Discriminated by characteristics so appropriate and so decisive that no observation of succeeding ages has been able to add anything essential or to subtract anything as superfluous from their insignia. At this moment the poet and the artist subsist on their sterling properties; and the greatest of the moderns could do no more than recompose from the birth of Minerva, the charms of Pandora, and the horrors of Scylla the origin, the beauty and the deformities of his Sin; and if, by the superhuman flight of his fancy, he snatched the attributes and shape of Death from a region yet unexplored by former wings, the being itself had not been unknown to the ancients: it carried off Alcestis and offered battle, in its gloom, to Hercules. But will it be denied that by personifying the *act* by which his heroes were to fall, and the *punishment* attendant on that act, Milton has, as far as lay in him, destroyed the *credibility* of his poem? Homer found the *abstractions* which he mingled with the real actors of his poem already personified, and to demand a belief in the existence of Minerva or Jupiter subjected his reader to no greater exertion than to believe in the existence of Achilles or Ulysses. Had credibility not been the great principle of Homer, had he introduced '*Wisdom*' seizing Achilles by the hair, and '*Beauty*' ravishing Paris from the combat, the Iliad, in what concerns the plan, would be little more than the rival of *Pilgrim's Progress*.

(*Analytical Review*, April 1796, review of Roscoe's *Lorenzo de' Medici*, signed Z. Z.—XXIII, p. 351. Knowles, I, pp. 136–7)

'*Gothic Bulls and Emblematic Nonsense*'

IT WERE to be wished that Mr. Tassie had excluded from his collection such pollutions of art, such contemptible dumbshow of stupidity, which to posterity can only prove that the eighteenth century was still an age of barbarians.

(*Analytical Review*, November 1791, review of Raspe's *Catalogue o Tassie's Gems*, signed R. R.—XI, p. 266)

Allegory and Mythology

NONE EVER escaped from himself by crossing seas; none ever peopled a barren fancy and a heart of ice with images or sympathies by excursions into the deserts of mythology or allegory.

All ornament ought to be allegoric.

(1788–1818—Aphorisms 163 and 166)

Local Colour

NONE BUT indelible materials can support the epic. Whatever is local or the volatile creature of the time, beauties of fashion and sentiments of sects, tears shed over roses, epigrammatic sparkling, passions taught to rave and graces trained to move, the antiquary's mouldering stores, the bubbles of allegorists—are all with equal contempt passed over by him who claims the lasting empire of the human heart.

(1788–1818—Aphorism 201)

The Timelessness of Epic Poetry

WHEN WE consider the magnificent end of epic poetry, to write for all times and all races, to treat of what will always exist and always be understood, the puny laws of local decorum and fluctuating fashions, by which the omission or modification of certain habits and customs, natural but obsolete, is prescribed, cannot come into consideration. Such laws may bind the meaner race of writers.

(Analytical Review, January 1793, review of Cowper's Homer, signed
Z. Z.—XV, pp. 1–2. Knowles, I, p. 82)

The Universal and the Transitory

MICHELANGELO APPEARED and soon felt that the candidate of legitimate fame is to build his works, not on the imbecile forms of a degenerate race, disorganised by clime, country, education, laws and society; not on the transient refinements of fashion or local sentiment, unintelligible beyond their circle and century to the rest of mankind; but to graft them on Nature's ever-lasting forms and those general feelings of humanity, which no time can efface, no mode of society obliterate; and in consequence of these reflections discovered the epic part of painting; that basis, that indestructibility of forms and thoughts, that simplicity of machinery on which Homer defied the ravages of time, which sooner or later must sweep to oblivion every work propped by baser materials and factitious refinements.

(1808—*History of Art*, p. 218)

Reynolds's claims to emulate Fuseli in devotion to Michelangelo

THE HIGHEST compliment ever paid by one artist to the style and memory of another, it must be owned, Sir J. pays to Michel-angelo, when he declares that 'were he now to begin the world again, he would tread in the steps of that great master: to kiss the hem of his garment, to catch the slightest of his perfections, would be glory and distinction enough for an ambitious man'. Yes, if that attempt were likely to be attended with applause and encouragement! But suppose the contrary: suppose the neglect of the great, the execration of the vulgar, the ridicule of the false critic and the invective of the hireling to be the conse-quence of that pursuit, would the author, young and unpro-tected, just beginning his career of active life, dare to stem the muddy torrent? Would he find resources in himself and the per-fections of his model sufficiently invigorating to brave the repeated checks of contempt, poverty and abuse? If Brutus was weak enough to pronounce at last that virtue was a phantom; is it probable that an artist, struggling with the fashions and prejudices of his age, should be content to wrap himself in ques-tionable excellence, and hug his own *virtù* for its sole reward?

246

The cautions, modifications and fears[1] mixed by the retiring sage, even now, with what may be called his apotheosis of Michelangelo leave room to suspect that the practice of the younger artist would not be uniformly stamped by that lofty and independent confidence in himself which at all times of life distinguished the mighty Tuscan from all his contemporaries.

(*Analytical Review*, May 1791, review of Reynolds's last Discourse, signed R. R.—X, pp. 4–5)

Michelangelo as master of the Allegorical-Sublime: the Sistine Chapel

ITS SUBJECT is *theocracy* or the empire of religion, considered as the parent and queen of man; the origin, the progress, and final dispensation of Providence, as taught by the sacred records. Amid this imagery of primeval simplicity, whose sole object is the relation of the race to its Founder, to look for minute discrimination of character is to invert the principle of the artist's invention: here is only God with man. The veil of eternity is rent; time, space, and matter teem in the creation of the elements and of earth; life issues from God and adoration from man, in the creation of Adam and his mate; transgression of the precept at the tree of knowledge proves the origin of evil, and of expulsion from the immediate intercourse with God; the economy of justice and grace commences in the revolutions of the Deluge, and the covenant made with Noah; and the germs

[1] 'That Michelangelo was capricious in his inventions cannot be denied; and this may make some circumspection necessary in studying his works; for though they appear to become him, an imitation of them is always dangerous, and will prove sometimes ridiculous. To me, I confess, his caprice does not lower the estimation of his genius . . . and however those eccentric excursions are considered, we must at the same time recollect that those faults, if they are faults, are such as never could occur to a mean and vulgar mind. . . .' Against these demurs of Reynolds Fuseli protests strongly in his *History of Art*: 'The principles, the style of Michelangelo are . . . either all true or all false, etc.' (*see below*, p. 317). In his own old age, however, Fuseli was to go much further than Reynolds in criticising Michelangelo, as will be seen in the following pages.

of social character are traced in the subsequent scene between him and his sons; the awful synod of prophets and sibyls are the heralds of the Redeemer, and the host of patriarchs the pedigree of the Son of Man; the brazen serpent and the fall of Haman, the giant subdued by the stripling in Goliath and David, and the conqueror destroyed by female weakness in Judith, are types of his mysterious progress, till Jonah pronounces him immortal; and the magnificence of the Last Judgment, by showing the Saviour in the judge of man, sums up the whole, and reunites the Founder and the race.

(1801—Lecture III, pp. 158-9)

The Beginnings of Michelangelo

MICHELANGELO APPEARS to have had no infancy; if he had, we are not acquainted with it. His earliest works are equal in principle and compass of execution to the vigorous proofs of his virility. Like an oriental sun, he burst upon us at once, without a dawn.

(1825—Lecture XI, pp. 21-2)

Michelangelo—the Salt of Art

SUBLIMITY OF conception, grandeur of form, and breadth of manner are the elements of Michelangelo's style. . . . As painter, as sculptor, as architect, he attempted, and above any other man succeeded, to unite magnificence of plan and endless variety of subordinate parts with the utmost simplicity and breadth. His line is uniformly grand: character and beauty were admitted only as far as they could be made subservient to grandeur. The child, the female, meanness, deformity, were by him indiscriminately stamped with grandeur. A beggar rose from his hand the patriarch of poverty; the hump of his dwarf is impressed with dignity; his women are moulds of generation; his infants teem with the man; his men are a race of giants. . . .[1]

---

[1] There is good reason to suppose that Fuseli attached greater importance to this passage, from 'His line . . .' to '. . . a race of giants', than to anything

He is the inventor of epic painting, in that sublime circle of the Sistine chapel which exhibits the origin, the progress, and the final dispensations of theocracy. He has personified motion in the groups of the cartoon of Pisa; embodied sentiment on the monuments of St. Lorenzo, unravelled the features of meditation in the Prophets and Sybils of the Sistine chapel; and in the Last Judgment, with every attitude that varies the human body, traced the master-trait of every passion that sways the human heart. . . . Such, take him all in all, was Michelangelo, the salt of art. . . .

(1801—Lecture II, pp. 84-7)

Fuseli on Michelangelo and God

A GREAT deal might be overlooked, but for his [Fuseli's] excessive vanity, which will not allow merit in others. He asserts that no man in England understands drawing but himself, and that Michelangelo was a greater man than God Almighty: alluding to the style of figures of that artist, which he is weak enough to think surpasses Nature.

(Edward Dayes, *Professional Sketches of Modern Artists*, published 1805 —quoted by Ruthven Todd in *Tracks in the Snow*, 1947)

The Breadth of Michelangelo

THE BREADTH of Michelangelo resembles the tide and ebb of a

else he ever wrote. It was probably written in 1788, as a part of the original version of the *Aphorisms*. It first appeared in print on pp. 76–8 of the additional quire of Volume I of William Seward's anonymously published *Anecdotes of Some Distinguished Persons* (1795), with an acknowledgment to 'one of the greatest ornaments of the present English School of Painting . . . Mr. Fuseli'; it was quoted at full length, together with Seward's complimentary introductory remarks, in Fuseli's own unsigned review of this work in the *Analytical Review* for May 1795 (Vol. XXI, p. 620). It was then incorporated not only into the first Lecture of 1801, but also, with interesting variants, into the eleventh Lecture of 1825, and then forms part of the 151st Corollary of the posthumously published *Aphorisms*.

mighty sea: waves approach, arrive, retreat, but in their rise and fall, emerging or absorbed, impress us only with the image of the power that raises, that directs them; whilst the discrepance of obtruding parts in the works of the infant Florentine, Venetian and German schools, distracts our eye like the numberless breakers of a shallow river, or as the brambles and creepers that entangle the paths of a wood, and instead of showing us our road, perplex us only with themselves. By breadth the artist puts us into immediate possession of the whole. . . .

(1805—Lecture V, pp. 250–1)

Late misgivings about Michelangelo

MICHELANGELO . . . had power, knowledge and life sufficiently great, extensive and long, to have fixed style on its basis, had not an irresistible bias drawn off his attention from the modesty and variety of Nature. . . .

(1825—Lecture XI, p. 5)

The Dotage of Michelangelo—his 'senile caprices'

HIS LINE became generic, but perhaps too uniformly grand. . . . This is the *terribil via*, this is that 'magic circle', in which we are told that none durst move but he. No, none but he who makes sublimity of conception his element of form. Michelangelo himself offers the proof: for the lines that bear in a mass on his mighty tide of thought the Gods and Patriarchs and Sybils of the Sistine Chapel, already too ostentatiously show themselves in the Last Judgment, and rather expose than support his ebbing powers in the Chapel of Paul. Considered as a whole, the Crucifixion of St. Peter and the Conversion of Paul, in that place, are the dotage of Michelangelo's style; but they have parts which make that dotage more enviable than the equal vigour of mediocrity.

(1825—Lecture XI, pp. 18–19)

Gothic and Classical Elements in Michelangelo

IN MORE advanced years, the Torso of Apollonius became his standard of form. But the Daemons of Dante had too early tinctured his fancy to admit in their full majesty the Gods of Homer and of Phidias.

(1825—Lecture XI, p. 20)

Raphael—The Master of Expression and the Painter of Humanity

THE INSPIRATION of Michelangelo was followed by the milder genius of Raphael Sanzio, the father of dramatic painting; the painter of humanity; less elevated, less vigorous, but more insinuating, more pressing on our hearts, the warm master of our sympathies. What effect of human connexion, what feature of the mind, from the gentlest emotion to the most fervid burst of passion, has been left unobserved, has not received a characteristic stamp from that examiner of man? Michelangelo came to nature, nature came to Raphael—he transmitted her features like a lucid glass, unstained, unmodified. We stand with awe before Michelangelo, and tremble at the height to which he elevates us—we embrace Raphael, and follow him wherever he leads us.

(1801—Lecture II, pp. 87–8)

Dramatic Invention in Literature and Painting

THE EXHIBITION of character in the conflict of passions with the rights, the rules, the prejudices of society, is the legitimate sphere of dramatic invention. It inspires, it agitates us by reflected self-love, with pity, terror, hope and fear. . . . Such is the invention of Sophocles and Shakespeare, and uniformly that of Raphael.

(1805—Lecture IV, pp. 195–6)

The Madonnas of Raphael

Fuseli had heard of the existence of the Sistine Madonna, but had never seen it. In the *Universal Museum* in February 1768 he just mentions in passing 'an altar-piece from St. Sisto at Piacenza, on canvas, *almost decayed*, in Dresden'.

THE MADONNAS of Raphael, whether hailed parents of a God, or pressing the divine offspring to their breast, whether receiving him from his slumbers, or contemplating his infant motions, are uniformly transcripts from the daily domestic images of common life and of some favourite face matronised: the eyes of his Fornarina beamed with other fires than those of sanctity; the sense and native dignity of her lover could veil their fierceness, but not change their language.

(1788–1818—Corollary to Aphorism 167)

The insipidity of Raphael's Madonnas, the character of his Magdalens

OF IDEAL female beauty, though he himself, in his letter to Count Castiglione, tells us that, from its scarcity in life, he made attempts to reach it by an idea formed in his own mind, he certainly wanted that standard which guided him in character. His Goddesses and mythologic females are no more than aggravations of the generic forms of Michelangelo. Roundness, mildness, sanctimony and insipidity, compose the features and air of his Madonnas: transcripts of the nursery, or some favourite face. The Madonna del Impanato, the Madonna Bella, the Madonna della Sedia, and even the longer proportions and greater delicacy and dignity of the Madonna formerly in the collection of Versailles, share more or less of this insipidity: it chiefly arises from the high, smooth, roundish forehead, the shaven vacuity between the arched semicircular eye-brows, their elevation above the eyes, and the ungraceful division, growth and scantiness of hair. This indeed might be the result of his desire not to stain the virgin character of sanctity with the

252

most distant hint of coquetry or meretricious charms; for in his Magdalens, he throws it with luxuriant profusion, and surrounds the breast and shoulders with undulating waves and plaits of gold. The character of Mary Magdalen met his,—it was the character of a passion. It is evident from every picture or design at every period of his art in which she had a part, that he supposed her enamoured when she follows the body of the Saviour to the tomb, or throws herself dishevelled over his feet, or addresses him when he bears his cross. The cast of her features, her forms, her action, are the character of love in agony. When character inspired Raphael, his women became definitions of grace and pathos at once.

(1825—Lecture XI, pp. 24–5)

Making common cause with Michelangelo

'The taste for pure and elegant composition was revived by Raphael and expired with him. Michelangelo was always for doing something better than well; and as such attempts excite the wonder and admiration of the ignorant; they are flattering to vanity and almost certain to become fashionable. Hence a puerile ambition for novelty and originality became the predominant principle of an imitative art, the business of which is to *copy*, and not *create*' (R. Payne Knight—Note to *The Landscape*)

WE ARE not a little concerned when we compare such trenchant criticism with the homage offered by the late president of the academy to the gigantic powers of Michelangelo: he held it honour enough to be allowed to kiss the hem of his garment. It would be as just to tax the ancients with the abortions of the tame craftsmen who inundate Italy and Germany in our days as Michelangelo with the caricatures of the madmen who, he predicted, would sally from his chapel and sacrilegiously scatter the limbs of his compositions. A comparison can no more take place between Michelangelo and Raphael, had he even excelled the ancients in design, than between the painter of the Lesche at

Delphi and the author of the Olympian Jupiter.[1] Homer might. give much to Sophocles, but could receive nothing in return. It is unnecessary to enlarge on the rest of the note: neither to 'copy' nor to 'create' is a proper term for an art, the business of which is to imitate and to invent.[2]

(*Analytical Review*, June, 1794, review of R. Payne Knight's *The Landscape, a didactic poem*, signed R. R.—XIX, p. 179)

An early comparison of Raphael with Michelangelo and Leonardo da Vinci

RAPHAEL . . . as the charms of novelty faded, saw that the soul would for ever elude the dissections of myology,[3] characters never fall under the denomination of colours, and sentiments be inexpressible to masks. Such a discovery, could it have been made by another than Raphael, would have led to despondence, mediocrity or servile imitation; but to the future painter of mankind it was the voice of genius. He at once felt his own superiority, whilst he pitied the waste of great talents, and enjoyed the perseverance with which masters and rivals had contrived and polished the instruments which he alone could

[1] Polygnotos of Thasos must have painted his famous *Fall of Troy* in the Lesche or hall of the Cnidians at Delphi some time before 467 B.C., while Phidias did not finish his statue of the Olympian Zeus till about thirty-five years later. Both works are discussed in Fuseli's first Lecture. It is Phidias, not Polygnotos, who is here regarded as corresponding to Michelangelo.

[2] In his early *Remarks on Rousseau* (1767) Fuseli had himself talked of the 'creation' of Raphael, Correggio and Titian, and as recently as May 1789, in describing his own painting of *Titania and Bottom*, he had employed the phrase: 'This is the *creation* of a poetic painter' (*see* p. 289). Fuseli's old Zurich mentors, Bodmer and Breitinger, who had at first claimed for artistic genius a certain figurative creatorship, were shocked at the more extravagant and literal interpretations of this conception which became current with the advance of the Storm-and-Stress movement, and repudiated them as blasphemous, just as Fuseli himself does in his third Lecture (*see above*, pp. 201-2).

[3] *Myology*—the science of muscles, here with reference to Michelangelo's over-emphasised anatomy. This sketch is based largely on Mengs' *Reflections*, which were still unpublished, but known to Fuseli in the original Italian manuscript.

manage. From that moment he without a sigh left to Vinci the magnificence of contrast; resigned to Angelo the demonstrations of anatomy; and the magic of light and colours to others, to grasp with success at the expression of character and mind. ... All the advantages Raphael might derive from Michelangelo could be no more than a cement to consolidate his system. Their materials differed as widely as their ends: the one contrived the soul for the body, the other subjected clay to spirit; the one bloated expression into grimace to entrap a muscle, the other courted physiognomy to touch the mind; that sacrificed his design to pomp of lumber and endless means, this valued means only as they led to his design. Michelangelo painted his *Last Judgment* to demonstrate the infinity of attitudes which precipitation and ascent may give; when Raphael opens the gates of Heaven, we bend with awe and are dissolved in rapture. ...

It is certain that the sweetness of his temper and a native ease of mind, ripened to gentility by world and study, kept up by female fondness, and by a court life polished into elegance, it is certain, I say, that so genial a character, contrasted with the savage independence, the proud shyness or rusticity of his rivals, procured to his days great part of the honours now paid pure to his genius. ...

Thus, like a torrent, passed the life of Raphael Sanzi, the painter of the soul and the friend of man; but though rapid, passed smooth, neither ruffled by adversity, nor turbid with passions.—He had run a race of glory ere the genius of other mortals starts, and left to time a name

For ever to be uttered with a sigh! [1]

(Unsigned article entitled *An account of Raphael Sanzi* in the *Universal Museum* for February 1768, pp. 81–3)

A later comparison of Michelangelo and Raphael

... there can, I believe, be but one opinion with regard to the methods adopted by Michelangelo and Raphael in the inven-

[1] Armstrong, *Art of Preserving Health*, IV, 217: *A name still to be utter'd with a sight.*

tion of the moment that characterises the creation of Eve: both artists applied for it to their own minds, but with very different success: the elevation of Michelangelo's soul, inspired by the operation of creation itself, furnished him at once with the feature that stamps on human nature its most glorious prerogative: whilst the characteristic subtlety, rather than sensibility of Raphael's mind, in this instance, offered nothing but a frigid succedaneum; a symptom incident to all, when after the subsided astonishment on a great and sudden event, the mind recollecting itself, ponders on it with inquisitive surmise. In Michelangelo, all self-consideration is absorbed in the sublimity of the sentiment which issues from the august Presence that attracts Eve; 'her earthly', in Milton's expression, 'by his heavenly overpowered', pours itself in *adoration*: whilst in the inimitable cast of Adam's figure, we trace the hint of that half conscious moment when sleep began to give way to the vivacity of the dream inspired. In Raphael, creation is complete—Eve is presented to Adam, now awake; but neither the new-born charms, the submissive grace and virgin purity of the beauteous image: nor the awful presence of her Introductor, draw him from his mental trance into effusions of love and gratitude; at ease reclined, with fingers pointing at himself and his new mate, he seems to methodise the surprising event that took place during his sleep, and to whisper the words 'flesh of my flesh'.

(1801—Lecture III, pp. 165–7)

The shortcomings of Michelangelo and Raphael

... it often requires no inconsiderable degree of mental power and technic discrimination to separate the sublimity of Michelangelo, and the pathos of Raphael from the total neglect or the incongruities of scenery and background, which frequently involve or clog their conceptions, to add by fancy the place on which their figures ought to stand, the horizon that ought to elevate or surround them, and the masses of light and shade indolently neglected or sacrificed to higher principles.

(1805—Lecture IV, pp. 222–3)

The Historic Painter and the 'fixed character of things'

FIRM HE rests on the true basis of art, imitation: the fixed character of things determines all in his choice, and mere floating accident, transient modes and whims of fashion, are still excluded. If defects, if deformities are represented, they must be permanent, they must be inherent in the character. Edward the First and Richard the Third must be marked, to strengthen rather than to diminish the interest we take in the man; thus the deformity of Richard will add to his terror, and the enormous stride of Edward to his dignity.

(1801—Lecture III, pp. 178–9)

SECTION THREE

DEGENERATION OF ART
AFTER MICHELANGELO
THROUGH THE SACRIFICE OF 'MIND'
TO MEDIUM AND TECHNIQUE

'That the Art has been in a gradual state of decline from the age of Michelangelo to the present, must be acknowledged,' says Reynolds in his fifteenth Discourse. Fuseli would have corrected this to a 'rapid state of decline'. For him even Titian, the 'master of colour', and Correggio, the 'master of *chiaroscuro*', who, according to mid-eighteenth-century standards, constitute together with Michelangelo and Raphael the great four of painting, are already branded with corruption and degeneracy, because colour and *chiaroscuro* themselves are inferior, sensual principles, hostile to 'mind' and 'subject'. Fuseli is the zealous champion of line as against colour, of the *porte-crayon* (our pencil) as against the *pencil* (our brush). In Fuseli's opinions on these questions we have certainly the chief source and inspiration of some of Blake's most startling utterances, such as: 'Till we get rid of Titian, and Correggio, Rubens and Rembrandt, We never shall equal Rafael and Albert Durer, Michael Angelo and Julio Romano.' 'These pictures . . . were the result of temptations and perturbations, labouring to destroy Imaginative power, by means of that infernal machine called Chiaro Oscuro, in the hands of Venetian and Flemish Demons, whose enmity to the Painter himself, and to all Artists who study in the Florentine and Roman Schools, may be removed by an exhibition and exposure of their vile tricks. They cause that everything in art shall become a machine. They cause that the execution shall be all blocked up with brown shadows. . . . Rubens is a most outrageous demon. . . . Correggio is a soft and effeminate, and consequently a most cruel demon. . . .' 'In a work of Art it is not Fine Tints that are required, but Fine Forms; Fine Tints without are nothing. Fine Tints without Fine Forms are always the Subterfuge of the Blockhead.' 'Venetian Attention is to Contempt and Neglect of Form Itself and to the Destruction of all Form or Outline Purposely and Intentionally. . . . Michelangelo knew and despised all that Titian could do.' In these and similar utterances Blake is carrying to the extremest possible lengths certain ideas of Fuseli, and omitting all the qualifications Fuseli, for all his air of recklessness, had always been careful to introduce—and, of course, Dürer would, in Fuseli's scheme of things, appear among the villains instead of among the heroes, as he does with Blake. It is something much more than the professional discretion of a Keeper of the Royal Academy that guides Fuseli in his dealings with the Venetians, with Correggio, with Rubens and with Dutch colour, and prevents him from making himself grotesque over them, as Blake does. Here was something which was not, indeed, in his line, but which he was sensitive to, whether he liked it or not. Hostility and involuntary admiration wrestle with one another in him, and he gives, in spite of himself, a curiously grudging, but penetrating account of what colour and *chiaroscuro* were to mean to later generations, for whom historic painting, the Grand Style, 'subject', 'story' and 'conception' as opposed to execution could only rank as obsolete curiosities. Shortly before his death he is even disposed to rank Titian and Tintoretto equal with Michelangelo.

The Principle of Synaesthesia. 'Colour affects or delights like sound' (Aphorism 176)

TITIAN'S EYE, as musical, if I may be allowed the metaphor, as his ear, abstracted here that colour acts, affects, delights, like sound; that stern and deep-toned tints rouse, determine, invigorate the eye, as warlike sound or a deep bass the ear; and that bland, rosy, gray and vernal tints soothe, charm and melt like a sweet melody.

(1810—Lecture VIII, pp. 340-1)

'Brilliancy is less required than unison' (Lecture VI)

COLOUR OWES its effect sometimes more to position and gradation than to its intrinsic value.

(Aphorism 184)

WHEN TREATING on Chiaroscuro, we have observed what may now be applied to Colour, that the primary tone depends on choice, and is arbitrary; but it decides all the rest, as the tone of the first violin in a regular concert tunes all the voices and all the instruments. Its effect entirely depends on the union of the surrounding tones with it, and has no other value but what it derives from contrast. By this the simplest tone, well managed, may become rich, splendid and harmonious; it is then the tone of nature; whilst the most brilliant colour, if contradicted or disappointed by the detail of inferior ones, may become heavy, leathern and discordant.

(1810—Lecture VIII, p. 343)

The colouring of the Dutch and Flemish schools

THE EYE tinges all nature with its own hue. The eye of the Dutch and Flemish schools, though shut to forms, tipped the cottage, the boor, the ale-pot, the shambles, and even the haze of winter, with orient hues and the glow of setting suns.

(1788–1818—Aphorism 174)

Mere colour

THERE ARE works whose effect is entirely founded on the contrast of tints, of what is termed warm and cold colour, and on reflected hues; strip them of this charm, reduce them to the principles of light and shade and masses, and, as far as the want of those can degrade a picture, they will be fit to take their places on sign-posts.

(1788–1818—Aphorism 191)

Line versus Colour

WHEN IT is the object of the Arts . . . to make sense the minister of mind. . . . *Design,* in its most extensive as in its strictest sense, is their basis; when they stoop to be the mere playthings, or debase themselves to be the debauchers of the senses, they make *Colour* their insidious foundation . . . It is not for me, (who have courted and still continue to court Colour as a despairing lover courts a disdainful mistress), to presume . . . to add . . . my opinion . . . But . . . it becomes me . . . to tell you, that if the principle which animates the art gives rights and privileges to Colour not its own . . . if what is claimed in vain by form and mind, it fondly grants to colour . . . then the art is degraded to a mere vehicle of sensual pleasure, an implement of luxury, a beautiful *but trifling* bauble, or a splendid fault.

(1810—Lecture VIII, pp. 332–4)

The 'Linear Method'—expressive line, as opposed to colour and grace, the master principle of all great art

. . . we may deduce . . . that the schools of Greece recognised all one elemental principle: that acuteness and fidelity of eye and obedience of hand form precision; precision, proportion; proportion, beauty; that it is the 'little more or less', imperceptible to vulgar eyes, which constitutes grace and establishes the superiority of one artist over another: that the knowledge of the degrees of things, or taste, presupposes a perfect knowledge of the things themselves: that colour, grace, and taste are ornaments, not substitutes of form, expression and character, and when they usurp that title, degenerate into splendid faults.

(1801—Lecture I, pp. 63–4)

The gaudy glories of Venice—colour and commerce

> 'Canova was spoken of. . . . Fuseli in his whimsical way said: "What could be expected from a man coming from Venice, in respect of correct design—where to know an *ankle* from a *gizzard* was the common extent of their observation and accuracy?" '
>
> (*Farington Diary*, 13 January 1804)

ADD TO this the character of the place and the nature of the encouragement held out to the Venetian artists. Venice was the centre of commerce, the repository of the riches of the globe, the splendid toy-shop of the time: its chief inhabitants were princely merchants, or a patrician race elevated to rank by accumulations from trade, or naval prowess; the bulk of the people, mechanics or artisans, administering the means, and in their turn fed by the produce of luxury. Of such a system, what could the art be more than the parasite? . . .—Such was, such will always be the birth-place and the theatre of colour: and hence it is more matter of wonder that the first and greatest colourists should have so long foreborne to overstep the modesty of nature in the use of that alluring medium, than that they yielded by degrees to its golden solicitations.

(1801—Lecture II, pp. 103–4)

Baroque profusion: depravity of taste

SPLENDOUR, CONTRAST and profusion are the springs of its invention. The painter, not the story, is the principal subject here. Dazzled by piles of Palladian architecture, tables set out with regal luxury, terraces of plate, crowds of Venetian nobles, pages, dwarfs, gold-collared Moors, and choirs of vocal and instrumental music, embrowned and tuned by meridian skies, what eye has time to discover, in the brilliant chaos, the visit of Christ to Simon the Pharisee, or the sober nuptials of Cana? but when the charm dissolves, though avowedly wonders of disposition, colour, and unlimited powers of all-grasping execution, if considered in any other light than as the luxurious trappings of ostentatious wealth, judgment must pronounce them ominous pledges of irreclaimable depravity of taste, glittering masses of portentous incongruities and colossal baubles.

(1805—Lecture IV, pp. 213–14)

Correggio[1]

SENSUALITY PERSONIFIED is the general character of his females, and the grace of his children less naïveté than grimace, the caricature of jollity.

(1788–1818—Corollary to Aphorism 218)

Tintoretto's 'Annunciation'

TINTORETTO HAS turned salutation into irruption. The angel bursts through the shattered casement and terrifies a vulgar female; but his wings are tipped in heaven.

(1788–1818—Corollary to Aphorism 167)

Tintoretto's 'Crucifixion of San Rocco'

THE MULTITUDINOUS rabble dispersed over that picture (for such, rather than composition, one group excepted, that assemblage of accidental figures deserves to be called,) he connected by a sovereign tone, ingulphing the whole in one mass of ominous twilight, an eclipse, or what precedes a storm, or hurricane, or earthquake; nor suffering the captive eye to rest on any other object than the faint gleam hovering over the head of the Saviour in the centre, and in still fainter tones dying on the sainted group gathered beneath the Cross.

(1805—Lecture VI, p. 295)

[1] For Fuseli's appreciation of Correggio's chiaroscuro, which greatly impressed him, *see below*, Part V, Section 4—*The Infinite*.

Paolo Veronese

'—that superior harmony on which the
Venetian school rests its superiority of
colour'

THE MOST technic comprehension of a magnificent whole, and
supreme command over the infinite variety of parts, equal
suavity, energy and ease of execution, go hand in hand with the
most chaotic caprice in the disposition and the most callous
tyranny over the character of the subject. Whatever relates to
the theory of colours, of solid, middle and aerial tints, to the
opposition of hues warm or cold, and the contrast of light and
dark masses, is poised with prismatic truth; the whole is a scale
of music.

(1802—from a note made on eight pictures of Veronese's in the
Louvre, printed from the manuscript by Knowles, pp. 263–4)

Rubens's 'Crucifixion' in St. Walburgha's, Antwerp

... Rubens came to his work with gay technic exultation, and,
by the magic of his palette, changed the terrors of Golgotha to
an enchanted garden and clusters of flowers.

(1810, Lecture IX, p. 367)

The incorrectness of Rubens

IT WAS not to be expected that correctness of form should be the
object of Rubens, though he was master of drawing, and even
ambitious in the display of anatomic knowledge; but there is
no mode of incorrectness, unless what directly militated against
his style, such as meagreness, of which his works do not set
an example. His male forms, generally the brawny pulp of
slaughtermen; his females, hillocks of roses in overwhelmed
muscles, grotesque attitudes, and distorted joints, are swept

along in a gulph of colours, as herbage, trees and shrubs are whirled, tossed and absorbed by inundation.

(1810—Lecture IX, p. 369)

Eleventh-hour revision of opinion in favour of the Venetian Colourists

OF THE great restorers of Art, the two we have considered[1] made Design and Style the basis of their plan, content with negative and unambitious colour; the two next inverted the principle, and employed Design and Style as vehicles of *colour* and *harmony*.[2] The style of Titian has two periods: he began with copying what was before him without choice, and for some time continued in the meagre, anxious and accidental manner of Giovanni Bellini; but discovering in the works of Giorgione that breadth of form produced breadth of colour, he endeavoured, and succeeded, to see Nature by comparison, and in a more ample light. That he possessed the theory of the human body needs not to be proved from the doubtful designs which he is said to have made for the anatomical work of Vesalio; that he had familiarised himself with the style of Michelangelo, and burned with ambition to emulate it, is . . . evident . . . from the elemental conceptions, the colossal style and daring foreshortenings which astonish in the *Cain and Abel*, the *Abraham and Isaac*, the *Goliath and David* on the ceiling of the fabric of Santo Spirito at Venice. Here, and here alone, is the result of that union of tone and style which, in Tintoretto's opinion, was required to make a perfect painter—for in general the male forms of Titian are those of sanguine health, often too fleshy for character, less elastic than muscular, or vigorous without grandeur. . . . A certain national character marks the brightest era of the Venetian school: however deviating from each other, Titian, Tintoretto,

[1] Michelangelo and Raphael.
[2] The fourth 'Restorer of Art' dealt with is Correggio, the discoverer of 'harmony'. Fuseli's estimate of Correggio remains to the last substantially unchanged.

Bassano and Veronese acknowledged but one element of imitation, Nature herself. This principle each bequeathed to his followers; and no attempt to adulterate its simplicity by uniting different methods distinguished their immediate successors. Hence they preserved features of originality longer than the surrounding schools, whom the vain wish to connect incompatible excellence soon degraded to mediocrity, and from that plunged to insignificance.

(1825—Lecture XI, pp. 27–9)

SECTION FOUR

THE DEGENERATION OF ART
AFTER MICHELANGELO
THROUGH THE SACRIFICE OF MIND
TO SOULLESS REALISM

In Fuseli's eyes any artist who does not specialise in the Grand Style, with its story-telling pictures of heroic action, is hardly a true artist at all. He grudgingly admits portrait and landscape as just within the pale, but is unwaveringly contemptuous of *genre* and still life. Whenever a painter employs figures which are not unmistakably based on Greek statues, or at least idealised both in form and feature on the analogy of Greek statues, Fuseli refuses to believe that he has done anything but slavishly copied from some chance model, without having anything of his own to express. Everywhere he is on the look-out for realistic elements, and wherever he finds them he roundly damns them as downright slavish naturalism. Dürer and Rembrandt are in his eyes the worst offenders. The one element in Rembrandt's work on which he is able to bestow ecstatic praise is not that which we should nowadays attach the chief importance to.

The Meanness of Realism

FRANCESCO BARBIERI broke like a torrent over the academic rules of his masters. As the desire of disseminating character over every part of his composition made Raphael less attentive

267

to its general effect, so an ungovernable itch of copying all that lay in his way made this man sacrifice order, costume, mind, to mere effects of colour: a mass of flesh, a pile of wood, a sleeve, a hilt, a feathered hat, a table-cloth, or a gold-tissued robe, were for Guercino what a quibble was for Shakespeare. The countenance of his Dido has that sublimity of woe which affects us in the Æeneid, but she is pierced with a toledo and wrapped in brocade; Anna is an Italian Duenna; the scene, the Mole of Ancona or of Naples, the spectators a brace of whiskered Spaniards, and a deserting Amorino winds up the farce. In his St. Petronilla the rags and brawny limbs of two gigantic porters crush the effect which the saint ought to have, and all the rest is frittered into spots. Yet is that picture a tremendous instance of mechanic powers and intrepidity of hand. As a firm base supports, pervades, unites the tones of harmony, so a certain stern virility inspires, invigorates and gives a zest to all Guercino's colour. . . . If his male figures be brought to the test of style, it may be said that he never made a man; their virility is tumour or knotty labour; to youth he gave emaciated lankness, and to old age little besides decrepitude and beards—meanness to all: and though he was more cautious in female forms, they owe the best part of their charms to chiaroscuro.

(1788–1818—Corollary to Aphorism 126)

Domenichino's 'Martyrdom of St. Agnes'—an example of realistic meanness

AT THE Martyrdom of St. Agnes, you saunter amidst the mob of a lane, where the silly chat of neighbouring gossips announces a topic as silly, till you find, with indignation, that instead of a broken pot, or a petty theft, you are to witness a scene for which Heaven opens, the angels descend, and Jesus rises from his throne.

(1788–1818—Corollary to Aphorism 98)

The Disgusting Naturalism of Dürer and Rembrandt

MEANNESS OF manner is the infallible consequence that results from the exclusive recourse to one model: why else are those who have most closely adhered to, and most devoutly studied the model, exactly the most incorrect, the most remote from the real human form? Can there be anything more disgusting to an eye accustomed to harmony of frame, than the starveling forms of Albrecht Dürer, unless it be the swampy excrescences of Rembrandt? The figures of the former, proportions without symmetry; those of the Dutch artist, uniform abstracts of lumpy or meagre deformity: and yet the German was a scientific man, had measured and, in his opinion, reduced to principles the human frame; whilst the Dutchman, form only excepted, possessed every power that constitutes genius in art, seldom excelled in invention and composition, and the creator of that magic combination of colour with chiaroscuro, never perhaps before, and surely never since attained.

(1810—Lecture VII, p. 314)

The anxious preciseness of Albrecht Dürer

ALBRECHT DÜRER was in my opinion a man of great ingenuity, without being a genius. He studied, and, as far as his penetration reached, established certain proportions of the human frame, but he did not invent[1] a style: every work of his is a proof that he wanted the power of imitation, of concluding from what he saw, to what he did not see, that he copied rather than selected the forms that surrounded him, and sans remorse tacked deformity and meagreness to fulness, and sometimes to beauty. Such is his design; in composition copious without taste, anxiously precise in parts, and unmindful of the whole, he has

[1] Fuseli contributed an earlier version of this account of Dürer to Seward's *Anecdotes* in 1795. One variant reading here is of special interest. Originally Fuseli had written 'he did not *create* a style'; this was altered to 'he did not *invent* a style' (*see above*, p. 202).

rather shown us what to avoid than what to follow. He sometimes had a glimpse of the sublime, but it was only a glimpse:
the expanded agony of Christ on the Mount of Olives, and the
mystic conception of his figure of Melancholy, are thoughts
of sublimity, though the expression of the last is weakened by
the rubbish he has thrown about her. His Knight attended by
Death and the Fiend is more capricious than terrible, and his
Adam and Eve are two common models shut up in a rocky
dungeon. If he approached genius in any part of art, it was in
colour. His colour went beyond his age, and as far excelled in
truth and breadth and handling the oil colour of Raphael as
Raphael excels him in every other quality.

(1801—Lecture II, pp. 115–17)

Dürer

THE FORMS of Albrecht Dürer are blasphemies on Nature, the
thwarted growth of starveling labour and dry sterility, formed
to inhabit his hell of paradise. To extend the asperity of this verdict beyond the forms of Albrecht Dürer would be equally unjust and ungrateful to the father of German art, on whom
invention often flashed, whom melancholy marked for her own.
. . . The felicity of his organs, the delicacy of his finger, the freedom and sweep of his touch have found an encomiast in the
author of the life prefixed to the Latin edition of his works.

(1788–1818—Corollary to Aphorism 151)

Rembrandt—'with every prejudice or superiority of taste and style against him'

NO ONE, of whatever period of art, of whatever eminence or
school, out-told Rembrandt in telling the story of a subject, in
the choice of its real crisis, in simplicity, in perspicuity: still, as
the vile crust that involves his ore, his local vulgarity of style,
the ludicrous barbarity of his costume, prepossess eyes less pene-

trating than squeamish against him, it requires some confidence to place him with the classics of invention.

(1788–1818—Corollary to Aphorism 170)

Rembrandt

THE FEMALE forms of Rembrandt are prodigies of deformity; his males are the crippled produce of shuffling industry and sedentary toil.

(1788–1818—Corollary to Aphorism 151)

'The gigantic but barbarous genius of Rembrandt' (Lecture IV)

REMBRANDT WAS, in my opinion, a genius of the first class in whatever relates not to form. In spite of the most portentous deformity, and without considering the spell of his chiaroscuro, such were his powers of nature, such the grandeur, pathos, or simplicity of his composition, from the most elevated or extensive arrangement to the meanest and most homely, that the best cultivated eye, the purest sensibility, and the most refined taste dwell on them, equally enthralled. Shakespeare alone excepted, no one combined with so much transcendent excellence so many, in all other men unpardonable faults—and reconciled us to them. He possessed the full empire of light and shade, and of all the tints that float between them: he tinged his pencil with equal success in the cool of dawn, in the noon-day ray, in the livid flash, in evanescent twilight, and rendered darkness visible. Though made to bend a steadfast eye on the bolder phenomena of Nature, yet he knew how to follow her into her calmest abodes, gave interest to insipidity or baldness, and plucked a flower in every desert. None ever like Rembrandt knew to improve an accident into a beauty, or give importance to a trifle.

(1801—Lecture II, pp. 121–2)

Salvator Rosa's paroxysms of fever

... his line is vulgar; his magic visions, less founded on principles of terror than on mythologic trash and caprice, are to the probable combinations of nature, what the paroxysms of a fever are to the flights of vigorous fancy. Though so much extolled and so ambitiously imitated, his banditti are a medley made up of starveling models, shreds and bits of armour from his lumberroom, brushed into notice by a daring pencil. Salvator was a satirist and a critic, but the rod which he had the insolence to lift against the nudities of Michelangelo, and the anachronism of Raphael, would have been better employed in chastising his own misconceptions.

(1801—Lecture II, pp. 102–3)

Jusepe Ribera

A SHRIVELLED arm, a dropsied leg, were to Ribera what a breast-plate and a gaberdine were to Rembrandt. As in objects of imitation he courted meagreness or excrescence, so in the choice of historic subjects he preferred to the terrors of ebullient passions features of horror or loathsomeness, the spasms of Ixion, St. Bartholomew under the butcher's knife. Nor are the few ideas of gaiety by which he endeavoured to soothe his exasperated fancy less disgusting: Bacchus and his attendants are grinning Lazaroni or bloated wine-sacks; brutality under his hand distorts the feature of mirth.

(1808—*History of Art*, p. 305)

SECTION FIVE

THE PLIGHT AND TASK OF ART
IN THE MODERN WORLD,
ESPECIALLY IN ENGLAND

Fuseli always took the gloomiest view of the prospects of art in his own day, especially in England—not that he ever gave signs of believing that matters looked better in any other country. What alone mattered in his eyes was the revival of the Grand Style, the return to Michelangelo and Raphael, above all to Michelangelo. If it had been only Raphael, he would have met with less opposition. One of the principal and quite unrealisable demands of Fuseli's programme was that portrait and landscape painting should be put very much in their place, and that place was, in his not always openly avowed opinion, less among the arts proper than among the highly skilled handicrafts. Cunningham writes: 'During the delivery of one of his lectures, wherein he calls landscape painters the topographers of art, Beechey admonished Turner with his elbow of the severity of the sarcasm; presently, when Fuseli described the patrons of portrait painters as men who would give a few guineas to have their own senseless heads painted, and then assume the air and use the language of patrons, Turner administered a similar hint to Beechey. When the lecture was over, Beechey walked up to Fuseli and said, "How sharply you have been cutting up us poor labourers in portraiture!" "Not you, Sir William," exclaimed the professor, "I only spoke of the blasted fools who employ you!" ' The reference is evidently to Lecture IV, delivered in 1805. The expressions quoted by Cunningham do not occur in the printed text of 1820, but there is no reason to suspect him of substantial inaccuracy. Fuseli certainly modified and amplified his lectures considerably for the press, and allowed himself to speak things he judged it discreeter not to print. He did not stand alone in his bitterness against the portrait painters —this was a party-division in the art world of his day. Haydon writes of his own "strong sense of individual wrong, as belonging to a class—that of historical painters—who had neither the rank, the power, nor the patronage of portrait painters. All which, it is my belief they would have had, if the Academy had not been founded . . ." (*Journal*, 31 December 1812). He dreams that he is making a 'capital speech' in defence of historical painters against portraitists (19 September 1824). On the occasion of Fuseli's death Haydon lashes out in his diary against 'this nest of portrait painters', who are 'enjoying the full fruits of their pernicious supremacy'. Repeatedly he returns to this theme, notably in an argument with Shee on 10 July 1826. Blake writes similarly: 'While Sir Joshua was rolling in Riches, Barry was Poor and Unemploy'd except by his own Energy, Mortimer was call'd a Madman, and only Portrait Painting applauded and rewarded by the Rich and Great. Reynolds and Gainsborough Blotted and Blurred one against the other and Divided all the English World between them. Fuseli, indignant, almost hid himself. I am hid' (Annotations to Reynolds' *Discourses*). All Fuseli's compliments to contemporary English portrait painters —and he paid many—have a sting in them. Little familiarity with Fuseli's terminology is needed to recognise in nearly every word of his phrase about Gainsborough, 'the dexterous singularities of original talent', a veiled insult. (Originality was, in his view, the prerogative of 'genius'.) Of Reynolds as a painter he was prepared to think somewhat more highly, but nothing he prints about him is inconsistent with what Cunningham records of a conversation in which he takes up Lawrence for comparing Reynolds with Raphael: ' "Blastation! you will drive me mad—Reynolds and Raphael!—a dwarf and a giant! why will you waste all your fine words!" He rose and left the room, muttering something about a tempest in a pint pot.' Not the least interesting point about the handsome compliment Knowles records him as having paid to Turner as 'the only landscape painter of genius in Europe' is the contempt implied in it for all the other landscape painters of the day, including Constable.[1] The only kind of landscape painting Fuseli could, in conformity with his general outlook, wholeheartedly approve of was the ultra-heroic landscape on the analogy of historic painting, and that was just what Turner provided him with. In Blake, more than in any other contemporary, he was prepared to recognise an artist after his own heart. Very revealing are the estimates of some of his own paintings

[1] Fuseli . . . thought it witty to call to the Academy porter, 'Strowger, bring me my umbrella, I am going to see Mr. Constable's pictures' (Redgrave, *Century of British Painters*).

which he contributed anonymously to the *Analytical Review* in 1788 and 1789.

Fuseli's 'doubts whether higher art will exist much longer'

OUR AGE, when compared with former ages, has but little occasion for great works, and that is the reason why so few are produced . . . everything that surrounds us tends to show us in private, is become snug, less, narrow, pretty, insignificant. We are not, perhaps, the less happy on account of all this; but from such selfish trifling to expect a system of Art built on grandeur, without a total revolution, would only be less presumptuous than insane.

(1825—Lecture XII, pp. 47–8)

Collecting mania, mere portrait and true art in England

. . . Britain never ceased pouring its caravans of noble and wealthy pilgrims over Italy, Greece and Ionia, to pay their devotions at the shrines of *virtù* and taste: not content with adoring the obscure idols, they have ransacked their temples, and none returned without some share in the spoil: in plaster or in marble, on canvas or in gems, the arts of Greece and Italy were transported to England, and what Petronius said of Rome, that it was easier to meet there with a god than a man, might be said of London. Without inquiring into the permanent and accidental causes of the inefficacy of these efforts with regard to public taste and support of art, it is observable, that, whilst Francis I was busied . . . to scatter the seeds of taste over France, . . . in England, Holbein and Torregiano under Henry, and Federigo Zucchero under Elizabeth, were condemned to Gothic work and portrait painting. Charles indeed called Rubens and his scholars to provoke the latent English spark, but the effect was intercepted by his destiny. His son, in possession of the cartoons of Raphael, and with the magnificence of

Whitehall before his eyes, suffered Verio to contaminate the walls of his palaces, or degraded Lely to paint the Cymons and Iphigenias of his court; whilst the manner of Kneller swept completely what yet might be left of taste under his successors: such was the equally contemptible and deplorable state of English art, till the genius of Reynolds first rescued from the mannered depravation of foreigners his own branch,[1] and soon extended his view to the higher departments of art. . . . The plans lately adopted and now organising within these walls for the dignified propagation and support of art, whether fostered by the great, or left to their own energy, must soon decide what may be produced by the unison of British genius and talent, and whether the painters' school of that nation which claims the foremost honours of modern poetry, which has produced with Reynolds, Hogarth, Gainsborough, and Wilson, shall submit to content themselves with a subordinate place among the schools we have enumerated.

(1801—Lecture II, pp. 127-9)

The Prince Regent's discouragement of Historic Painting

HE NEVER can be great who honours what is little. Grandeur of style and execution do not exclusively depend upon dimensions: but in an age and amidst a race who have erected littleness or rather diminutiveness of size to the only credentials of admissibility into collections, . . . that which ennobled the age of Pericles, of Julio, and Leone, must be content to look to posterity for its reward. If it were physiognomically true, that the structure of every human face bears some analogy to that of some brute, it might reasonably surprise, that an individual[2] marked

[1] *Reynolds' own branch* is, of course, portrait-painting, which Fuseli always refused to acknowledge as one of the pure or 'higher departments' of art.

[2] Fuseli does not name the individual here referred to. There can, however, be little doubt that the Prince Regent is intended. Haydon writes in his *Journal* in December 1812: 'Do you really expect to raise art by encouraging pictures two feet long and three feet wide? Do you also agree with

by nature with no very remote resemblance to a hippopotamus, should be considered as the legislator of a taste equally noted for tameness of conception and effeminate finish; but as it is improbable that one individual, however favoured by circumstances or endowed with all-persevering activity, or arrogance, could stamp the taste of a nation exclusively with his own, it may be fairly surmised that he did no more than find and rear the seeds of that Micromania which infects the public taste.

(1788–1818—Aphorism 238 and Corollary)

The prospects of Historic Painting in England

'James Moore I met. He sd. Fuseli continues very loud in His declaration that Historical Painting will never be encouraged in this Country'. (*Farington Diary*, 4 June 1809)

WHAT, THEREFORE, can be urged against the conclusion, that, as far as the public is concerned, the Art is sinking, and threatens to sink still deeper, from the want of demand for great and significant works? Florence, Bologna, Venice, each singly taken, produced in the course of the sixteenth century alone, more great historic pictures than all Britain taken together, from its earliest attempts at painting to its present efforts. What are we to conclude from this? That the soil from which Shakespeare and Milton sprang is unfit to rear the Genius of Poetic Art? Or are we to find the cause of this seeming impotence in that general change of habits, customs, pursuits and amusements, which for near a century has stamped the national character of Europe with apathy or discountenance[1] of the genuine principles of Art?

(1825—Lecture XII, p. 56)

the Edinburgh reviewers that Raphael would have deserved more praise had he painted pictures of more moderate dimensions?' The government was repeatedly approached with schemes for the encouragement of large historical paintings, but always unsuccessfully.

[1] *Discountenance* as a substantive, in the sense of 'the act or fact of discountenancing'—an obsolete usage; see *New English Dictionary*.

Academies the homes of lost causes

ALL (Academies), whether public or private, supported by patronage or individual contribution, were and are symptoms of Art in distress, monuments of public dereliction and decay of Taste. But they are at the same time the asylum of the student, the theatre of his exercises, the repositories of the materials, the archives of the documents of our art, whose principles their officers are bound now to maintain, and for the preservation of which they are responsible to posterity, undebauched by the flattery, heedless of the sneers, undismayed by the frown of their own time.

(1825—Lecture XII, p. 58)

Modern Art

MODERN ART, reared by superstition in Italy, taught to dance in France, plumped up to unwieldiness in Flanders, reduced to 'chronicle small beer' in Holland, became a rich old woman by 'suckling fools' in England.[1]

(1788–1817—Aphorism 150)

Trouncing the Rev. Robert Anthony Bromley

WHEN WE add to this that the whole is delivered in the style and with the somnific loquacity of a drowsy homily, generally without perspicuity or grammar, and frequently with foreign constructions in English words, the reader will forgive us if we refuse to enter into a more circumstantial analysis of a work which to us appears to have hardly any other title to grave con-

---

[1] One needs perhaps to be familiar with Fuseli's outlook to be able to follow this aphorism, which is concerned entirely with the 'subjects' of painting, from devotional Italian painting through Dutch *genre* to English portrait-painting. Fuseli regarded the predominance of portrait, as opposed to historic painting, as marking the intrinsic inferiority of English art.

sideration than its size, and to contain scarcely a period not obnoxious to censure.[1]

(*Analytical Review*, July 1793, review of Bromley's *Philosophical and Critical History of the Fine Arts* . . ., signed Z. Z.—XVI, p. 242)

Fuseli and Blake on Reynolds' 'Discourses'

It is remarkable that two men who not only appear to have so much in common, but were also each of them conscious of having so much in common with one another as Fuseli and Blake should have differed so completely as they did in their estimates of Reynolds' *Discourses*, a book that raised most of the questions both had particularly at heart. Fuseli ranks them once at least above everything else written on art, Blake's comment is: 'This man was hired to depress art.' It turns out, however, that Fuseli's admiration and assent are by no means unqualified, while Blake's ferocious dissent is from time to time interrupted with involuntary enthusiastic agreement, expressed, indeed, sometimes in such characteristic terms as these: 'Somebody Else wrote this page for Reynolds. I think that Barry or Fuseli wrote, or dictated it.' It must be taken into consideration also, that we have Blake's comments only on Reynolds' first volume, from which the seven last Discourses, to which Fuseli attached special importance, are missing. Certainly Fuseli goes further in his praise and Blake in his condemnation of Reynolds than one would expect of either, if there had been no extraneous circumstances to influence them. Such extraneous circumstances there

---

[1] Bromley had given bitter offence not only to Fuseli, but to a large faction in the Royal Academy by his praise of Benjamin West. Fuseli quotes at length the offending passage, in which Bromley instances West's notorious *Death of Wolfe* as 'the one, though the only one' perfect historic picture; in which he speaks of West as the 'master who has introduced Britain to a taste in the histŏric line, which was very new to the acquaintance of her own artists'. Bromley describes West's *Death of Wolfe* as 'one of the most genuine models of historic painting in the world'. He defends West for that use of contemporary costume which Fuseli in particular had so violently condemned: 'Equally just, but equally new to the historic pencil, is the character of the dress in which these victorious men are exhibited.' It has been stated in the *Listener* (25 May 1950) that Fuseli 'acknowledged the perfection of West's academic revolution'. But this is hardly borne out by Knowles' cautious statement that he spoke of the *Death of Wolfe* 'in qualified terms of praise' (p. 62). How qualified this praise was, the veiled insults in the allusion to it as a work which 'respect forbids me to name' (third Lecture) sufficiently disclose.

were. At the age of twenty-seven Fuseli could write to Lavater: 'Here is a bit of unadorned vanity for you: to be the greatest painter of my age, says Reynolds, I need only to go to Italy for a few years' (6 May 1768). Of Blake we find recorded that when, at the age of twenty-three or so, he in his turn showed some of his sketches to Reynolds, all he met with was discouragement and the advice 'to work with less extravagance and more simplicity, and to correct his drawing'. For the rest, Fuseli and Blake, in spite of all they had in common, were very far from being in complete agreement with one another all along the line. *See* Introduction, pp. 56–57.

Reynolds as Art Critic

... unsystematic and loose as the discourses of our great countryman appear to be, they abound with more real information, with grander principles, more practical instruction and less prescribed sentiments than most of the elementary philosophical or biographical works that have been published on art and artists, from the times of Leonardo da Vinci to those of Mengs ...

(*Analytical Review*, September 1789, unsigned review of Reynolds' *Discourse* of December 1788—V, p. 41)

Reynolds as Critic

TO COMPARE Reynolds with his predecessors would equally disgrace our judgment and impeach our gratitude. His volumes can never be consulted without profit, and should never be quitted by the student's hand but to embody by exercise the precepts he gives and the means he points out.

(1820—Introduction to *Lectures*, p. 15)

The Merits of Sir Joshua Reynolds' 'Discourses' and of his paintings

THEY CONTAIN what can be taught by precept, and they direct taste where precept ceases. They are not, indeed, equal; timorous caution sometimes, and sometimes whim deviate from the simplicity and grandeur of the general principles, but neither frequently nor with sufficient persuasion to mislead a mind ardently intent on art. And when it is considered, that he who delivered these discourses was and must be chiefly celebrated for having obtained a high rank only in a secondary class of art, the impartiality and resignation which dictated precepts so noble must place in our admiration the man even above the artist!

(Analytical Review, July 1797, unsigned review of The Works of Sir Joshua Reynolds—XXVI, p. 3)

Reynolds as Colourist—his 'Infant Hercules' in the Academy of 1788

> '—a work which may properly be called the triumph of professional execution—of execution which not only disdains, but rejects or tramples on every other help.'

TO LOOK for hope or fear among the wilds of mythology has long been considered as the refuge of the cold and the lame ... Little solicitous about the perplexities of vulgar eyes, he has enchanted the higher connoisseur with the magic hues of ideal colour, and uninterrupted torrents of harmonious hues. Juno, Amphitryon, Alcmene, Iphicles, Tiresias and every attendant figure are indiscriminately swept along in a 'flood of glory'; mere vehicles of one superior principle, they vanish and emerge as it winds or pours its masses of dazzling light or transparent shades. Here may be seen what the steady pursuit of one principle can do in art. The pathos of the subject is in its colour; the colour agitates the eyes, the hearts that scorn the frigid actors.

(Analytical Review, June 1788, unsigned account of the Royal Academy Exhibition for 1788—I, p. 219. Twenty-five years later, in 1813, Fuseli wrote another critique of this picture, which is printed on pp. 387–8 of Knowles's Biography.)

Sir Joshua Reynolds' 'The Cottagers', Thomson

THIS INSIPID scene, equally destitute of beauty, passion, forms and chiaroscuro, subsists on the canvass by an opposition of tints, but must perish by the monotony of white and black when put to the test of the graver.

(*Analytical Review*, July 1789, unsigned account of Macklin's Gallery —IV, p. 370)

Sir Joshua Reynolds' painting, 'The Vestal', from an Ode to Meditation by the Rev. Mr. Gregory

IT IS not necessary to know that the *Vestal* is the portrait of Mrs. B——ll, to discover the whole is an irony. The humid side-leer of this eye can as little issue from the face of chastity, as a vestal from such a mother. But the picture, as a composition of certain beauties and certain characters, its expression, tones and forms (the vestal's arm and hand excepted), the veiled light which decoys the mind into voluptuous reveries, never let us once remember that it ridicules what it pretends to celebrate.

(*Analytical Review*, July 1789, unsigned account of Macklin's *Gallery*— IV, p. 369)

Gainsborough's Art[1]—'not History—a humble, more individual imitation of nature'

> 'He affected not to know the Christian name of Gainsborough . . . he was grossly unjust also to that elegant artist's merits . . .' (Cunningham's *Life of Fuseli*)

IF THE dexterous singularities of original talent are among the

---

[1] The following anecdote illustrates Gainsborough's opinion of Fuseli's art: 'Garvey sd. that when Fuseli exhibited his large picture of Macbeth at the little Royal Academy, he went there with Gainsborough who on seeing it sd. He shd. not like to be in a one Horse Chaise before that picture . . . On the contrary Sir Joshua was sd. to approve it in some respects' (*Farington Diary*, 18 February 1804).

proper objects to which the eye of youth ought to be directed, what could more properly command the attention of an auditory of artists and students (no matter of what nation) than the name and example of our lamented Gainsborough? . . . After pronouncing it 'difficult to determine whether he excelled most in portraits, landscapes, or fancy pictures', the author commends him for that judgment and modesty which never allowed him to overstep his own limits; and contrasts him with those who, not content with excelling in their own department, ridiculously attempted to figure away in spheres not their own, or destroyed the unity of their effects by a medley of heterogeneous materials. Here we meet with the names of *Hogarth* and *Wilson*, and might, without surprise, have met with more.

(*Analytical Review*, September 1789, unsigned review of Reynolds'
Discourse of December 1788—V, pp. 38–40)

Gainsborough's 'Lavinia', from Thomson's 'Autumn' in Macklin's Gallery

THIS IS a faithful transcript of the forms and hues of nature, and the forms and hues of nature never leave the mind indifferent. We may venture to say more with regard to the general tone: the sensibility of the artist has produced a harmony, which a meaner mind could not have conceived, all inspiring a sympathy with the poor child before us; but is this the sympathy that would seize our breast at the sight of such an infant as Lavinia? The figure before us is the offspring and immediate heir of poverty; the stumpy shortness of her form, the raggedness of her garb and air take nothing indeed from her innocence, but never can allow her to be mistaken for the 'lovely young Lavinia that once had friends, and on whose birth fortune deceitful smiled' . . .

(*Analytical Review*, July 1789, unsigned—IV, p. 368)

Biography and History—Portrait and Historical Painting

COULD Mr. M. confound plans and ends so dissimilar as those of biography and history? Whilst this admits the man only in his public character, in his official garb; the prince, the leader, the statesman; the features, the actions which connect him with the interests of society and the fate of nations at large; that conducts us to the inmost recesses of his habitation, examines his form, his physiognomy, and shows the father, the son, the husband, in domestic dishabille. To demand from the calm anatomist of the individual at rest and unobserved the pathos of him who observes him in action and under the sway of passions, is to demand of the painter of portrait the vigorous imitation of the historic or dramatic artist. . . . The points of sight, at which the historian and the biographer fix their reader, vary not more than the fidelity which is prescribed to both. The motives from which the former bids his hero act, or the speeches which he delivers from his lips, are more the offspring of analogy than reality, it is sufficient that both be characteristic; but the biographer has little to do with motives, and confines himself to literal tradition,[1] or the words he heard.

(*Analytical Review*, November 1793, review of Murphy's *Tacitus*, signed Z. Z.—XVII, p. 244)

The Inferiority of mere Portrait

THE PORTRAIT I mean is that common one, as widely spread as confined in its principle; the remembrancer of insignificance, mere human resemblance, in attitude without action, features without meaning, dress without drapery, and situation without propriety. The aim of the artist and the sitter's wish are confined to external likeness; that deeper, nobler aim, the personification of character, is neither required, nor, if obtained, recognised. The better artist, condemned to this task, can here only distin-

[1] i.e. written records.

guish himself from his duller brother by execution, by invok-
ing the assistance of background, chiaroscuro and picturesque
effects, and thus sometimes produces a work which delights the
eye, and leaves us, whilst we lament the misapplication, with a
strong impression of his power; him we see, not the insignificant
individual that usurps the centre, one we never saw, care not if
we never see, and if we do, remember not, for his head can per-
sonify nothing but his opulence or his pretence; it is furniture.

(1805—Lecture IV, pp. 215–16)

Landscape, tame and sublime[1]

TO PORTRAIT painting, thus circumstanced, we subjoin, as the
last branch of uninteresting subjects, that kind of landscape
which is entirely occupied with the tame delineation of a given
spot; an enumeration of hill and dale, clumps of trees, shrubs,
water, meadows, cottages and houses, what is commonly called
Views. These, if not assisted by nature, dictated by taste, or
chosen for character, may delight the owner of the acres they
enclose, the inhabitants of the spot, perhaps the antiquary or
the traveller, but to every other eye they are little more than
topography. The landscape of Titian, of Mola, of Salvator, of
the Poussins, Claude, Rubens, Elzheimer, Rembrandt and Wilson, spurns all relation with this kind of map-work. To them,
nature disclosed her bosom in the varied light of rising,
meridian, setting suns; in twilight, night and dawn. Height,
depth, solitude, strike, terrify, absorb, bewilder in their scenery.
We tread on classic or romantic ground, or wander through the

---

[1] Fuseli would seem to have been comparatively insensitive to landscape,
just as he was contemptuous of those who took an interest in nature when
she was not engaged in gala performances. One of the few recorded instances
of his responding enthusiastically to a landscape impression is the following
in Farington's diary: 'Fuseli was last week at Clifton near Bristol and raved
abt. the romantic scenery, saying "It was the finest thing in the kingdom—
sublime etc." ' (*Farington Diary*, 28 February 1808). Striking landscape impressions do also occasionally appear amongst his sketches, especially from
his seaside holidays. Paul Ganz reproduces some of these in his volume
of *Zeichnungen* (1947).

characteristic groups of rich congenial objects. The usual choice of the Dutch school, which frequently exhibits no more than the transcript of a spot, borders, indeed, nearer on the negative kind of landscape; but imitation will not be entitled to the pleasure we receive, or the admiration we bestow, on their genial works, till it has learnt to give an air of choice to necessity, to imitate their hues, spread their masses, and to rival the touch of their pencil.

(1805—Lecture IV, pp. 217–18)

Landscape-painting

LANDSCAPE IS either the transcript of a spot, or a picturesque combination of homogeneous objects, or the scene of a phenomenon. The first pleases by precision and taste; the second adds variety and grandeur; the third may be an instrument of sublimity, affect our passions or wake a sentiment.[1]

(1788–1818—Aphorism 236)

Wright's picture for Act IV of 'The Tempest'—the Dignity of History

WE CANNOT help thinking that the figures occupy too small a space in the disposition of this picture for the dignity of history. It has been observed by the biographer of Milton (Dr. Johnson) that 'no man forgets his original trade. . . .' Poetry and passions, when treated by the landscape painter or the painter of still life,

---

[1] It is interesting to compare these views of Fuseli with the following utterance of Wordsworth's on the same subject, recorded by Farington: 'Wordsworth said he thought Historical subjects shd. never be introduced into Landscape, but where the Landscape was to be subservient to them. Where the Landscape was intended principally to impress the mind, figures, other than such as are general, are injurious to the effect which the landscape shd. produce as a scene founded on the observation of Nature' (*Farington Diary*, 28 April 1807).

become mere attendants on the favourite objects—mere expletives of the situation.

(*Analytical Review*, May 1789, unsigned account of Boydell's *Shakespeare Gallery*—IV, p. 109)

Fuseli on Blake

FUSELI CALLED on me last night and sat till 12 o'clock. He mentioned Blake, the Engraver, whose genius and invention have been much spoken of. Fuseli has known him several years and thinks he has a great deal of invention, but that fancy is the end and not a means in his designs. He does not employ it to give novelty and decoration to regular conceptions, but the whole of his aim is to produce singular shapes and odd combinations.

(*Farington Diary*, 24 June 1796)

TO THE eyes of the discerning . . . the merit of Mr. Blake . . . need not be pointed out; and while a taste for the arts of design shall continue to exist, the original conception, and the bold and masterly execution of this artist cannot be unnoticed or unadmired.

(Unsigned Advertisement to Blake's illustrations for Young's *Night Thoughts*, dated 22 December 1796 and usually attributed to Fuseli)

On Blake's illustrations to Blair's Grave

THE AUTHOR of this moral series before us endeavoured to awake sensibility by touching our sympathies with nearer, less ambiguous, and less ludicrous imagery than what mythology, Gothic superstition, or symbols as far-fetched as inadequate could supply. His invention[1] has been chiefly employed to spread a familiar and domestic atmosphere round the most important of all subjects; to connect the visible and the invisible world, without provoking probability; and to lead the eye from

[1] Cunningham, in reprinting this passage, reads 'His *avocation* has been chiefly employed . . .'; Gilchrist reads *invention* instead of *avocation*.

the milder light of time to the radiations of eternity. Such is the plan and the moral part of the author's invention. The technic part and the execution of the artist, though to be examined by other principles, and addressed to a narrower circle, equally claim approbation, sometimes excite our wonder, and not unseldom our fears, when we see him play on the very verge of legitimate invention. But wildness so picturesque in itself, so often redeemed by taste, simplicity and elegance, what child of fancy, what artist would wish to discharge? The groups and single figures, on their own basis, abstracted from the general composition and considered without attention to the plan, frequently exhibit those genuine, unaffected attitudes, those simple graces, which nature and the heart alone can dictate, and only an eye inspired by both discover. Every class of artist, in every stage of their progress or attainments, from the student to the finished master, and from the contriver of ornament to the painter of history, will find here material of art and hints of improvement.

(1805, Preface to Blair's *Grave* with Blake's illustrations)

For three other utterances on Blake, recorded only by the not always reliable Gilchrist, *see* Introduction, p. 43. Fuseli's admiration of Blake had perhaps somewhat narrower limits than Gilchrist suggests.

Fuseli on his own 'Theseus receiving the Clue from Ariadne', a finished sketch

MYTHOLOGY CAN claim little of this performance besides the name. Its sentiment springs in every age, and dwells in every breast. That this Theseus was not fed with roses, that this Ariadne is worthy to be courted by a God, is their smallest praise. If this be a sketch, it will be difficult to find a finished picture in the room.

(*Analytical Review*, June 1788, unsigned account of the Royal Academy Exhibition of 1788—I, p. 220)

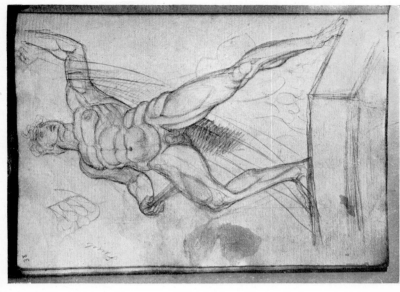

Horse-tamer ("opus Phidiae"), Monte Cavallo, Rome,
and one of Fuseli's sketches from it

Fuseli on some of his own paintings for Shakespeare

(*a*) *Midsummer Night's Dream, Act IV, Scene 1*

THIS IS the creation of a poetic painter, and the scene is peculiarly his own; a glowing harmony of tone pervades the whole;
and instead of being amused by mere humour, an assemblage
calculated to delight the simple correct taste, which sensibility
has refined, bursts on us to relax the features without exciting
loud laughter. The moment chosen by the painter, when the
queen, with soft languor, caresses Bottom, who humorously
addresses her attendants, gave him licence to create the fanciful
yet not grotesque group, which he has so judiciously contrasted
as not to disturb the pleasurable emotions the whole must ever
convey to a mind alive to the wild but enchanting graces of
poetry. The elegant familiar attendants seem to be buoyed up
by the sweet surrounding atmosphere, and the fragrant nosegay
bound together with careless art, yet so light, that the rude wind
might disperse the 'insubstantial pageant'. The soft and insinuating beauty, the playful graces here displayed, would, without
reflection, scarcely be expected from the daring pencil that
appears ever on the stretch to reach the upmost boundary of
nature.

(*b*) *Macbeth, Act I, Scene 3*

THIS IS a sublime scene and the figure of Macbeth uncommonly
grand: a character too great to be daunted by an extraordinary
event betrays no sign of fear or even astonishment; the slumber-
ing fire of ambition is roused, and the firmly-nerved hand of
power raised to command those to stay and say more, from
whom a dastard would have fled. At this moment only one
passion agitated the soul of Macbeth: a daring hope was labouring for birth in a shape he had but a glimpse of; as the bubbles
melted into air, in a moment, he reflected, undisturbed by jar-
ring emotions, and darted towards his future grandeur. The
figure and attitude of Banquo appear rather strained and
inferior to the rest of the composition, which, like a stupendous
feature in nature, seizes the whole mind, and produces the

concentred calm of admiration, instead of the various dilated pleasurable sensations which arise from contemplating grace and beauty.

(c) Lear renouncing Cordelia, Act I, Scene 2

PERHAPS THERE is not a picture in the room that tells the story more directly and faithfully than the renunciation of Lear. Our poet's words may be repeated: 'Yes, every inch a king.' The ungoverned rage of a man accustomed to see all things bend so quickly to his will, that he never considered why they did so, contrasts with the rough earnestness of Kent, who, by an abrupt interposition, irritates the wrath he wished to appease, and makes the cloud burst with tenfold fury over the slight impediment that stopped without allaying the storm. Goneril and Regan, with unblushing fronts, stand erect; but we own we expected to see the gentle Cordelia with downcast eyes, shrinking from the anger which terrified even while it wounded her ingenuous mind. The contempt which the hypocrisy of her sisters inspired might naturally dictate her answer; but at the moment the painter has chosen she may be supposed to be overwhelmed with fear and tender compassion for her still dear, but mistaken father.

(d) Hamlet, Act I, Scene 4

THE UNIFORM sweep of gloom that quietly diffuses itself over this picture seems in unison with the still horror of impatient curiosity which reflection had sharpened and puzzled. The ardour of rational courage braces Hamlet's nerves; his eyes already have flown to the shade, who strides with majestic dignity, and looks a king. The position of the moon preserves the prevailing tone, and prevents the playfulness of its beams from disturbing the harmony of the whole by introducing the tranquil yet cheerful sensations they usually produce. This is a happy effort of genius to cut a gordian knot and substitute a beauty for a defect.

(*Analytical Review*, May 1789, unsigned account of Boydell's *Shakespeare Gallery*—IV, pp. 110–12)

Fuseli on his own 'Beatrice' in the Royal Exhibition, 1789

THE TONE of colouring *Mr. Fuseli's Beatrice* . . . strikingly contrasts with the gaudy glare of unblended masses which surround it on every side. Hero is a princess; and now for the first time, we see a Beatrice: she starts forward, as if still tripping with silent haste on her light fantastic toe, eager to listen to the important secret, which works, as she drinks it in, a strange revolution in her mind. Her animated attitude displays the sprightliness of her mind; but it is not the levity of a wanton which appears; on the contrary, in a voluptuous form we trace the chastened playfulness of innocent gaiety, which dreams not of the wishes it inspires. An air of propriety and dignity reminds us that we are looking at a female, whose rank and education have equally secured her from transgressing the bounds prescribed by modesty or acquiring vulgarity of manners.

> (*Analytical Review*, May 1789, unsigned account of the Royal Exhibition—IV, pp. 106–7)

Fuseli on his own painting of 'Macbeth with the Witches at the Cauldron'

YOU HAVE another of my best poetical conceptions. . . . I have endeavoured to supply what is deficient in the poetry. To say nothing of the general arrangement of my picture, which in composition is altogether triangular, (and the triangle is a mystical figure), I have endeavoured to shew a colossal head rising out of the abyss, and that head Macbeth's likeness. What, I would ask, would be a greater object of terror to you, if, some night, in going home, you were to find yourself sitting at your own table, either writing, reading or otherwise employed? would not this make a powerful impression on your mind?

> (After 1805—utterance addressed to and recorded by John Knowles, pp. 189–90. The painting in question was produced 1793–4)

PART FIVE

NON-CLASSICAL IMPULSES

BURSTING THROUGH

THE CLASSICAL HUSK

By no process of manipulation can that central body of aesthetic doctrine which Fuseli to the last so energetically insists on be represented as anything but classical. Yet Fuseli himself was, both in his personality and in his work, anything but the Classical type. The representative Classical taste of his age, both in England and in Germany, either rejected him downright, or accepted him only with considerable qualifications—thus Reynolds only approved of his *Macbeth* 'in some respects'. It was in the non-classical camp, and especially among the younger English Romantic painters, that he found his most enthusiastic following. Nobody seems really to have believed in his Classicism except himself. 'His imagination, though he seemed not aware of it, was essentially Gothic,' writes Cunningham; 'his mind dealt with the poetry and superstitions of Christendom; he talked about, but seldom drew the gods and goddesses of Olympus.' Irrepressible non-Classical impulses manifest themselves strongly and repeatedly in his actual painting and in his personal bearing and manner (in all of which they easily predominate) and also, though less conspicuously, in his theoretical utterances on art. Not only does he always express even his most classical convictions with a most unclassical vehemence; he is also for ever mingling with them ideas of a very different provenance and character, ideas that only the most acrobatic dialectics, quite divorced from all real experience, could ever reconcile with such dogmas as the classical Canon of Proportion or the completely de-individualised and delocalised principle of generalisation. It is surely better to accept this phenomenon as a great unresolved contradiction than to aim at rescuing Fuseli's consistency by interpreting away all the incisive contours of his assertions, and trimming them into a semblance of symmetry. One certainly goes too far behind his back, if one assumes that in all his classical declarations he simply misunderstood himself or really meant something different from what he said, and was in truth nothing but a Romantic expressing himself in a misleading way. It is not even justifiable to designate all the non-classical elements in his nature and in his artistic theory and practice as 'Romantic', unless one can demonstrate that everything which is not Classical necessarily must be Romantic—a two-party system, which, like so many other two-party systems, has long since lost validity. Fuseli was not altogether blind to the Romantic developments going on around him, and sufficiently clearly dissociated himself from them, even where he also parted company with the Classicists. He rejected the mystical and transcendental, was sceptical about the cult of the Infinite, and censured as 'Mannerism' or 'oddity' all contemporary strivings after uniqueness or originality except his own. He is ultimately a pure individualist, too pure an individualist to belong so much as tacitly or by implication to any party, even to the party which had made individualism one of the chief points of its programme. Classical doctrine itself, as he upheld it, was just an ingredient in his particular brand of individualism, but as such it was all-important to him.

It would go far towards extricating Fuseli from quite discredited and absurd-looking old artistic conventions, if we could represent him as having believed not in Historical Painting, but rather in Poetic Painting—as, indeed, all his most memorable pictures can far more aptly be called poetic than historic. According to Reynolds this is, indeed, a distinction without a difference: 'In conformity with custom', he writes, 'I call this part of the art History Painting; it ought to be called Poetical, as it really is' (IVth Discourse, 1771). Usage was uncertain. Fuseli himself, in demolishing Bromley, particularly rates him for using such a term as 'poetic painting' at all: 'Unacquainted with the comprehensive system which allots to painting the epic, the dramatic and the historic department, he cuts it short into what he calls poetic and historic painting. Such is his theory' (*Analytical Review*, July 1793, review of Bromley's *History of the Fine Arts*). Twelve years later, however, Fuseli is himself found using the term *Poetical Painting*, a thing he very rarely does: 'Fuseli has little hope of *Poetical* painting finding incouragement in England. The People are not prepared for it. Portrait with them is everything. —Their taste and feelings all go to *realities*.—The ideal does not operate on their minds.—*Historical* painting, viz.: matter of fact, they may encourage' (*Farington Diary*, 24 July 1805). Most often, however, when Fuseli speaks of *Historical Painting*, it can be assumed that he understands the term very comprehensively, and that it is either synonomous with or at least includes Poetic Painting.

SECTION ONE

BEAUTY AND EXPRESSION

Winckelmann, in his *History of the Art of the Ancients* (1764) had established it as a great aesthetic principle that 'expression detracts from beauty'. Beauty should be 'a figure belonging neither to this nor to that particular person, and not expressing any state of mind or feeling of passion, because these mingle foreign elements with beauty and disturb the unity'. This distinction between beauty on the one hand and expression or character on the other, was given very wide currency two years later by Lessing, who maintained in his *Laocoon* that, in the plastic arts, expression should always be sacrificed to beauty. This soon became a central tenet of eighteenth-century Classicism. Goethe violently attacked it in his youth, but became himself one of its chief defenders in his classical phase. In 1772 Reynolds said in his fifth Discourse: 'If you mean to preserve the most perfect beauty *in its most perfect state*, you cannot express the passions, all of which produce distortion and deformity, more or less, in the most beautiful faces.' There is perhaps no better test for unimpeachable classical orthodoxy than a man's reaction to this particular doctrine. The German Romantics did not like it. Blake wrote in the margin against the passage just quoted from Reynolds: 'Passion and Expression is Beauty Itself. The Face that is incapable of Passion and Expression is deformity Itself. . . . Reynolds cannot bear Expression.' Fuseli, going further still, says that beauty without expression is nothing at all. Admittedly he is concerned in the first place with the limited question of the treatment of faces in historic paintings; admittedly he can and does appeal to the authority of another classical aesthete, Mengs, at least for making Expression an end to be pursued in art, though, of course, not for sacrificing Beauty to Expression, a possibility which Mengs does not envisage. But the energy and boldness with which Fuseli speaks on this theme make it legitimate to give his words a wider application and to see him as in his own way standing for that very antithesis of classicism, the expressionistic view of art. It fits in with this that those who have in our days rediscovered Fuseli and recognised deep affinities between his work and their own are most of them Expressionists or heirs of Expressionism.

Whether the source of beauty and sublimity is in mind or in matter . . .

THE AUTHOR of the ingenious work before us attempts to prove that all those appearances of nature, or works of art, which are the objects of taste, derive their power of exciting emotions in us, not from qualities inherent in themselves as material forms, but from some association with our feelings, habits or modes of life. . . . He denies that matter is fitted to produce any emotion in the mind, but supposes that material objects, by means of their colour or form, affect us as arbitrary signs of those qualities with which we have observed them combined. He likewise allows a *resemblance* between the sensations they excite and our emotions; in doing which we think he has allowed all that an advocate of the opposite system would wish to have granted. Thus he says there is a *resemblance* between the lively sensation of sunshine and the emotion of joy; but what is this, if it is not saying that sunshine is fitted to *produce* joy? . . . The author will not allow anything terrible in the roaring of a lion, or the growl of a tiger, or pleasant in the notes of birds, except so far as we have been habituated to consider them as expressions of the habits of those different animals. In this most of his readers will probably think he has warped his natural feelings by the love of system; as well as where he asserts that colours have nothing intrinsically beautiful or expressive. Is not everyone sensible, for instance, of the brilliancy, beauty and even cheerfulness given to a winter landscape covered with snow, though the associated ideas are all gloomy, dreary and cheerless? The author even asserts that the blind may receive the same delight from the ideas which they associate with colours that they do who see;

which he instances in Dr. Blacklock.[1] Surely this is going contrary to the common sense of all mankind. When Blacklock in his poems speaks of the glow of the evening sky, or of the purple year, can he feel the emotions Thomson did, when he had been feasting his eyes with the varied tints that accompany the setting sun, or the warm colouring spread over the face of vernal nature? The blind poet may, by long habitual association, use the terms with propriety, but it is a kind of working with unknown quantities. Who does not see that he wants, not an adventitious idea, but the very source and spring of all the beauty his terms are conversant about?

(*Analytical Review*, May 1790, review of Alison's *Essays on the Nature and Principles of Taste*, signed Y. Y.—VII, pp. 27-8)

Beauty and the advance of the Human Mind

A GENUINE perception of Beauty is the highest degree of education, the ultimate polish of man; the master-key of the mind, it makes us better than we were before.

(1825—Lecture XII, p. 41)

Beauty

WHATEVER BE your powers, assume not to legislate on beauty: though always the same herself, her empire is despotic, and subject to the anarchies of despotism, enthroned to-day, dethroned to-morrow: in treating subjects of universal claim, most has been done by leaving most to the reader's and spectator's taste or fancy . . . The Apollo and Medicean Venus are not by all received as the canons of male and female beauty; and Homer's Helen is the finest woman we have read of, merely because he has left her to be made up of the Dulcineas of his readers.[2]

(1788–1818—Corollary to Aphorism 41)

[1] *Dr. Blacklock*: the blind north country poet, Thomas Blacklock (1721–91), was still living when Fuseli alluded to him in the present passage.
[2] Cp. Burke *On the Sublime and Beautiful* (1756), V, 5, where the account of Helen in the third Iliad is thus commented on: 'Here is not one word said

ON *beauty* I do not mean to perplex you or myself with abstract ideas,[1] and the romantic reveries of Platonic philosophy, or to inquire whether it be the result of a simple or complex principle. As a local idea, beauty is a despotic princess, and subject to the anarchies of despotism, enthroned to-day, dethroned to-morrow. The beauty we acknowledge is that harmonious whole of the human frame, that unison of parts to one end, which enchants us; the result of the standard set by the great masters of our art, the ancients, and confirmed by the submissive verdict of modern imitation.

(1801—Lecture I, pp. 21–22)

THOSE WHO have assigned to the plastic arts beauty, strictly so called, as the ultimate end of imitation, have circumscribed the whole by a part. . . . Beauty alone fades to insipidity; and, like possession, cloys.

(1788–1818—Aphorisms 40 and 42)

Beauty and Expression—Winckelmann and the Germans

ABOUT THE middle of the last century the German critics established at Rome began to claim the exclusive privilege of teaching the art, and to form a complete system of antique style. The verdicts of Mengs and Winckelmann became the oracles of Antiquaries, Dilettanti and artists from the Pyrenees

of the particulars of her beauty; nothing which can in the least help us to any precise idea of her person; yet we are much more touched by this manner of mentioning her than by those long and laboured descriptions of Helen, whether handed down by tradition or formed by fancy, which are to be met with in some authors.' And also Reynolds' VIIIth Discourse (1778): 'A great part of the beauty of the celebrated description of Eve in Milton's *Paradise Lost* consists in using only general, indistinct expressions, every reader making out the detail according to his own particular imagination.'

[1] This is aimed against Mengs and Winckelmann, especially against the opening chapter of Mengs' *Reflections on Beauty and Taste*, in which Plato's definition of Beauty as a reminiscence of supreme perfection is quoted from the *Phaedrus*.

to the utmost North of Europe, have been detailed, and are not without their influence here. Winckelmann was the parasite of the fragments that fell from the conversation or the tablets of Mengs.[1] . . . He reasoned himself into frigid reveries and Platonic dreams on beauty. As far as the taste or the instructions of his tutor directed him, he is right, whenever they are, and between his own learning and the tuition of the other, his history of art delivers a specious system and a prodigious number of useful observations. He has not, however, in his regulation of epochs, discriminated styles and masters with the precision, attention and acumen, which, from the advantages of his situation and habits, might have been expected; and disappoints us as often by meagreness, neglect, and confusion, as he offends by laboured and inflated rhapsodies on the most celebrated monuments of art. To him Germany owes the shackles of her artists, and the narrow limits of their aim; from him they have learnt to substitute the means for the end, and by a hopeless chase after what they call beauty, to lose what alone can make beauty interesting, expression and mind.

(1820—Introduction to *Lectures*, pp. 13–14)

Beauty and Expression

EXPRESSION ALONE can invest beauty with supreme and lasting command over the eye. On beauty, unsupported by vigour and expression, Homer dwells less than on active deformity; he tells us in three lines that Nireus[2] led three ships, his parentage, his form, his effeminacy; but opens up in Thersites a source of comedy and entertainment. Raphael not only subjected beauty to expression, but, at the command of invention, degraded it into a handmaid of deformity: thus the flowers of infancy and youth, virility and old age, are scattered round the temple-gate, to impress us more by comparison with the distorted beings that

[1] Winckelmann himself acknowledged in a published letter known to Fuseli that Mengs had given him great assistance in the whole technical part of his *History of the Arts of the Ancients*.

[2] Nireus, the handsomest of the Greeks before Troy; *see Iliad*, II, 671.

crawl before and defy the powers of every other hand but the one delegated by Omnipotence.[1]

(1788–1818—Aphorism 99 and Corollary)

'Proportion' or 'expression' the secret of Greek superiority in art?

Innumerable longer passages in Fuseli's *Lectures* appear with no variations at all, or with only immaterial variations, also in the *Aphorisms*. In the present case, however, the difference between the two versions is remarkable: that of the *Aphorisms* shows Fuseli substantially conforming in his attitude towards Greek art with the conventional Neo-Classical views of the Winckelmann school, while the version of the same passage in the *Lectures* shows him strongly dissociating himself from those views. It is impossible to establish which is the earlier, which the later version, owing to the very long period over which Fuseli is known to have worked on the text of the *Aphorisms*. Probably the version of the *Aphorisms* is here the later one.

THE PRE-EMINENCE of ancient art ... was less the result of superior powers than of simplicity of aim and uniformity of pursuit. The Helladic and the Ionian schools appear to have concurred in directing their instruction to the grand principle of *form and expression*: this was the stamen[2] which they drew out into one immense connected web.

(1801—Lecture II)

THE SUPERIORITY of the Greeks seems not so much the result of climate and society as of the simplicity of their end and the uniformity of their means. If they had schools, the Ionian, that of Athens and of Sicyon appear to have directed their instruction to one grand principle, *proportion*: this was the stamen which they drew out into one immense connected web; whilst modern

---

[1] Raphael's cartoon of St. Peter and St. John healing the lame man before the Temple.

[2] *Stamen*—the warp of a textile fabric; a favourite word of Fuseli's.

art, with its schools of designers, colourists, machinists,[1] eclectics, is but a tissue of adventitious threads.

(1788–1818—Aphorism 148)

Classical Art as an art of Expression[2]

'Yesterday after dinner Northcote had a contest with Fuseli, who insisted that all modern artists, even Raphael, were weak in the power of giving expression to their figures. Northcote upheld a contrary opinion. He said the discriminations of character were better given by the moderns, but by the ancients, as far as we know of their work, little of that kind was to be seen. . . . Fuseli became impatient and left the room' (*Farington Diary*, 12 April 1807)

THE EXPRESSION of the ancients, from the heights and depths of the sublime, descended and emerged to search every nook of the human breast; from the ambrosial locks of Zeus, and the maternal phantom fluttering round Ulysses, to the half-slain mother, shuddering lest the infant should suck the blood from her palsied nipple, and the fond attention of Penelope dwelling on the relation of her returned son.

The expression of the ancients explored nature even in the mute recesses, in the sullen organs of the brute; from the Argus of Ulysses, to the lamb, the symbol of expiatory resignation, on an altar, and to the untameable feature of the toad.

[1] *Machinists*—really scene-painters; Fuseli regularly alluded to the painters now known as *Baroque* by this uncomplimentary term, and it enjoyed a certain currency in this sense up to the middle of the nineteenth century. Fuseli takes the term over from Mengs.

[2] Winckelmann had established it as one of the main axioms of the new classicism that ancient art consistently sacrificed expression to beauty. Fuseli stands isolated in his age with his paradoxical reversal of this axiom. Preference for expression and character in art, as opposed to beauty, normally went hand in hand with a preference for mediaeval as against ancient art. Fuseli has never anything but contempt for mediaeval art, but he contrives to make ancient Greek art mean *for him* what mediaeval art meant for those who rejected the new classicism and all its works.

The expression of the ancients roamed all the fields of licit and illicit pleasure; from the petulance with which Ctesilochus exhibited the pangs of a Jupiter delivered by celestial midwives, to the libidinous sports of Parrhasius, and from these to the indecent caricature which furnished Crassus with a repartee.

(1788–1817—Corollary to Aphorism 92)

Character or Pathos as opposed to Beauty—the painter as the teller of a tale

PERFECT BEAUTY he has not represented; no face of Raphael's is perfectly beautiful; no figure of his, in the abstract, possesses the proportions that could raise it to a standard of imitation: form to him was only a vehicle of character or pathos, and to those he adapted it in a mode and with a truth which leaves all attempts at emendation hopeless. . . . His expression, in strict unison with and decided by character, whether calm, animated, agitated, convulsed, or absorbed by the inspiring passion, unmixed and pure, never contradicts its cause, equally remote from tameness and grimace: the moment of his choice never suffers the action to stagnate or to expire; it is the moment of transition, the crisis big with the past and pregnant with the future.—If, separately taken, the line of Raphael has been excelled in correctness, elegance, and energy; his colour far surpassed in tone, and truth, and harmony; his masses in roundness, and his chiaroscuro in effect—considered as instruments of pathos, they have never been equalled; and in composition, invention, expression, and the power of telling a story, he has never been approached.

(1801—Lecture II, pp. 88–9)

Expression and Characterisation

TO MAKE a face speak clearly and with propriety, it must not only be well constructed, but have its own exclusive character.

Emblematic Frontispiece
to Fuseli's *Remarks on Rousseau*

Though the element of the passions be the same in all, they neither speak in all with equal energy, nor are circumscribed by equal limits. Though joy be joy, and anger anger, the joy of the sanguine is not that of the phlegmatic, nor the anger of the melancholy that of the fiery character; and the discriminations established by complexion are equally conspicuous in those of climate, habit, education, and rank. Expression has its classes .... The tremulous emotion of Hector's breast when he approaches Ajax, is not the palpitation of Paris when he discovers Menelaus; the frown of the Hercynian Phantom may repress the ardour, but cannot subdue the dignity of Drusus; the fear of Marius cannot sink to the panic of the Cimber who drops the dagger at entering his prison, nor the astonishment of Hamlet degenerate into the fright of vulgar fear.

(1805—Lecture V, pp. 256–7)

The metamorphic workings of extreme passion

ONLY THEN, when passion and suffering become too big for utterance, the wisdom of ancient art has borrowed a feature from tranquillity, though not its air. For every being seized by an enormous passion, be it joy or grief, or fear sunk to despair, loses the character of its own individual expression, and is absorbed by the power of the feature that attracts it. Niobe and her family are assimilated by extreme anguish; Ugolino is petrified by the fate that swept the stripling at his foot, and sweeps in pangs the rest. The metamorphoses of ancient mythology are founded on this principle, are allegoric. Clytia, Biblis, Salmacis, Narcissus, tell only the resistless power of sympathetic attraction.

(1805—Lecture V, pp. 259–60)

Exaggeration

> 'Conscious of not having all the strength he
> wished, he endeavoured to make up for
> it by violence and pretension. He carried
> this so far as to look fiercer than usual,
> when he sat for his picture. . . . His notion
> of repose was like that of Pistol: "Now,
> Pistol, lay thy head in Fury's lap" ' (Leigh
> Hunt on Fuseli in *Lord Byron and Some of His
> Contemporaries*)

THE FEAR of not being understood, or felt, makes some invigorate expression to grimace.[1]

(1788–1818—Aphorism 79)

---

[1] Fuseli has here taken up into the *Aphorisms* a phrase from his anonymous
article in the *Universal Museum* of February 1768, where Michelangelo is
charged with having 'bloated expression into grimace'. This circumstance
helps to establish the correctness of the attribution of that article to Fuseli.

SECTION TWO

NATURE AND ART

Fuseli's partisanship for the classical Canon of Proportion and his notorious words 'Nature always puts me out!' might, taken by themselves, lead one to suppose that he either, like such classicists as Mengs, Winckelmann and Reynolds, looked down on nature with the superiority of the complacent believer in abstract mind and in human civilisation, or else, like Blake, repudiated her with mystical abhorrence as 'Satan's Wife' (Blake's *Laocoon* sheet). In reality Fuseli is very far from rejecting nature either classically or romantically, either as a poor makeshift or as a diabolical machination. He surprises us by again and again proclaiming the absolute supremacy of nature over art and genius, and even by championing 'warm, fleshy, genial life'. He is able to make room for these conceptions inside his classical theory (though not really to reconcile them with it) by appealing to Pliny's anecdote of Lysippus and the 'school of nature'. Often, indeed, he insists so emphatically and exclusively on the heroic idealising function of art, that the least deviation into anything like realism must necessarily appear a betrayal and an abomination—then nature is nothing more than a 'collective idea'. Often, however, he becomes, in theory at least, the advocate of an unequivocally realistic procedure in art. The realism he thus defends is usually assigned a modest position among the 'inferior branches' of art, but it can also sometimes happen that he exalts it above idealisation altogether, dismissing the idealiser as a mere 'mannerist', or deploring Michelangelo's departures from the 'modesty and variety of Nature'. He is sometimes unmistakably conscious of his own inconsistency in this connexion, disturbed by it and anxious to straighten it out with the intermediary conception of 'imitations of essential nature' (*see* pp. 230–5). What is curious is that he remains quite unaware how effectively all his arguments in favour of the

307

'school of nature' might be used to defend much in modern art that he has unhesitatingly condemned and still continues to condemn. He exhorts the artist to 'dive in the crowd' but still cannot forgive Rembrandt and many other great painters for having dived into the crowd. It never seems to occur to him that the realistic principle he sometimes upholds might be applicable to modern art, nor does he ever give a single example from among the moderns to illustrate what he has in mind. He is concerned only with the vanished paintings of Lysippus, as he reconstructs them in his imagination, with the so-called *Gladiator* of Agasias, and, it may well be assumed, with some of his own experimental drawings.

The Method of Lysippus

IF WE mistake not, Pliny tells us that Lysippus adopted a method of his own, and yet untried by his predecessors, to excel. They, said he, made men as they *are*; that is, they gave the substance of the human frame. A figure had been produced by Polycletus, called the canon or standard rule, which probably united the principles of design of the schools that preceded Lysippus. The exclusive imitation of these principles introduced a squareness of forms, a stern way of marking, which soon deviated into manner; all their figures were in fact one man; the discriminations of character and surface, those resources of variety, were lost in a kind of monumental style. Such seems on the whole to have been the state of art, when Lysippus inquired of Eupompus, what method of his predecessors he advised him to imitate, and musing on the painter's answer, which pointed out nature herself instead of her representative, he soon discovered what way was left for him to become original and, in some respects, superior to former artists. *In some respects*, we say, because the method he pursued, being less ideal, could not excel the sublimity of Phidias or Polycletus. This method was to flatter the eye with illusion by imitating the graces of flesh and surface, to disguise the transition of muscle to muscle, the insertion of limb into limb, and to clothe the bones more genially; thus, diffusing an air of reality over his figures, he pronounced himself, with truth, the first who made man as he *appears*. His figures were probably to those of Phidias, Polycletus and perhaps even Praxiteles what the Gladiator, as he is miscalled, of Agasias, and the Apollo are to the Dioscuri on Monte Cavallo,[1] or to the Lapithae and the groups on the friezes of the temples at Athens.

(*Analytical Review*, June 1794, review of R. Payne Knight's *The Landscape, a Didactic Poem*, signed R. R.—XIX, pp. 177–8)

Originality, the classical canons and the variety of Nature

THE LEADING principle of Eupompus may be traced in the advice which he gave to Lysippus (as preserved by Pliny), whom, when consulted on a standard of imitation, he directed to the contemplation of human variety in the multitude of the characters that were passing by, with the axiom 'that Nature herself was to be imitated, not an artist'. Excellence, said Eupompus, is thy aim, such excellence as that of Phidias and Polycletus; but it is not obtained by the servile imitation of works, however perfect, without mounting to the principle which raised them to that height; that principle apply to thy purpose, there fix thy aim. He who, with the same freedom of access to Nature as another man, contents himself to approach her only through his medium, has resigned his birth-right and originality together; his master's manner will be his style. If Phidias and Polycletus have discovered the substance and established the permanent principle of the human frame, they have not exhausted the variety of human appearances and human character; if they have abstracted the forms of majesty and those of beauty, Nature, compared with their works, will point out a grace that has been left for thee; if they have preoccupied man as he *is*, be thine to give him that air with which

[1] The statues on Monte Cavallo were of the greatest importance to Fuseli, especially in the anatomical proportions and the attitudes he cultivated. By generally accepted standards he greatly overrated these works. His judgments on them and on other outstanding works of classical sculpture fluctuate curiously. *See above*, Part IV, Section 1.

he actually *appears*. Such was the advice of Eupompus: less lofty, less ambitious than what the departed epoch of genius would have dictated, but better suited to the times, and better to his pupil's mind.

(1801—Lecture I, pp. 59–60)

The School of Nature

DIVE IN the crowd, meet beauty: follow vigour, compare character, snatch the feature that moves unobserved and the sudden burst of passion—and you are at the school of nature with Lysippus.

(1788–1818—Aphorism 139)

Warm, fleshy, genial life

IT IS to life we must recur,—to warm, fleshy, genial life,—for animated forms. To Nature and life Zeuxis applied, to embody the forms of Polycletus and Alcamenes: and what was the prerogative of Lysippus, but to give the air, the *morbidezza*, the soft transitions, the illusions of palpitating life, to bronze and marble? The pedantry of geometrically *straight* lines is not only no idealism, it is a solecism in Nature. *Organisation*, your object, is inseparable from *life*; *motion* from organisation: where organisation and life are, there is a seat of life, a *punctum saliens*, acting through veins and branching arteries, consequently with *pulsation*, and by that, undulating and rounding the passages of parts to parts. Of the milliards of commas, or points, that Nature mediately or immediately produces, no two are alike; how, then, could she produce straight lines,[1] which are all similar, and by their nature cut, divide, interrupt, destroy?

(1825—Lecture X, p. 388)

---

[1] Cp. Blake: 'They say there is no straight line in Nature; this is a lie, like all that they say' (Additional Passage to *Public Address*).

The Mannerist and Nature

A MANNERIST is the paltry epitomist of Nature's immense volume; a juggler, who pretends to mimic the infinite variety of her materials by the vain display of a few fragments of crockery.

(1810—Lecture VII, pp. 322–3)

Art and the general processes of History

NATURE HERSELF has set her barriers between age and age, between genius and genius, which no mortal overleaps. . . .

(1825—Lecture XII, p. 55)

Nature and Art

TO ASSERT the claims of nature against the usurpations of art . . . is the preceptive part of the poem. . . . This our author has executed in a manner . . . which oftener destroys than establishes, and rather lops than restrains the hand of art. This perhaps was inseparable from the present state of the subject; the meretricious taste of the age might deserve a censor not less rigid; and the author would be considered as having done much, had he done no more than persuaded us to recur to the simple appearances of nature, before we listened to the hireling suggestions of art. . . . But after all, time is the great specific for re-obtaining in their former simplicity the shorn or sophisticated graces of nature. . . .

(*Analytical Review*, June 1794, review of R. Payne Knight's *The Landscape, a Didactic Poem*, signed R. R.—XIX, p. 174)

*Time the only legitimate mellower—the faked patina
of Parmigiano*

WITH INCREDIBLE force of chiaroscuro, he united bland effects
and fascinating hues, but their frequent ruins teach the important lesson, that the mixtures which anticipate the beauties of
time are big with the seeds of premature decay.

(1801—Lecture II, p. 106)

SECTION THREE

THE PRAISE AND THE PROBLEMS
OF GENIUS

Even in an age which was at bottom principally occupied with defining and glorifying genius, Fuseli stands out as a man with something of his own to say on that theme and a unique way of saying it. After his disappointment in Rousseau, he firmly set his face against the predominant tendency, which, in Germany in particular, assumed more and more exalted forms, to regard the man of genius as an incarnate god and to establish around him a new religion. 'It is ludicrous', he insists, 'to give a consequence to the arts which they can never possess.' 'To say that a mean or vicious character cannot arrive at eminence in art, is to say that a villain cannot possess exquisite organs' (*see above*, Part II, Section 7). Again and again he dwells on 'that unaccountable weakness incident to the greatest powers' (Lecture II). He does not even spare Michelangelo, the man of genius he venerates most and in whom he so often sees his own ideal self. At the same time, however, he carefully avoids all myths of the Prometheus or Lucifer type in speaking of the afflictions, dangers and tragedies of genius; the Dionysian and daemonic hyperbole of such works as Goethe's *Faust*, Hölderlin's *Empedocles* or Byron's *Manfred* is quite missing from all his utterances on these themes. But while always denying that there is anything supernatural or superhuman about genius, Fuseli pays to it the most glowing tributes for what it achieves, and also for what it unsuccessfully aspires towards, within the limits of nature and humanity. Like Blake, he thoroughly dislikes Reynolds's sober conception of genius. 'Reynolds . . . had the affectation to deny genius', Knowles records him as saying. It is remarkable, however, that he in his later years came near to accepting Reynolds's view, saying that 'without unwearied toil . . . genius is a 'bubble'. His declaration in the *History of Art*, that the true artist may be said to owe his power to study and not to nature, is by no means the piece of irony one might at first suspect it to be. Here also Fuseli's views fluctuated considerably.

The Language of Genius

THERE ARE, in the walks of science, certain characteristics of true genius. Suppose it even employed in the highroads of argument or composition—there is a light of method, a chain of truths, a nerve of expression, so candid a manner, the style glows so genially, palpitates so warmly, faints away so pallid, or mixes so meltingly with your heart, that you cry out: 'There is more than head, art, memory—there is truth, sentiment, soul!' Such is the language of genius; and do you think it employs another, when virtue is the theme? Nothing is so easily found out as moral copies and originals. Memory is not genius; in that soil genius grows not. . . . 'Twas the heart, 'twas strength of mind, 'twas the enthusiasm of benevolence that scattered flowers over *Emile*.

(1767—*Remarks on Rousseau*, pp. 49–50)

Exalted aims defended against the advocates of mediocrity

THE STRINGS of the soul can never be wound up to an extreme; they slacken by themselves. A mediocrity of models blasts virtue, as it does genius. The musician forms himself upon the loftiest flights of winged voice, the deepest thunders of the bass, or explores the labyrinths of symphony. The painter roams over the Elysium of ideal beauty, and dips his pencil in the rainbow. The poet's eye

in a fine frenzy rolling,
Does glance from heaven to earth, from earth to heaven.

314

Whoever told a young poet not to study Homer, or a philosopher to lay by Plato, because there was rather no hope of their rivalling them? Is the warrior to cock his eye at the wall with Coeur de Lion, to break his head against it with Charles XII, or, with Frederick at Planian, to calculate what millions of drops of blood will run down a perpendicular rock of battle, and how many will dung its soil, and be imbibed by its hemlock and nightshade?[1] Nay, even the nestling of a shop, does he glow for anything on this side of a plum,[2] or meditate bankruptcy? And why will you, under pretence of high-soaring impossibility, forbid man to study himself, his elements? Why drown in your catscalls the legislation of humanity? Why insinuate to fathers and mothers that the heir of quality and estate need not be a man; that in Rome's politest days nobody was sure of giving his dinner, no subscriber to the assembly in Caesar Street, St. Romulus's, of enjoying either ball or supper, however advertised to be opened at eight and to be on the table exactly at twelve, as long as that eternal Cato's brow smote good company and pleasure with his horrid stern *je ne sais quoi*?

(1767—*Remarks on Rousseau*, pp. 41–3)

Natural limitations not to be transcended by the imitation of great models

A comment on Uvedale Price's suggestion that the landscape gardeners should ennoble their taste by studying the great painters of Landscape.

WE CONFESS our doubts about the efficiency of such helps as are pointed out to them in the works of the great masters of land-

---

[1] Three discouraging examples of military failure and disaster: Richard Lion-heart's abandonment of the siege of Jerusalem in 1191; the killing of Charles XII of Sweden by a cannon-ball at the siege of Frederikshald in 1718; and an anecdote of Frederick the Great scratching figures in the sand with his stick at Nimburg (*not* at the nearby Planian) after his serious defeat at Kolin in 1757.

[2] *A plum*—obsolete slang term for a fortune of £100,000.

scape. *Recti cultus pectora roborant*[1] may be an useful axiom in taste as well as in morals, where hearts are found to feel and heads to apply; but when we reflect that Albert Durer gave to his Adam the breast and feet of a Mercury or Meleager, whilst he borrowed for him a pair of arms from a cobbler; that he set his Eve on a body, legs and feet not unworthy of a nymph, and applied to a scullion or laundress to furnish her with arms, wrists and hands; when we discover in every print of Andrea Mantegna the imitation of some antique, coupled with excrescences of clumsiness or meagre deformity; when it cannot be disguised that Andrea del Sarto and Jacopo da Pontormo, from pupils of the ancients and Michelangelo, shrunk into tame copyists of the haggard style exported from Nuremberg to Tuscany; when we reflect on all this, we are tempted to consider the study of Claude and Poussin as extremely uninteresting to men guided by precedent and fashion; though we seriously think the public owe gratitude to the writer who so ably endeavours to correct their taste.

> (*Analytical Review*, November 1794, review of Uvedale Price's *Essay on the Picturesque*, signed R. R.—XX, p. 266)

Genius, Imitation and Nature

IT WOULD be injustice to suppose that ... our author could mean to depreciate the benign influence of original genius or to insinuate aught against the necessity of its periodical appearance. ... Who better than our historian knows that, if nature be inexhaustible in her resources and productions, and genius be merely a power of seizing and representing with clearness some of her features, the appearance of one man of genius can no more check the perceptions than preclude the existence of another? He who takes Homer or Michelangelo for his model, adopts him merely as his medium to see nature more distinctly or on a grander scale; he imitates without copying. ...

> (*Analytical Review*, December 1796, review of Roscoe's *Lorenzo de' Medici*, signed Z. Z.—XXIV, p. 564; Knowles, I. pp. 144–5)

[1] Horace, *Odes*, IV, 4—a favourite quotation of Fuseli's, who very freely translates it himself in the third chapter of his *Remarks on Rousseau*, 'and liberty to virtue steel the soul'.

Genius

OF *genius* I shall speak with reserve, for no word has been more indiscriminately confounded; by genius I mean that power which enlarges the circle of human knowledge, which discovers new materials of nature or combines the known with novelty, whilst *talent* arranges, cultivates, polishes the discoveries of genius.

(1801—Lecture I, p. 23)

Genius: the one-sidedness of all human greatness

A CHARACTER of equal universal power is not a human character—and the nearest approach to perfection can only be in carrying to excellence one great quality with the least alloy of defects.

(1805—Lecture VI, pp. 277–8)

No Laodicean compromises with the absolutist claims of great genius

THE MORE finished a character, the more discriminated by his actions and turn of thought from his contemporaries, he pursues paths of his own so much the more he attracts, so much the more he repels; the ardour of the one is equal to the violence of the other: he is not merely disliked, he is detested by all who have no sense for him; whilst by those who enter his train of thought, or sympathise with him, he is adored. Indifference has no share in what relates to him, it is a softer word for antipathy . . . Where yes or no must decide, the mouth that can form neither, rejects. The principles, the style of Michelangelo are of that so closely-connected magnitude, that they are either all true or all false: pretended gold is either gold or not . . . If Michelangelo did not establish art on a solid basis, he subverted

317

it; he can claim only the heresies of paradox and receive their reward—disgust.

(1808—*History of Art*, pp. 219–20)

Aphorisms on Genius

HEAVEN AND EARTH, advantages and obstacles, conspire to educate genius (Aphorism 11).

GENIUS WITHOUT bias is a stream without direction: it inundates all, and ends in stagnation (Aphorism 14).

MISCONCEPTION OF its own powers is the injurious attendant of genius, and the most severe remembrancer of its vanity. Much of Leonardo da Vinci's life evaporated in useless experiment and quaint research. Michelangelo perplexed the limbs of grandeur with the minute ramifications of anatomy; Raphael forsook humanity to people mythologic deserts with clumsy gods and clumsier goddesses; Shakespeare, trusting time and chance with Hamlet and Othello, revised a frozen sonnet[1] or fondled his Adonis; whilst Milton dropped the trumpet that had astonished Hell, left Paradise, and introduced a pedagogue to Heaven. When genius is surprised by such lethargic moments, we can forget that Johnson wrote *Irene*, and Hogarth made a solemn fool of Paul (Aphorism 19 and Corrollary).

DISTINGUISH BETWEEN genius and singularity of character; an artist of mediocrity may be an odd man: let the nature of works be your guide (Aphorism 31).

HE HAS more than genius—he is a hero—who can check his powers in their full career, merely not to crush the feeble on his road (Aphorism 113).

[1] In his review of Steevens's *Shakespeare* Fuseli quotes without dissent the editor's words: 'We have not reprinted the sonnets of Shakespeare, because the strongest act of parliament that could be framed would fail to compel readers into their service' (*Analytical Review*, XIX, 350).

A COPIOUS measure of will is sometimes assigned to ordinary and contracted minds; whilst the greatest faculties as frequently evaporate in indolence and languor (Aphorism 128).

HE IS a prince of artists and of men who knows the moment when his work is done. Next to him who can finish, is he who has hid from you that he cannot (Aphorisms 130 and 131).

GENIUS KNOWS no partner. All partnership is deleterious to poetry and art: one must rule (Aphorism 137).

THE LESSONS of disappointment, humiliation and blunder, impress more than those of a thousand masters (Aphorism 140).

MEDIOCRITY DESPATCHES and exults; the man of talent congratulates himself on the success of his exertions; Genius alone mourns over defeated expectation (Aphorism 205).

THERE ARE moments when all are men, and only men, and ought to be no more; but the artist who, when his daily task is over, can lock his meditation up with his tools, ranks with mechanics (Aphorism 229).

(1788–1818—*Aphorisms*)

Genius

IT IS the lot of Genius to be opposed, and to be invigorated by opposition. All extremes touch each other: frigid praise and frigid censure wait on easily attainable or common powers; but the successful adventurer in the realms of Discovery, in spite of the shrugs, checks and sneers of the timid, the malign and the envious, leaps on an unknown or long lost shore, ennobles it with his name, and grasps immortality.[1]

(1825—Lecture XI, p. 18)

[1] This passage, in a somewhat shorter form, constitutes the thirteenth of Fuseli's *Aphorisms*.

The Artist and the World

... NOTHING that ennobles a man was ever produced by gold.
... No geniune work of Art ever was or ever can be produced,
but for its own sake; if the artist do not conceive to please himself, he never will finish to please the world.

(1825—Lecture XII, p. 54)

Invariable Rules

IF ART be a complete system of invariable rules, he only is a
master of Art who substantiates its precepts by equal uniformity
of execution and taste; and ... he can only be said ... to be
indebted to 'study' and not to 'nature', if he put himself at last
in possession of it.

(1808—*History of Art,* p. 256)

Genius and hard work

... remember that, though even the best directed labour cannot supply what Nature has refused, still it remains an experiment uniformly sanctioned by time, that without unwearied
toil, obstinate perseverance and submissive resignation, neither
the theory nor the practice of the art can be fully acquired, and
that without them genius is a bubble and talent a trifle.

(1825—Lecture X, pp. 386-7)

SECTION FOUR

THE ARTIST'S PERSONALITY
IN RELATIONSHIP TO HIS WORK

'But, of course, only those who have personality and emotions know what it means to want to escape from these things' (T. S. Eliot)

One of the classical doctrines to which Fuseli attached particular importance was that of the impersonal character of great art. He can hardly have failed to realise that everything he himself drew or wrote was marked by extreme idiosyncrasy; indeed, there can be no doubt that he consciously cultivated his own peculiarities. But on principle he was opposed to the obtrusion of personality in art. He recommends as an ideal model the objective style of Caesar; but cannot help feeling himself in practice much more strongly attracted by the highly subjective manner of Tacitus, to which he nevertheless expressly denies the 'highest praise', just because it is so personal. This discrepancy arises again and again in Fuseli's critical judgments, both on the plastic arts and on literature. Homer is perhaps the only artist amongst those to whom he is devoted, in whose work the immediate irresistible appeal he feels is in full conformity with his abstract standard of what *should* be. One is never quite convinced that the 'impersonal' Apollo of Belvedere really means as much to him as the extremely personal work of Michelangelo—and yet in theory he is prepared, as he necessarily must be prepared, to subordinate Michelangelo himself to the Apollo, if it comes to the point, and to find him wanting, because he has not the serene impersonal detachment of the classical ideal: 'The Daemons of Dante had too early tinctured his fancy to admit in their full majesty the Gods of

Homer and Phidias.' As a rule, admittedly, he prefers to ignore this particular dilemma—the oddness one is conscious of in his utterances on Michelangelo, and also in his criticisms and illustrations of Shakespeare and Milton, arises largely from his generally ignoring their distinctive personalities as far as possible, and treating their art as though it really were classically impersonal—which results, of course, not in truly impersonal interpretations of them, but in their being totally, often most incongruously dyed with the peculiar tincture of Fuseli's own temperament. Classical impersonality is certainly the last thing anybody will nowadays find or want to find in Fuseli's own work. It is by his eccentricity—anything but a classical quality —that he lives now, and it was by his eccentricity also that he fascinated or repelled his contemporaries. This is true both of those who, like Haydon and Hunt, felt a curious discrepancy between the impression his actual presence made and that produced by his paintings, and of those who, with Farington and Hoppner, found him a very forcible instance' of 'Men being like their works' (*Farington Diary*, 13 May 1803). Even in his theoretical writings Fuseli is once at least forced, in spite of his belief in impersonal standards, to consider the possibility that nothing remains but 'to transpose *yourself* into your subject', to 'paint one's own mind'.

Personal intervention of the poet in his work

IT WERE to be wished, the example of Homer, whose own feelings on what he relates never exceed the single exclamation of νήπιος, who nowhere appears himself, had been better attended to by his followers: even Paradise Lost would have acquired additional dignity by such conduct. Not that we should be willing to sacrifice to the observation of this rule those pathetic digressions with which the blind bard has endeared himself to our memory. We mean the unbecoming epithets, the Christian's indignation descending to vulgar passion, which even he has too much indulged. . . .

(*Analytical Review*, June 1792, review of Cumberland's *Calvary*, signed R. R.—XIII, p. 126)

The seeming anonymity of the greatest art

TO HAVE leisure to think of the author, when we read, or of the artist, when we behold, proves that the work of either is of an inferior class; we have neither time to inquire after Homer's birth-place or rank, when Andromache departs from her husband, nor stoop to look for the inscription of the artist's name when we stand before the Apollo.

> (*Analytical Review*, January 1793, review of Cowper's *Homer*, signed Z. Z.—XV, p. 2. Knowles, I, p. 83)

Personality in Literature and Art

TACITUS SPEAKS like a man who has power. . . . With readers of mere taste and whom circumstances preclude from making use of his precepts, he leaves, however, more an impression of himself, than of the facts he relates; he is read and studied not so much for what he tells, as for the manner in which he tells it; and that this in works of literature and art is not the highest praise, we believe needs no proof.

> (*Analytical Review*, November 1793, review of Murphy's *Tacitus*, signed Z. Z.—XVII, p. 243)

Advice on Style

FUSELI SPOKE of James Moore's acct. of the War in Spain. . . . The letters of Sir John Moore He sd. are admirable. 'They are like the writing of Caesar, and as good, simple, clean and classical.' . . . 'I wish,' sd. He, 'that James Moore[1] cd. write as well; but He has done very well. I recommended Him not to allow *Himself* to appear in the work, but to suppress His feelings.'

> (*Farington Diary*, 3 July 1809)

---

[1] James Moore (1762–1860), brother of Sir John Moore of Corunna. Fuseli was a great friend of the Moore family.

The intrinsic and the acquired qualities of an artist[1]

JUDGE NOT an artist from the exertions of accidental vigour or some unpremeditated flights of fancy, but from the uniform tenor, the never-varying principle of his works: the line and style of Titian sometimes expand themselves like those of Michelangelo; the heads and groups of Raphael sometimes glow and palpitate with Titian's tints; and there are masses of both united in Correggio: ... But these sudden irradiations, these flashes of power are only exceptions from their wonted principles; pathos and character own Raphael for their master, colour remains the domain of Titian, and harmony the sovereign mistress of Correggio.

(1788–1818—Aphorism 170 and Lecture II)

Individuality and absolute standards in Art

EVERY ARTIST has, or ought to have, a character or system of his own; if, instead of referring that to the test of nature, you judge him by your own packed notions, or arraign him at the tribunal of schools which he does not recognize—you degrade the dignity of art, and add another fool to the herd of Dilettanti.

(1788–1818—Corollary to Aphorism 18)

Individual excellence

IF FINISHING be to terminate all the parts of a performance in an equal degree, no artist ever finished his work. A great part of conception or execution is always sacrificed to some individual excellence which either he possesses or thinks he possesses. The colourist makes lines only the vehicle of colour; the designer subordinates hue to his line; the man of breadth or

---

[1] This is based on a passage in Article VI in the third section of Mengs' *Reflexions on Beauty and Taste*.

chiaroscuro overwhelms sometimes both and the subject itself to produce effect.

(1788–1818—Aphorism 132)

The Painter of Oneself

IN FOLLOWING too closely a model, there is danger in mistaking the individual for Nature herself; in relying only on the schools, the deviation into manner seems inevitable: what then remains, but to transpose *yourself* into your subject?

(1788–1818—Aphorism 144)

The Painter of his Own Mind

NO PAINTER ever painted his own mind so forcibly as Michelangelo Amerigi, surnamed Il Caravaggi. To none nature ever set limits with a more decided hand. Darkness gave him light; into his melancholy cell light stole only with a pale reluctant ray, or broke on it, as flashes on a stormy night. The most vulgar forms he recommended by ideal light and shade, and a tremendous breadth of manner.

(1801—Lecture II, p. 100)

SECTION FIVE

INWARDNESS, IMAGINATION
AND THE INFINITE

As early as 1775 Fuseli singled out the too exclusive and immediate cult of inwardness, of disembodied floating emotions, moods and intuitions, as the great weakness and danger of contemporary German poetry, and it is this that he still has in mind, when he in 1820 inveighs against the evil consequences for German art of Winckelmann's 'frigid reveries and Platonic dreams of beauty'. Against all such tendencies—and they may fairly be designated as specifically Romantic tendencies—he sets up the conception of the 'Image' and of 'Expression'. Within these limits, however, the inward still retains great importance for him—only he always insists that it must be fully 'embodied', that is to say, set forth in sharply outlined expressive form.[1] Knowles records of him: 'Fuseli frequently invented the subjects of his pictures without the aid of the poet or historian . . . these he denominated "philosophical ideas made intuitive, or sentiment personified".' This terminology is prosaic to the point of pedantry, but it is Fuseli's characteristic way of formulating his qualified belief in inwardness as the true source of artistic production. Imagination is a term which he is more at home with, and readily employs with a certain flourish. It is remarkable, however, that he, the great painter of dreams and nightmares, living in a time which was, especially in Germany, very much occupied with the mysteries of the dream-world, only once touches on these questions in his theoretical writ-

[1] R. H. Wilenski, who sees in Fuseli nothing but an imitator of Reynolds, John Brown and Blake, expressly denies him just that *power to externalise experience* which he himself valued and cultivated above all things (*English Painting*, 1933; p. 234 in 1947 reprint).

326

ings, and then has very little to say about them. The Infinite or, as he sometimes terms it, 'Immensity' is for him always felt as the background of all life and activity, and as a goal, legitimate or illegitimate, of human aspiration, sometimes also as an immediate object of human experience, but, unlike the Romantics, he refuses to admit that it can be either represented in art or taken possession of by genius. All such artistic raids on the infinite are as suspect to him as the portrayal of the deity or the belief that art is creation. As far as *grandeur* and the *sublime* art may legitimately go, ought indeed to go, but *immensity* is the prerogative of Nature. Some slight concessions he is willing to make in these matters to Michelangelo's *Creation of Adam* and *Creation of Eve*, and also, though, not without irony, to the cupolas of Correggio, an artist he otherwise shows little enthusiasm for.

The outward and the inward

THE UNINTERRUPTED undulation of outward forms, the waves of life, originate within, and, without being traced to that source, instruct less than confound. The real basis of sight is knowledge, and that knowledge is internal. . . .

(1810—Lecture VII, pp. 320–1)

Imagination and the world of fact

REALITY TEEMS with disappointment for him whose sources of enjoyment spring in the elysium of fancy. The ear absorbed in harmonies of its own creation, is deaf to all external ones.

(1788–1817—Aphorisms 20 and 120)

'Big with the very elements of dreams'

ONE OF the most unexplored regions of art are dreams, and what may be called the personification of sentiment: the Prophets, Sibyls and Patriarchs of Michelangelo are so many branches of one great sentiment. The dream of Raphael is a characteristic representation of a dream; the dream of Michelangelo is moral inspiration, a sublime sentiment.

(1788–1818—Aphorism 231)

327

The finiteness of art, the infinity of nature

'The imagination of the Finite succumbs to Infinity . . .' (Letter of Fuseli's, November 1765)

IF WHAT is finite could grasp infinity, the variety of Nature might be united by individual energy; till then, the attempt to amalgamate her scattered beauties by the imbecility of Art will prove abortive. Genius is the pupil of Nature; perceives, is dazzled by and imperfectly transmits one of her features: thus saw Michelangelo, Raphael, Titian, Correggio; and such were their technic legacies, as inseparable from their attendant flaws, as in equal degrees irreconcilable. That Nature is not subject to decrepitude, is proved by the superiority of modern over ancient science; what hinders modern Art to equal that of classic eras, is the effect of irremovable causes.

(1825—Lecture XI, pp. 7–8)

NATURE FINISHES all, but an attempt to mimic nature's universality palsies the hand of art.

(1806—Lecture IV, p. 234)

Nature and Man

IT IS the privilege of Nature alone to be equal. Man is the slave of a part; the most equal artist is only the first in the list of mediocrity.

(1788–1818—Aphorism 155)

Ambition and the sense of the Infinite

> 'He was a slave to his love of fame, and to nothing else' (Cunningham)

'Digito monstrarier', *'Ille ego'*, *'Dicier hic est'*[1] have, God knows, engendered more glorious deeds for nature, religion and the state, infinitely more, than the idea of the intrinsic beauty of such actions ever would have done. However fleeting the echoes of posthumous fame may be—they still tickle us, and what are certain kinds of tickling other than a profusion of pleasurable sensations, beneath whose buoyant spell all consciousness of succession is lost, whence beatitude arises? Give me the *all-things-at-once sensation* and keep the grovelling pleasure of succession for yourself. . . .

> (Letter to Dälliker, November 1765—Muschg, p. 109, German)

Michelangelo's 'Creation of Adam and Eve'

WHO CAN be so frigid to misconstrue this double image of Omnipotence into mere apposition? Here is the measure of immensity.

> (1801—Lecture III; contracted in the 1820 reprint to: 'Here apposition is the symbol of immensity'—Knowles, II, p. 161; in Fuseli's own *Creation of Eve* for the *Milton Gallery* God is not represented at all)

Correggio's chiaroscuro—'Reality and immensity at once'

IF, STRICTLY speaking, he was not the inventor of . . . *chiaroscuro*

---

[1] Tags from the satire on ambition in *Persius*, I, 28 seq., thus translated by Dryden:

> Oh, but *'tis brave to be admired, to see*
> The crowd with pointing fingers cry *'That's he'* . . .

This letter of Fuseli's contains another allusion to the same passage in *Persius*, see p. 109.

... he fully spanned its measure, and expanded the powers of its harmony through Heaven and earth; in his eye and hand it became the organ of sublimity; the process of his cupolas made it no longer a question whether an art circumscribed by line and figures could convey ideas of reality and immensity at once. Entranced by his spell, and lapped in his elysium, we are not aware of the wide difference between the conception of the medium, the place, space, and mode in which certain beings ought, or may be supposed to move, and that of those beings themselves; and forget, though fully adequate to the first, that Correggio was unequal to the second; that though he could build Heaven, he could not people it.

(1805—Lecture VI, pp. 297–8)

The contemplation of infinity and the conformation of the organs

AND THOUGH perhaps we should be nearer truth by ascribing the cause of Correggio's magic to the happy conformation of his organs, and his calm serenity of mind, than to Platonic ecstasies, a poet might at least be allowed to say 'that his soul, absorbed by the contemplation of infinity, soared above the sphere of measurable powers, knowing that every object whose limits can be distinctly perceived by the mind, must be within its grasp; and however grand, magnificent, beautiful, or terrific, fall short of the conception itself, and be less than sublime'—In this, from whatever cause, consists the real spell of Correggio.

(1805—Lecture VI, p. 299)

On Count Stolberg's description of the Rhine-falls at Schaffhausen

HE WHO attempts to communicate his feelings on a phenomenon of such magnitude furnishes the reader with a measure of himself. The grandeur of mind which, on entering the domain of

330

liberty,[1] raised Stolberg above national pride, rendered him a fit spectator of nature's uncontrolled scenery. To see the simple object before us unite with immensity overpowers, no doubt, every mind; but why 'the manifest omnipotence of God' should be more perceptible to a philosopher in the thunders and foam-clouds of a cataract than in the whisper of a gentle breeze is not easily discovered.

(*Analytical Review*, December 1797, review of Count Stolberg's *Travels*, signed Z. Z.—XXVI, p. 548)

[1] On crossing the frontier from Germany to Switzerland.

SECTION SIX

THE ENTOMOLOGICAL SUBLIME

> '—a science which gave serenity to my earlier days——' (Fuseli's *Advertisement* to his own translation of his brother Caspar's *Archives of Entomology*, 1795)

Contemptuous though he is of Stolberg for needing a foaming cataract to give him a sense of the infinite, Fuseli himself seldom reacts strongly to anything but the monumental, grandiose or overwhelming, unless it appear in female guise. He remains faithful to the end to the motto adopted in his youth: 'I do not wish to build a cottage, but to erect a pyramid' (Knowles, p. 396). He 'needs space, height, depth, length'; he despises Gessner's rivulets and 'whatever is strictly called rural'; he has no use for 'tears shed over roses'. Flowers count for very little in his vision of existence. There is only one form in which he can hold infinity in the palm of his hand, and that is, characteristically enough, the form of the insect, the beetle, the spider, or at best the butterfly. Hardly anybody who knew him well wrote about him without dwelling on his entomological hobby, which, Cunningham says, he specially indulged in his fits of despondency. He had a distaste for the 'pure physical sciences', Knowles tells us, and was ignorant of them, but on entomology he could speak as an authority with anybody. 'By skill and care he sometimes reared in his house some of the rarer English insects, among them the *Sphinx atropos*, *Sphinx uphorbiae* and others. His great love of entomology induced him occasionally to introduce moths into his pictures, which he painted with great care and fidelity . . .' (Knowles). He taught himself Dutch in order to be able to read and review J. Christian Sepp's *Beschouwing der Wonderen Gods in de minstgeachte Schepselen*. This enthusiasm mirrors itself in his writings on painting and literature.

332

The Michelangelo of Insects

HE WHO seeks the grand will find it in a trifle; but some seem made to find it only there. Rösel[1] saw man like an insect, and insects as Michelangelo men.

(1788–1818—Aphorism 156)

The Ichneumon-wasp

WHAT AN idea of evanescent diminutiveness presents the egg of an animal destined to live, to feed, to grow to its full size, to pass through all its changes—within another egg more minute than a common pin's head!

(*Analytical Review*, March 1789, review of J. C. Sepp's *Insects of the Netherlands*, signed R. R.—III, p. 260)

In Defence of Insects

TO ANSWER such untutored nonsense would be ludicrous, as comic as to ask Mr. Coxe what he means by the distinction of 'brutes' from 'insects'. Will he inform us what size, what organisation discriminates the line between them? The ant-hunter, the spider and the bee are surely as much nearer to man in contrivance and instinctive power than the sheep or ass, as they are farther removed from him in organisation or size. After the discoveries of the microscope, who can allow expression to a *horse* and refuse it to a *beetle*, or as our author calls it, to a *cockchafer*? Man, formed for mediocrity, generally judges only from size; but size, whether immensely great or small, is a relative idea, and supposes somewhere an organ capable to

---

[1] August Johann Rösel (1705–59), a Nuremberg miniature-painter, published 1746–51 a great serial illustrated work on entomology, *Die Insektenbelustigung*, which Fuseli studied with great enthusiasm in his boyhood.

judge of it, though the friend of Mr. Coxe should 'never before have heard of it'.

(*Analytical Review*, February 1790, review of Coxe's *Travels in Switzerlaud*, signed R. R.—VI, pp. 156–7)

Butterflies and Beetles

... of all insects, the class of *lepidoptera* or *feather-winged* is and always must be the favourite of the public, of male and female dilettanti; the delicate finger, that shrinks with horror from the beetle, mounts the head with ribbons *en papillon*, and stains the ostrich and the heron feather with the hues of iris and machaon.[1]

(*Analytical Review*, December 1795, review of W. Levin's *The Papilios or Butterflies of Great Britain*, signed R. R.—XXII, p. 583)

Human kindness and insect-hunting

MR. S. SUMMONS all his pathos in describing the exertions and means employed to resuscitate a larva of this beautiful species (*monacha*), to all appearance drowned by venturing too far into some water, in which the oak branch it fed on had been kept to preserve its freshness. If the Humane Society boast of more ingenious contrivances, they seldom can of happier results. Gentle heat, with patience and blotting paper, triumphed over apparent death, and a beautiful male moth was obtained from the larva in the sequel. The parent, it must be owned, appears to have been saved from perishing in water, only that the offspring might have the honour of expiring on the red-hot steel of Mr. Sepp.

(*Analytical Review*, August 1797, review of J. C. Sepp's *Insects of the Netherlands*, signed Z. Z.—XXVI, pp. 120–1)

---

[1] *Iris* and *machaon* are here, of course, both technical terms of the entomologists, employed to analyse the markings and indicate the genera of butterflies.

The Picturesque Spider

IF THE picturesqueness of objects be increased in proportion to their roughness of surface and intricacy of motion, two spiders, such as the *avicularia*, not to descend to too diminutive a scale, caressing or attacking each other, must, in point of picturesqueness, have greatly the advantage over every athletic or amorous *symplegma*[1] left by the ancients.

(*Analytical Review*, November 1794, review of Uvedale Price's *Essay on the Picturesque*, signed R. R.—XX, p. 265)

Insects Homerically viewed

THE DISCOVERIES of entomology approach immensity. Every day discomposes the cobweb labours of precipitate classification, and the systems erected on the fragments of former observation totter already on the ruins. The framer of an entomologic system resembles a wanderer who, invited by the overhanging woods and wide-shading luxuriance of an opposite shore, mistakes an arm of the sea for a fordable river, enters the current and is irresistibly swept to the ocean. If the classes of Linné, still triumphant, rear their heads and stand unshaken, his divisions and subdivisions are crumbling every hour into dust amid the incessant shock of discovery and new arrangement. The reason is obvious: nature dictated the classes, transient appearances, and frequently whim, the subordinate parts. Of this the genus *papilio* offers indisputable proof. Its pompous divisions into Greek and Trojan demi-gods; the race of Helicon and Parnassus; into bands of Danai and Nymphal trains, with their gorgeous trappings and attendant Plebeians, proved weak auxiliaries in a system of realities. Round, angular, indented, tailed wings, scallops and sinuosities, ensanguined or variegated spots, are characteristics too fleeting and uncertain to form

[1] *Symplegma*—close interlocking of two bodies, here as a subject for the sculptor. Fuseli disapproves of Price's theory of the picturesque, which he is, of course, in the present passage, reducing to absurdity.

divisions, or establish rank. Accordingly, the catalogues of his successor,[1] armed with ampler means of comparison, broke and continue to break in upon his orders, and to degrade his heroes. Patroclus has leapt among the *noctuae*; Achilles, Nestor, Philoctetes, Telemachus and a long etc. now join the nymphal train of *Ursulas* and *Atalantas*, who, in their turn, are doomed to give up numbers to the new Fabrician order of *satyrs*.

And what has science gained by all this systematic havoc?

(*Analytical Review*, January 1798, review of James Edward Smith's
Rarer Lepidopterous Insects of Georgia, signed R.—XXVII, pp. 1–2)

---

[1] *Fabricius, Johann Christian* (1745–1808), entomologist at Kiel University, whose classification still holds good.

PART SIX

THE

OLDER FUSELI

ON

LITERATURE

SECTION ONE

THE OLDER FUSELI
ON LITERATURE

The historical approach to literature was one of the characteristic innovations carried out by the generation to which Fuseli belonged, especially in Germany. Fuseli himself was not only familiar with the Bible, with much of ancient Greek and Latin literature and of the literature of the four principal modern European languages, but also with the learning of his day in its bearing on these questions, and with general history. The conditions, it would seem, were all fulfilled for his participating in the historical way of interpreting poetry and seeing the individual writer and work in relationship to their particular age and place and cultural phase, and the whole of literature as one continuous texture, inextricably united by countless reciprocal influences, material and spiritual. Of this there is, however, hardly a trace in his writings. He commends Herder's *Ideen zur Philosophie der Geschichte der Menschheit,* but the fervent visionary estimate of historical processes is not for him, with his sceptical view of all civilisation and of human nature. It is as though he were only prepared to recognise as really valid, either in literature or in the plastic arts, those phenomena which he can conceive of as substantially independent of historical processes and conditions—and of these he sees very few, fewer and fewer the older he grows. He picks out his giants, eliminates as blemishes everything in their work that, in his opinion, bears the mark of the period and country to which they belonged, and sees the alone valid residue as something timeless, delocalised, apart. Such a radical distinction between *giants* and *dwarfs* (his own favourite terms) necessarily disrupts the historical continuity of literature and art, and discredits the historical approach to these things just at that point where it should most decidedly prove its value. Sceptical

339

though he is as to whether there are any universally valid standards in art or in anything else, it is such absolute standards alone that he is prepared to acknowledge, that he unwaveringly postulates and seeks, and nothing will induce him to put up with, still less to welcome enthusiastically, any relative standards instead. Thence his classicism or pseudo-classicism, his demand for a 'canon'. The historical approach, in so far as it involves the admission that all aesthetic standards are relative and dependent on place, period, antecedents and nationality, could never commend itself to him. If the absolute standard must be abandoned, then he would emphatically prefer purely individual and incommensurable standards for each giant capable of asserting them, to fluctuating historical standards—mere 'fashions' they would be, in his terminology—which are valid only for one place and period. It is in keeping with this attitude that he refuses to recognise any fundamental difference between Greek mythology, Shakespearean folklore and Miltonic allegory (*see above*, pp. 242-4). Real poetry worth the name has become for him, in his old age, a matter of four or so giants, all of whom had been favourites with him in his youth, when the world's literature still presented itself to him in comparatively even breadth. What Phidias, Michelangelo and Raphael were to him in the plastic arts, Homer, Dante, Shakespeare and Milton were to him in literature; and though Homer's relationship to his age counts for something with him, he attaches very little importance to the fact that Dante lived in the Middle Ages, Shakespeare in the Elizabethan period, and Milton during the Puritan Revolution. This is certainly due not to an unconscious limitation of vision, but to deliberate choice. His *History of Art in Italy* and his *Lectures* show that he can use the historical method if he chooses, but he chooses to do so only in dealing with the dwarfs. His selection of great poets shows amongst other things how little affinity he ultimately had to pure lyric, and how strong his bias was towards epic—even Shakespeare he tends to see epically rather than dramatically. In a copy of Johnson's *Lives* he indignantly wrote in the margin against the stricture: 'We read Milton for instruction, retire harassed and overburthened, and look elsewhere for recreation; we desert our master and seek for companions——' 'I DO NOT'. His intimate knowledge of Shakespeare was remarked upon again and again by his contemporaries, and he pays his own tribute to it in his review of the *Remarks on Rousseau* (*see* p. 136). Nearly always, when he talks about literature, he has a right to be heard and something worth while to say. Of Dante, who certainly meant much to him, he speaks strangely seldom. His disappointing attitude to contemporary German literature after 1770, and to contemporary English literature after 1790, is dealt with in the Introduction.

The Epic-Sublime: Homer's 'Iliad'

THE EPIC painter depicts . . . the elements with their own simplicity, height, depth; the vast, the grand; darkness, light; life, death; the past, the future; man, pity, love, joy, fear, terror, peace, war, religion, government: and the visible agents are only engines to force *one* irresistible idea upon the mind and fancy. . . . Homer, to impress one forcible idea of *war*, its origin, its progress, and its end, set to work innumerable engines of various magnitude, yet none but what uniformly tends to enforce this and only this idea; gods and demigods are only actors, and nature but the scene of war; no character is discriminated but where discrimination discovers a new look of war; no passion is raised but what is blown up by the breath of war, and as soon absorbed in its universal blaze;—As in a conflagration we see turrets, spires, and temples illuminated only to propagate the horrors of destruction, so through the stormy page of Homer, we see his heroines and heroes but by the light that blasts them.

(1801—Lecture III, pp. 157–8)

Homer

HE HAS done much in art who raises your curiosity; he has done all, who keeps it up restless and uniform; prostrate yourself before the genius of Homer.

(1788–1818—Aphorism 123)

On translating Homer—Cowper

THE ENGLISH Jupiter perhaps shakes his ambrosial curls not with the full majesty of the Greek; the plaintive tones of Andromache do not perhaps melt, or the reverberated bursts of Hector's voice break on our ear with their native melody or strength; the stone of modern Sisyphus oppresses not with equal

341

weight, or rebounds with equal rapidity as that of old. The hoarseness of northern language, bound in pebbly monosyllables and almost always destitute of decided quantities, must frequently baffle the most vigorous attempt, even if no allowance were made for the terror that invests a celebrated passage, and dashes the courage of the translator with anxiety and fear.

(*Analytical Review*, January 1793, review of Cowper's *Homer*, signed Z. Z.—XV. p. 2. Knowles, I, p. 84)

Dante

THERE WAS but one instance in which Dante betrayed a failure in moral feeling. It is when Frate Alberigo, lying in misery in Antenora, implores him to remove the ice from his face. Dante promises to do so, on this condition—that the sinner shall first inform him who he is, and for what crime he is punished. But after Alberigo has fulfilled the conditions, the poet refuses to render him the service he had promised. That is bad, you know; faith should be kept, even with a poor devil in Antenora.

(Oral utterance, recorded by Knowles, p. 360)

Sonnets and other artificial verse forms

THE WING, the harp, the hatchet, the altar of Simmias[1] were the dregs of a degraded nation's worn-out taste; but it is a matter of surprise that a race[2] celebrated for susceptibility of sentiment should have submitted to lisp their first accents and continued to breathe their full raptures of love in the trammels of a sonnet.

(*Analytical Review*, April 1796, review of Roscoe's *Lorenzo de' Medici*, signed Z. Z.—XXIII, p. 349. Knowles, I, p. 134)

[1] Simmias, a poet of Rhodes, represented in the Greek Anthology by poems in emblematic figures like those found also occasionally among the English metaphysical poets.
[2] The Italians, with a special view to Petrarch.

Fuseli and English Literature

NOTWITHSTANDING THE predilection which Fuseli had for the ancients, particularly for Homer, yet he considered the first three acts of *Hamlet* and the second book of *Paradise Lost* to be the highest flights of human genius. . . . 'England,' he once said, 'has produced only three genuine poets, Shakespeare, Milton and Dryden.' A friend asked, 'What do you say of Pope?'— 'Pope never shewed poetic genius but once, and that, in the *Rape of the Lock*. A poet is an inventor; and what has Pope invented, except the Sylphs? In the *Dunciad* he flings dirt in your face every minute. Such a performance may be witty, but can never be esteemed a first-rate poem.'—He then called his *Eloisa to Abelard* hot ice. . . . For Gray, however, he had a high admiration; and when his opinion was asked by one who imagined that he held him cheap, he said, 'How! do you think I condemn myself so much as not to admire Gray? Although he has written but little, that little is done well.'

(Knowles, *Biography*, pp. 358–9)

Shakespeare's 'Intuition into the sudden movements of nature'

. . . by this radiant recollection of associated ideas, the spontaneous ebullitions of nature, selected by observation, treasured by memory, classed by sensibility and judgment, Shakespeare became the supreme master of passions and the ruler of our hearts: this embodied his Falstaff and his Shylock, Hamlet and Lear, Juliet and Rosalind. By this power he saw Warwick uncover the corpse of Gloster, and swear to his assassination and his tugs for life; by this he made Banquo see the weird sisters bubble up from earth, and in their own air vanish; this is the hand that struck upon the bell when Macbeth's drink was ready, and from her chamber pushed his dreaming wife, once more to methodize the murder of her guest.

(1801—Lecture III, p. 145)

343

The source of Shakespeare's power

CONSIDER IT as the unalterable law of Nature that all your power upon others depends on your own emotions. Shakespeare wept, trembled, laughed first at what now sways the public feature; and where he did not, he is stale, outrageous or disgusting.

(1788–1818—Aphorism 200)

On emending Shakespeare's text

AMONG THE peculiarities of Shakespeare's diction there are some of which the anomalies of construction bid defiance to grammar, whilst at the same time the meaning of the sentence is too obvious for misconception. Such is the following observation in the *Tempest*, Act I, Scene ii:

> —*like one,*
> *Who having unto truth, by telling of it,*
> *Made such a sinner of his memory,*
> *To credit his own lie . . .*

Such, in our opinion, as one of our author's 'wood-notes wild' emendation ought to pass submissively and with respect. But there are passages, which, by a certain coquetry of expression, equally allure and baffle the critic, promise to all and pledge themselves to none. Such, from the contest of the commentators, appears to be the celebrated couplet in *Love's Labour's Lost*, Act IV, Scene iii:

> *And when Love speaks, the voice of all the gods*
> *Makes heaven drowsy with the harmony.*

(*Analytical Review*, August 1794, review of Steevens's *Shakespeare*, signed Z. Z.—XIX, pp. 357–8)

344

Shakespeare and Milton

FUSELI, speaking of Shakespeare, sd. that if *Macbeth* only was put against all the works that had been since produced by a succession of Poets, *Dryden* and *Pope* included, it shd. be preserved, though the whole were to be sacrificed for it.—Hoare said and *Milton into the bargain*. This was instantly opposed by Fuseli and Opie—Fuseli sd. the speech of Adam to His Creator requiring a Mate was equal to anything.

(*Farington Diary*, 26 March 1804)

SHAKESPEARE IS to Sophocles what the incessant flashes of a tempestuous night are to daylight. Things came to Raphael and Shakespeare; Michelangelo and Milton came to things.

(1788–1818—Aphorisms 214 and 215)

In Defence of Milton's Sin and Death [1]

WITHOUT PRETENDING to decide on the admissibility of allegory or a mystic sense in epic poetry, we congratulate the author on having assigned a local habitation and a real part to death. Not to have been seduced by the feeble sophistry of Addison and Johnson, quibbling on a name, heedless of the laws of all narration, and insensible to the most sublime image that ever burst from human fancy, proves the discernment with which he, in this instance, penetrated the meaning of his great predecessor. The Sin and Death of Milton are real actors, and have nothing allegorical but their names. The poet unskilfully gave to positive beings names adopted by theology and common language to convey notions of mental qualities, ideas of privation. The portress and guardian of the infernal gates are not more allegoric than Force and Labour, when they chain Prometheus, or the grim feature which Euripides introduced in his Alcestis; not more than the twin brothers that convey Sarpedon's corpse

[1] Cf. pp. 243–4.

from the field of battle in Homer, or the dream that visits Agamemnon.

> (*Analytical Review*, June 1792, review of Cumberland's *Calvary*, signed R. R.—XIII, p. 123)

Intricacy and roughness as ingredients of the Picturesque

... INTRICACY APPEARS, however, sometimes, completely to destroy what roughness had established, and not to mention inferior painter or poets, let us in proof of it produce one passage from Milton. Describing the ground on which Satan stood, he says:

> *And such appeared in hue, as when the force*
> *Of subterranean wind transports a hill*
> *Torn from Pelorus, or the shattered side*
> *Of thundering Etna.*

Who will deny that these images, however sublime, are picturesque in the highest degree? Now add what follows:

> *Whose combustible*
> *And fuelled entrails thence conceiving fire,*
> *Sublimed with mineral fury, aid the winds,*
> *And leave a singed bottom, all involved*
> *With stench and smoke.*

This is so intricate that it might pass for an exemplification of it. And what is the effect? Smoke, languor, and a groan, that the mind capable of rending the promontory and convulsing the mountain should have sneaked into a miner's jacket and anatomised their loathsome entrails.

> (*Analytical Review*, November 1794, review of Uvedale Price's *Essay on the Picturesque*, signed R. R.—XX, p. 265)

Anti-Augustanism

THE EPOCH of rules, of theories, poetics, criticisms in a nation, will add to their stock of authors in the same proportion as it diminishes their stock of genius: their productions will bear the stamp of study, not of nature; they will adopt, not generate; sentiment will supplant images, and narrative invention; words will be no longer the dress but the limbs of composition, and feeble elegance will supply the want of nerves.

HE 'lisped not in numbers, no numbers came to him',[1] though he count his verses by thousands, who has not learnt to distinguish the harmony of two lines from that of a period— whom dull monotony of ear condemns to the drowsy psalmody of one recurring couplet.

(1788–1818—Aphorisms 110 and 111)

Richardson

FUSELI EVER considered Richardson a man of great genius, and one who had a key to the human heart, and was very indignant, in the latter period of his life, with a gentleman who spoke contemptuously of Clarissa Harlowe. This person said in his presence, 'No one now reads the works of Richardson.' 'Do they not?' said Fuseli, 'then by G—d they ought. If people are now tired of old novels, I should be glad to know your criterion of books. If Richardson is old, Homer is obsolete. Clarissa, to me, is pathetic—is exquisite; I never read it without crying like a child.'

(Knowles, *Biography*, p. 13)

---

[1] This quotation from the *Epistle to Arbuthnot* makes it sufficiently clear that it is Pope himself who is being attacked here. Nevertheless Fuseli was not only very familiar with Pope's poetry, but also himself imitated it in his unpublished *Dunciad of Painting* (*see above*, p. 28).

Beckford's 'Dreams, Waking Thoughts and Impressions'

FUSELI I called on. Beckford of Fonthill some years ago proposed to publish his travels,[1] Johnson printed them in quarto. They were written with genius—full of reflections on individuals and on nations—malevolent and expressive of a bad heart.— The descriptions of landscapes etc. were admirable.—Throughout the whole there was a spirit like champagne prevailing— sparkling everywhere. Fuseli had half a dozen pages of the letter-press, which he gave to Edwards of Pall Mall—Beckford had been prevailed on to suppress the book, as it would have made him enemies everywhere. . . . He (Beckford) is an actor, but no gentleman, said Fuseli; he speaks many languages, dances, sings, mimicks, you see the character is irregular by looking in his countenance, there is a twist in his look.

(*Farington Diary*, 22 January 1797)

Cowper

FUSELI THINKS Cowper the best of all the Poets of his period above Hayley etc., and even Darwin. He had imagery and his stile was more perfect and pure.

(*Farington Diary*, 28 May 1803)

---

[1] Beckford's *Dreams, Waking Thoughts and Impressions* were printed in 1783 and then suppressed. They appeared in an expurgated form in 1835, but the full original text was not published until 1891.

BIBLIOGRAPHICAL NOTE

FUSELI'S WRITINGS

Remarks on the Writings and Conduct of John James Rousseau. (London, 1767, anonymous, so far not reprinted.)

Life and Writings of Henry Fuseli, John Knowles (3 volumes).
(London, 1831; contains for the first time the *Aphorisms*, the *History of Art in Italy* and a few odd letters and notes; supplemented here with the first edition of the three original *Lectures*, which contains some interesting variants.) .

Heinrich Füssli: Briefe, edited by Walter Muschg (Basel, 1942).

Arnold Federmann: Heinrich Füssli, Dichter und Maler (Zurich, 1927).
(Contains some letters not in Muschg's edition, and Fuseli's early poems and *Complaints*; also a large series of valuable reproductions.)

Uncollected writings—*see* Appendix II.

Of the works translated by Fuseli the two following are of special interest:

Reflections on the Painting and Sculpture of the Greeks, etc., translated from the German Original of the Abbé Winckelmann (London, 1765).

Aphorisms on Man, translated from the original manuscript of the Rev. John Caspar Lavater, Citizen of Zuric (London, 1788).

WORKS ON FUSELI

Specially to be recommended, in addition to the publications of Knowles, Federmann and Muschg (whose introduction to the letters is very valuable), are the following:

Allan Cunningham's life of Fuseli, in *The Lives of the Painters*.
(1829, and variously reprinted.)

The Farington Diary, edited by James Grieg.
(London, 1922–8, eight volumes, containing many important references to Fuseli.)

Catalogues to the *Zurich Fuseli Exhibitions* of 1926 and 1941:

J. H. Füssli: Ausstellung von Gemälden, Zeichnungen und Kupferstichen. Introduction by W. Wartmann (Kunsthaus Zürich, 1926).

J. H. Füssli: (bicentary Exhibition Catalogue). Introduction by W. Wartmann (Kunsthaus Zürich, 1941).

Das römische Skizzenbuch von J. H. Füssli. Marcel Fischer (Kunsthaus Zürich, 1942).

Paul Ganz: Hans Heinrich Füsslis Zeichnungen (Bern-Olten, 1947).

Ruthven Todd: Tracks in the Snow.

(London, 1947; the well-illustrated essay *The Reputation and Prejudices of Henry Fuseli* contains much new material and forms an admirable and spirited introduction to Fuseli.)

Federmann gives a detailed bibliography up to 1927. This can be supplemented from the ample selected bibliography of Ganz. A complete Fuseli bibliography is badly needed. It would necessarily prove voluminous.

Fuseli's additions to Pilkington's *Lives of the Painters* (1805 and 1810) have not been utilised in the present volume, because such passages as would have been suitable recur in the *Lectures, Aphorisms* and *History of Art*. Fuseli is a writer who repeats himself a great deal, often for long passages without a single variant.

The twenty-one hitherto unknown poems of Fuseli referred to above on page 28 have since been published as a *Neujahrsblatt der Zürcher Kunstgesellschaft* (1951), with a detailed study of Fuseli as a lyrical writer by the editor of the present volume.

APPENDIX I

THE PRINCIPAL DATES
IN FUSELI'S LIFE

1741 Birth of Fuseli in Zurich on 6 February.

1761 In spring he is ordained and preaches his first sermon.

1762 Attacks Grebel in the pamphlet *The unjust magistrate*, written in collaboration with Lavater and Felix Hess.

1763 Leaves Zurich in February with Lavater, Hess and Sulzer; Leipzig; Berlin; six months in Barth (Pomerania) as Spalding's guest; back to Berlin in October (the *Complaints*); German translation of Lady Mary Wortley Montague's *Letters* published.

1764 Leaves Berlin for England, calling on Klopstock in Quedlinburg in March. Arrival in London about the end of March.

1765 Publishes English translation of Winckelmann's *Reflections*; becomes tutor to Lord Chewton, accompanying him to France in December.

1766 Shortly before or after 1 January Fuseli meets Rousseau in Paris. Some months in Lyons, where he quarrels with his pupil. Some months in Tours. Back in London about October. Intensive journalistic work for the next eighteen or so months.

1767 *Remarks on Rousseau* published on 23 April.

1768 About April or May of this year Fuseli shows Reynolds his drawings, and is encouraged by him to take up painting as a career. First attempts in oils. Journey to Rome planned.

1769 Translation of Dragonetti's *Treatise on Virtues and Rewards*, dedicated to Lord Chewton. Work on the *History of German Poetry*.

351

1770   Fire at Joseph Johnson's premises on 8 January destroys nearly everything Fuseli possesses. With the help of Coutts he sets out for Italy by long sea route in April, together with Armstrong. Breach with Armstrong in Genoa. Reaches Rome in May. Remains in Rome (with journeys to Naples, Venice, etc.) till autumn 1778. Drawings for Lavater's *Physiognomy*. A fever in 1772 leaves him with white hair and trembling hands.

1778   Arrives in Zurich in October, and stays there about six months. Self-portrait with Bodmer. Portrait of Magdalena Hess. In love with Anna Landolt; rejected as a suitor by her father. Inception of *Three Confederates*, completed 1781.

1779   March—separation from Anna Landolt and Lavater in Baden. April—return to London by Ostend. Reconciliation with Armstrong, who lies on his deathbed.

1780   Begins to exhibit regularly in the annual Exhibitions of the Royal Academy.

1782   First great success with *The Nightmare*. About this time he must have made the acquaintance of Blake.

1786   Begins his collaboration with Cowper in the translation of Homer. Boydell starts the *Shakespeare Gallery*.

1787   About this year Fuseli and Blake become more intimate. Macklin's *Poet's Gallery*.

1788   *Aphorisms on Man*, translated from a manuscript of Lavater's, published. Publication of Fuseli's own *Aphorisms on Art* announced, but prevented by a fire at the printer's. Fuseli works intermittently on these *Aphorisms* down to 1818, perhaps even later, and they are not published till six years after his death 30 June, Fuseli marries Sophia Rawlins. 'His wife is said to have been a young woman who had served him as a model; but her conduct was highly exemplary in the situation to which he elevated her.' (Clarke's *Georgian Era*, 1834). This year he is elected an Associate of the Academy. In May 1788 the *Analytical Review*, to which Fuseli contributes regularly till its suppression in 1798, begins to appear.

1789   Friendship with Mary Wollstonecraft, which continues till the end of 1792.

1790   Fuseli elected a Member of the Royal Academy—temporary friction on this account with Sir Joshua Reynolds, who was supporting another candidate. In this year Fuseli forms the project for his *Milton Gallery*, on which he is engaged for the next ten years.

1795   Contributions to Seward's *Anecdotes*.

1797   Coutts, Lock, Roscoe, Steevens, Seward and Johnson form a scheme to support Fuseli financially, so as to enable him to complete the Milton Gallery.

1799 Elected Professor of Painting. Milton Gallery (40 paintings) opened and proves a failure.

1800 Milton Gallery reopened with seven additional paintings—again a failure. (Very few of these paintings are known to survive.)

1801 *Lectures on Painting* (first three) published. Death of Lavater.

1802 28 August–10 October: Fuseli and various other Academicians are in Paris to see the art treasures accumulated by Napoleon.

1804 Fuseli elected Keeper to the Royal Academy.

1805 Fuseli's second course of three Lectures (*not* 1806, as Knowles states). Acquaintance with Knowles begins. Advertisement for Blake's illustrations to Blair's *Grave* written. Haydon becomes Fuseli's pupil. First revision of *Pilkington* published.

1806 Fuseli's *Ugolino* attacked in *Bell's Weekly Messenger* and defended by Blake in the *Monthly Magazine*.

1807 A silver vase presented to Fuseli from his pupils by Haydon.

1808 Work on the *History of Art in Italy* (published posthumously).

1810 Fuseli re-elected Professor of Painting. His third course of three Lectures. Another, more thorough revision of *Pilkington* published.

1815 Friendly relationship to Canova, who is now on a visit to England.

1816 At Canova's instance the Academy of St. Luke, Rome, confers on Fuseli a diploma of membership of the first class.

1820 Republication of the *Lectures*, with the addition of the three held in 1805 and of an Introduction: *A Characteristic Sketch of the Principal Technic Instruction, Ancient and Modern, which we possess*.

1825 In January Fuseli delivers his last three Lectures. On 16 April he dies after a brief illness at the Countess of Guildford's house, Putney Hill. His health had been gradually declining for some years, but his mental powers remained vigorous to the last.

1829 Cunningham publishes his life of Fuseli in the *Lives of the Painters*.

1830 Knowles publishes the second series of *Lectures*.

1831 Knowles publishes his *Life and Writings of Henry Fuseli* in three volumes.

(The editor wishes here to acknowledge his debt to Arnold Federmann's similar chronological table on page 167 of his book on Fuseli.)

APPENDIX II

FUSELI'S CONTRIBUTIONS
TO MAGAZINES

THE PRECEDING chronological table (Appendix I) indicates some, but by no means all of the miscellaneous journalistic enterprises Fuseli is known to have been engaged in as a translator and a writer of 'Advertisements', Dedications, Prefaces, etc. How many reviews and essays he contributed anonymously to periodicals in England and elsewhere it is impossible to say—probably more than anybody will ever succeed in identifying. Some of his magazine articles can, however, be traced with comparative certainty, and of these ample use has been made in the present volume. A list is here given of all the articles the editor has been able to identify. Fuseli's peculiar style, his favourite phrases and quotations, themes and ideas make it possible to determine his authorship beyond reasonable doubt in most cases, though a few border-line cases remain uncertain.

(a) 1767–9. *External evidence:* '. . . he returned to London to dedicate his pen to the daily toils of literature—to translations, essays and critiques. Of such pieces he wrote nearly an hundred. . . .' (Cunningham, of the years after Fuseli's return from France in October 1766).

'I am enclosing two or three of the papers I have contributed to some of the London magazines . . .' (Fuseli to Lavater, 6 May 1768).

Probably Fuseli had begun such journalistic work in London in the years 1764–5, before his departure for France. For the years 1767–8 the following articles have been traced—all of them unsigned:

Critical Review, May 1767, *Remarks on Rousseau* reviewed.

354

Universal Museum,	March	1767	Essay on the expression of the passions in painting, translated from Algarotti.
„	„	Sept.	1767	A Character (Nicodemo Tardi).
„	„	Feb.	1768	Description of Apollo in Belvedere (freely adapted from Abbé Winckelmann's History).
„	„	„	1768	Account of Raphael Sanzi.
„	„	March ⎱ April ⎰	1768	Literary Correspondence—dedication in French and English of a fictitious work, *La philosophie du sage* (in two instalments).
„	„	Oct.	1768	Anecdotes of the *Portefeuille de Lucifer* (Anti-Voltaire).
„	„	Dec.	1768	(?) Critical Remarks on Genius.

(Neither the British Museum nor the Bodleian have the *Universal Museum* for the years 1766 or 1769; Fuseli almost certainly began contributing to it before March 1767 and went on doing so after December 1768.)

(*b*) 1788–98. *External evidence:* 'In May 1788 the *Analytical Review* was commenced by Mr. Johnson. . . . Fuseli, of course, was among the number; and he wrote, during the progress of that work, which continued till December 1798, upwards of eighty articles, some of which were long and laboured criticisms, while others were only brief notices of the contents of the books. As his knowledge was general and extensive, he was employed in several departments of literature, and reviewed works on the classics, history, the *belles lettres*, physiology, geography and the fine arts. . . . (His) articles . . . are easily distinguished by the peculiarity of their style; and they generally have the initials Z. Z. affixed' (Knowles, pp. 80 and 383).

The number of articles in the *Analytical Review* signed Z. Z. turns out to be only 14; and of these, the earliest, on Dalrymple's *History of Christ* (May 1789), is quite certainly not by Fuseli. It is only in the fourteenth volume of the *Analytical Review*, in October 1792, that Fuseli is for the first time found using the signature Z. Z. Far more often, and over a far longer stretch of time, he is found using the signature R. R., which occurs about 27 times from February 1789 to June 1798 (R. in January 1798 is almost certainly a misprint for R. R., as the article in question is certainly Fuseli's, while the signature single R. is normally used by someone else). The signatures R. R. and Z. Z. account therefore between them for about 40 of Fuseli's contributions to the *Analytical Review*. Some articles with no signatures at all can be confidently attributed to him. Signatures he

355

occasionally makes use of are Y. Y., U. U., V. V. and (pretty certainly) L. L.—though this last signature is used by somebody else too. In the years 1789–92 there are a few reviews on favourite topics of Fuseli's, occasionally recalling his phraseology, signed M. and W. ; these are quite certainly not by him, but by Mary Wollstonecraft, who was in these years very much under his influence. It is impossible to make out whether Fuseli contributed any of the summaries of articles from the *Jenaische Allgemeine Literaturzeitung* which appear each month, classified, with other items from the foreign press, under the heading Literary Intelligence; one is sometimes inclined to suspect it. As the *Analytical Review* is made up entirely of reviews and critiques, without any original contributions, short titles of the works reviewed, or of the subjects of the critiques, are all that is given in the following table. Probably Fuseli wrote much for various periodicals after the suppression of the *Analytical Review* in December 1798—it will be a matter of searching.

FUSELI'S CONTRIBUTIONS TO THE
ANALYTICAL REVIEW

			Sign.	Vol.	Page
May	1788	(?) Zimmermann's Visit to the King of Prussia	—	1	97
June	1788	(?) The Arts	—	1	216
June	1788	Exhibition of Royal Academy	—	1	218
Oct.	1788	The Arts: Boydell's *Shakespeare Gallery*	—	2	234
Feb.	1789	Mémoires de M. le Duc de St. Simon	R. R.	3	147
March	1789	Christian Sepp: Beschouwing der Wonderen (I)	R. R.	3	257
May	1789	Secret History of Court of Berlin (two works)	R. R.	4	80
May	1789	The Arts: Exhibition. Boydell's Catalogue	—	4	106
July	1789	Supplement to Memoirs of Duc de St. Simon	R. R.	4	354
July	1789	The Arts: Catalogue of Macklin's *Gallery*	—	4	368
Sept.	1789	Rev. M. Madan's literal translation of *Juvenal*	R. R.	5	25
Sept.	1789	Reynolds's Academy Discourse on Gainsborough	—	5	38
Dec.	1789	Holcroft's version of Lavater's *Physiognomy*	Y. Y.	5	454
April	1790	(The same concluded)		6	421
Dec.	1789	Coxe's *Travels in Switzerland*	R. R.	5	462
Feb.	1790	(The same concluded		6	154

			Sign.	Vol.	Page
March	1790	Observations on Present State of the Royal Academy	—	6	330
March	1790	Alexander Bicknell: *Painting Personified*	R. R.	6	331
April	1790	To Correspondents (Apologies for inaccuracies in the Coxe and Holcroft reviews)	—	6	471
May	1790	Rev. A. Alison on the Nature and Principles of Taste	Y. Y.	7	26
July	1790	*Tracts, Philological, etc*, by late John Jortin	R. R.	7	241
Oct.	1790	James Stewart's *Antiquities of Athens* (II)	R. R.	8	121
Nov.	1790	Bell's *New Pantheon*	R. R.	8	291
April	1791	Jerningham's *Shakespeare Gallery*	R. R.	9	443
May	1791	Reynolds's last Discourse	R. R.	10	1
May	1791	Roemer's *Genera insectorum*	R. R.	10	56
Nov.	1791	Raspe's *Catalogue of Tassie's Gems*	R. R.	11	258
Dec.	1791	*Transactions of Linnaean Society* (Vol. I)	R. R.	11	397
June	1792	Richard Cumberland: *Calvary or the Death of Christ*	R. R.	13	121
Aug.	1792	Samuel Shaw: *Physiognomy* (Lavater abridged)	—	13	427
Oct.	1792	Hickey: *History of Painting and Sculpture*	R. R.	14	161
Oct.	1792	S. Foote: *Reform, a Farce*	Z. Z.	14	186
Nov.	1792	*Modèle des jeunes gens* (Winterthur)	—	14	332
Jan.	1793	Cowper's *Homer* (reprinted by Knowles)	Z. Z.	15	1
May	1793	Benjamin West: Presidential Discourse	R. R.	16	49
June	1793	*Love's Victims: or the Hermit's Story*, by the author of *The Prize, No song, no supper*, etc.	Z. Z.	16	163
July	1793	Rev. R. A. Bromley: *Philosophy and Critical History of the Fine Arts*	Z. Z.	16	241
Sept.	1793	Dalzel's Chevalier's *Description of Plain of Troy*	R. R.	17	1
Nov.	1793	Murphy's translation of *Tacitus*	Z. Z.	17	241
Feb.	1794	(The same concluded)		18	121
June	1794	History of principal rivers of Gt. Britain (Farington's *River Thames*)	Z. Z.	19	113
June	1794	R. Payne Knight: *The Landscape*, a Didactic Poem	R. R.	19	174
July	1794	*Transactions of Linnaean Society* (Vol. II)	R. R.	19	248
Aug.	1794	Steevens's *Shakespeare*	Z. Z.	19	350

			Sign.	Vol.	Page
Oct.	1794	Beresford's translation of *Virgil*	—	20	113
Nov.	1794	Uvedale Price: *Essay on the Picturesque*	R. R.	20	259
Dec.	1794	(?) Memoirs of Science and Arts	U. U.	20	365
May	1795	J. C. Fusely: *Archives of Etymology* (work of Fuseli's brother, translated by Fuseli)	Z. Z	21	523
May	1795	[Seward:] *Anecdotes of Some Distinguished Persons*	—	21	524
June	1795	W. Beloe: *Attic Nights of Aulus Gellius*	R. R.	21	609
Sept.	1795	W. Levin: *The Birds of Great Britain*	Z. Z.	22	244
Dec.	1795	W. Levin: *The Papilios or Butterflies of Great Britain*	R. R.	22	583
March	1796	(Henry Tresham) *The Sea-sick Minstrel*	—	23	282
April	1796	Roscoe: *Life of Lorenzo de' Medici*	Z. Z.	23	337
Dec.	1796	(The same concluded) (reprinted by Knowles)		24	561
June	1796	Stewart and Revett: *Antiquities of Athens* (III)	R. R.	23	561
July	1796	Professor Camper: *Anatomy and Drawing*	R. R.	24	1
Jan.	1797	(?) Selections from the French Anas	—	25	88
July	1797	Works and Life of Sir Joshua Reynolds	—	26	1
Aug.	1797	J. C. Sepp: *Wonders of God* (II)	Z. Z.	26	119
Dec.	1797	Fr. Leopold Count Stolberg: *Travels through Germany, Switzerland, Italy and Sicily*	Z. Z.	26	545
Jan.	1798	J. E. Smith: *Rarer Lepidopterous Insects of Georgia*	R.	27	1
Feb.	1798	(?) Florian's *Estelle*, translated by Susanna Cummins	V. V.	27	203
Feb.	1798	(?) Retrospect of the Active World: *Painting*	—	27	220
April	1798	(?) *The Castle on the Rock, or the Memoirs of the Ellerland Family*, by the author of *Derwent Priory*	V. V.	27	418
April	1798	Helen Maria Williams: *Tour in Switzerland*	R. R.	27	561
Aug.	1798	(?) Goethe: *Stella and Clavigo*	L. L.	28	170
Sept.	1798	*Transactions of Linnaean Society* (1797)	Z. Z.	28	237
Oct.	1798	(?) Uvedale Price: *Essay on the Picturesque* (Vol. II)	—	28	389
Oct.	1798	(?) Schiller: *Don Carlos* (two translations)	—	28	408
Dec.	1798	(?) Corancez: *Anecdotes of Rousseau*	L. L.	28	609

This represents a total of 67 items, one of which, being only a note of apology, can be ignored. Of the remaining 66 items, ten are doubtful. This leaves 56 fully reliable attributions. If Fuseli condensed occasional articles from the *Jen. Allg. Lit. Zeit.* for the Literary Intelligence of the *Analytical Review*, as he is likely to have done in the case of subjects he was specially interested in, this might account for some of the contributions still not identified.

At first sight one is puzzled to find Fuseli reviewing some of the works above listed. One of his practices was to review books containing references to himself, and to quote the passages in which his name occurred, especially if the reference was a complimentary one. Several instances of this might be quoted.

Remarkable is the review of the poem *Love's Victims* in June 1793. The excerpts show clearly enough that the poem was quite worthless, but the reviewer praises it very highly; and there can be no doubt that it is Fuseli writing here. Doubtless he knew the author of the poem and was giving a helping hand. Other instances of such procedures can be found—as, for example, where Fuseli says of the 'young friend' who designed the frontispiece to Seward's *Anecdotes*: 'He requires only the mediocrity of Raphael with respect to rank and to fortune, to enable him to become the rival of that great master in the noblest efforts of his genius and of his knowledge.' As a rule Fuseli reviewed only the graver type of publication, but he was probably responsible for the notices of *Estelle* and *The Castle on the Rock* (February and April 1798) as well as for that on *Love's Victims*. Careful search would probably show his hand in a few more of the innumerable short notices on novels and popular poems in the *Analytical Review*.

APPENDIX III

GOETHE'S ATTITUDE
TOWARDS FUSELI

ON 5 FEBRUARY 1774, one day after saying in a letter to Herder, how admirably Fuseli and Goethe would match one another, Lavater wrote to Goethe himself, telling him he ought to meet Fuseli, but adding that he regards Goethe as 'ten times more of a friend and a human being than Fuseli'. Soon after 16 November of the same year, Lavater, with a view, as he said, to rousing Fuseli's interest in Goethe and Herder, sent off a parcel of newly published books to him in Rome: Goethe's *Götz von Berlichingen* and *Werther*; Herder's *Die älteste Urkunde des Menschengeschlechts* and *Auch eine Philosophie der Geschichte*; and Klopstock's latest *Odes*. Some three months elapsed before Fuseli replied; but his answer, when it came, in March 1775, was one of the most impressive things he ever wrote (see pp. 92–3, 114, 118). He begins by saying, 'Thank you for the books', —but on the subject of Goethe's and Herder's writings he has not a single word to say. Instead he speaks all the time about Klopstock's odes, which he pulls to pieces with great savagery, concluding in general from them that the new German literature is completely on the wrong lines. One might suppose that he had not yet found time to look at the other, so much more important books Lavater had sent him—but one of them at least he had certainly read, Goethe's *Götz*, for although he does not mention it at all, still less express an opinion on it, he quotes from it—and what he quotes is the notorious impolite message of defiance. This is the only time that Fuseli, who so much revelled in quotations, is found quoting Goethe. In so far as Lavater had hoped, by sending the books to Fuseli, to rouse his interest in Goethe and Herder, he seemed to have failed. But Fuseli's letter made up for this in other ways, especially by the magnificent defence of the image in poetry, and Lavater sent it straight off to Goethe. Goethe passed it on at once to Herder, on 25 March, with the comment: 'Here, dear brother, is a magnificent letter of Fuseli's, from Lavater. What fire and fury the man has in him!'

Writing to Lavater in June 1777, Fuseli gives vent to his irritation about a number of things (*see* pp. 139–40) in the *Physiognomy*, which has just appeared, and then picks out as the best item in the publication the chapter on Homer; this chapter turned out, however, to be an unsigned contribution from Goethe, and not by Lavater at all. On 21 May 1779, in writing of the suicide of Lavater's secretary, who had been too much affected by reading *Werther*, Fuseli adds: 'Poor Goethe!' This is the only time Goethe's name occurs in any letter of Fuseli's known to survive.

In November 1779 Goethe came to Zurich, eagerly looking forward, as he writes (on 28 October), to seeing all the work of Fuseli's that Lavater can show him. Lavater had much to show him, for Fuseli had left many of his Roman drawings with him, before turning his back on Zurich for London six months earlier. These drawings make a great impression on Goethe, and Lavater gives him several of them, which Goethe carefully treasures down to his death. They are still in Weimar. Just before leaving Zurich Goethe writes to his friend Knebel in Weimar: 'I have, *per fas et nefas*, got hold of some paintings and drawings of Fuseli's, which will give you a shock' (30 November 1779). The outstanding document that shows how Fuseli's art had moved him is an undated letter to Lavater which must have been written soon after this, in which he asks Lavater to persuade Fuseli to make a design for a monument to be erected in Weimar—a plan of which nothing comes. He gives full rein to his admiration of Fuseli, speaks of his 'vast riches' and is prepared to go to any lengths to secure his collaboration. All his own ideas for the monument may go by the board, if it comes to the point: 'Fuseli . . . will certainly express the idea more forcefully, grandly, appropriately and originally. . . . However he visualises it, it will be all right.' Fuseli is one who 'fuses everything together with spirit and fire'. But this enthusiasm is short-lived. When the Fuseli pictures arrive in Weimar he acknowledges them briefly and without comment. It looks as though on second thoughts they have given him as great a shock as anybody. Seventeen years elapse before he is found speaking of Fuseli again—and during those years much has happened: he has dropped Lavater out of impatience with his Christian beliefs, which he mercilessly satirises; he has spent a long time in Rome, and fully developed the classical creed of his middle years; and he has found a new Swiss friend, Heinrich Meyer, like Lavater and Fuseli a man of Zurich, and as it happened, one who served his apprenticeship as a painter under Fuseli's father. About 1797 Goethe, Schiller and Heinrich Meyer, now professor of art in Weimar, form a league to combat the new Romantic attitude towards the plastic arts and to uphold against it the pure classical doctrines of Winckelmann. And in this connexion Goethe's attention again falls upon Fuseli, whose drawings he must have had out for inspection more than once in this year. He sees some kind of relationship between Fuseli's art and Romanticism, and attacks the two together. It is curious that in these anti-Romantic publications on the plastic arts, which now begin and continue intermittently over twenty years, Goethe himself is never found using Fuseli's name, which indeed nowhere appears in his officially published works. It is only in Goethe's letters, diaries, conversations and unpublished papers that Fuseli's name occurs[1]— when he is publicly criticised now, it is either without being named, or, if he is named, it is by Heinrich Meyer and not by Goethe himself.

On 27/28 May 1798 Goethe sent to his publisher Cotta a list of 'writings some of them complete, some more or less so and needing only a little time to revise and put the finishing touch to'. One item on this list is an article on 'the work of Henry Fuseli, with reference to his painting in Zurich and to the well-known engravings after him'. The draft for this projected article and a fragmentary opening to it still exist—but they were written towards the end of July 1797, *before* Goethe had seen the painting of the *Three Confederates* in Zurich, and also *before* he had seen some of the engravings evidently referred to in the list for Cotta. What Goethe jotted down on Fuseli in July 1797 was chiefly concerned with the drawings in his own collections—but between then and 27 May 1798 he had, as we shall see, on at least two different occasions been confronted with Fuseli's more official work, and he evidently now thinks of amalgamating these newest impressions with his earlier notes. These notes of July 1797 are brief but illuminating; the draft runs:

Estimate of Fuseli's work.   Bizarre.
Conflict between poetry and painting.   Tragic.   Humorous.
Manner.   Drawing.

The only part of this draft that Goethe tried to work out is the heading 'Conflict between poetry and painting'—and this he does in a

---

[1] Most of the passages in question are difficult to trace. Ernst Beutler brings together nearly all of them in his article on Fuseli in the quarterly, *Goethe*, 1939 (Vol. IV, No. 1), but gives none of the dates or sources, which detracts somewhat from the value of his work. All but two of the utterances he quotes the present writer has succeeded in tracing. One major inaccuracy in reproducing Goethe's original, which has already been taken over from Beutler by Ganz, may here be drawn attention to: in the fragment '*Ueber die Gegenstände der bildenden Kunst*' Goethe wrote: 'Der bildende *Künstler* soll dichten . . .', not 'Der bildende *Dichter* . . .'

fragment headed '*On the subjects of the plastic arts*', presumably written also immediately before he left Weimar for Frankfort on 31 July 1797. Setting out with some general reflections on the importance of clearness and objectivity in the plastic arts, Goethe comes to his own quarrel with Fuseli for his 'erroneous application of poetry to painting': 'It is all right for the plastic artist to invent poetically, but he ought not to "poeticise" (*Der bildende Künstler soll dichten, aber nicht poetisieren*), that is to say, *his* medium being one of direct sensuous representation, he has no business addressing himself to the imagination in the same way as the poet does, who in *his* art must first rouse the imagination, before he can produce any effect at all. Most of Fuseli's works offend in this way.' From this paraphrase of Goethe's words (a close translation would convey hardly any meaning at all) one can see what it was that scandalised his classical taste in Fuseli's work now. He felt—and very rightly felt—that in Fuseli's drawings all the dynamic qualities and energies of images evoked only before the mind's eye, as by poetry, are superimposed upon actual sensuous images presented to the physical eye, and this double assault is too much for him, is a kind of violation of his mental harmony. This is not simply a question of subject-matter—it is rather a question of style, of the tremendous intensity of Fuseli's style: certain kinds of emphasis, Goethe says, are legitimate in poetry, because the poet has *only words* to operate with, but the same kinds of emphasis in painting, where the eye is already directly affected in any case, are intolerable. For the rest, Goethe's mind moves along exactly the same lines in dealing with Fuseli as it does in these same weeks in dealing with Hölderlin, whom he and Schiller were trying to bring into a more salutary frame of mind by urging him to write 'little poems on humanly interesting subjects' instead of indulging in philosophical ideas and subjective visions. Another theme for a possible essay jotted down by Goethe within a day or two of that on Fuseli is: 'Advice to young poets about objectivity.'

Three months after the jottings on Fuseli's art, on 24 October 1797, Goethe was in Zurich, where he saw in the town hall Fuseli's painting of the *Three Confederates*—a picture in which he was interested not only on account of the artist, but also because his mind was at this time occupied with the story of William Tell. In January 1798 Goethe obtained a copy of Erasmus Darwin's *Botanical Garden*, and writes on the 26th to Schiller that the book is 'embellished with crazily allegorical engravings by Fuseli'. It is four months after this that he writes to Cotta of publishing an article on Fuseli with special reference to the painting and the engravings he has seen since the previous July. This article was never written, but very much of what should have gone into it was incorporated into the little art manifesto in novel form, *Der Sammler und die Seinigen* (*The Collector and his kith and kin*), begun as a result of a conversation with Schiller of

19 or 20 November 1798, completed in May 1799, and published soon after in the *Propyläen*. Fuseli is not here named—nor is any other individual artist named—but there is no doubt that the strictures on the 'sketcher' (*Skizzist*), the 'imaginer' (*Imaginant*) and the 'characteriser' (*Charakterist*) are all chiefly aimed at him; he is referred to about this time as a 'perfect example of the wrong thing' (quoted by Beutler, without date or source). So it is especially of Fuseli that Goethe is thinking, when he writes in *The Collector*: 'The sketcher on the other hand usually has too much imagination; he has a hankering after poetic, nay, fantastic subjects and is always a little exaggerated in his expression.' Or, of the 'Imaginers': 'Some termed them "poeticisers", because, instead of understanding the poetic element in the plastic arts, they try to emulate the poet, and strive after his prerogatives, overlooking and forfeiting their own advantages. . . . The "Imaginer" does infinite harm to plastic art, by chasing her beyond all her boundaries. . . .' It is significant, and in view of a later event particularly interesting, that when a collection of drawings, the most remarkable amongst them by Fuseli, was offered to Goethe in August 1799, he refused to buy it. It is worth noting that *in theory* Fuseli was as much opposed to subjectivity in art as Goethe himself at this stage was.

On 2 May 1800 Goethe saw in Leipzig a copy of Boydell's *Shakespeare Gallery*, and made the following observations on it in his diary: 'One may say of Fuseli, as of every mannerist of genius, that he parodies himself. In nearly all the other engravings in the *Shakespeare Gallery*, the composition and treatment are trivial and characterless.' The word *mannerist* had already played a considerable part in *The Collector and his kith and kin*—it was the term with which Fuseli was regularly dismissed by those who felt repelled by him. He himself is much given to defining and condemning 'mannerism'. It is to be noted, however, that, even here, Goethe does not deny Fuseli's genius—that he never does; he only shakes his head over it as genius misdirected and abused.

When Fuseli's first three Lectures were published, Goethe read them with great interest and care, though with no sympathy, both in the original English (1801) and in Eschenburg's German translation (1803). He entrusted the actual reviewing of the book to Heinrich Meyer, who was largely his mouthpiece, only adding a penetrating criticism of Eschenburg's shortcomings as a translator. In 1809 the sight of some engravings reminds him of Fuseli, whom he says he had almost forgotten, and he writes to Meyer, on 9 September of this year: 'I forgive Herr Fuseli his awful pronouncements on art, because I can after all learn a good deal that is historically interesting from him.' In 1818 Meyer condemns the Shakespeare illustrations of Fuseli for their wildness and ghastliness in an article in *Kunst und Altertum* attacking Romantic ideas of painting; this article, entitled *Neudeutsche religiös-patriotische Kunst*, was for a time mistakenly attributed to Goethe.

On 31 December 1823 Soret records how he dined with Goethe; when the meal was over, Soret says, Goethe 'showed me a portfolio of drawings, amongst which the beginnings of Fuseli were specially noteworthy'. This phrase is echoed just a year before Goethe's death, when he writes to Meyer and tells him that he has decided to buy a collection of Swiss drawings that has been offered to him: 'We shall have a regular treasure for those who can think and contemplate calmly. The drawings of Henry Fuseli alone are worth the money and more. Where else can one find such striking beginnings of an extraordinary man?' (7 March 1831—falsely dated 1832 by Federmann). This is Goethe's last word on Fuseli. He has moved a considerable distance from the dogmatic classicism of his middle years and is able to recapture something of the impression Fuseli's drawings had made on him at the age of thirty.

Heinrich Meyer's review of Fuseli's 'Lectures' in the 'Jenaische Allgemeine Literaturzeitung', 7, 8 and 9 February 1804

This review is signed W. K. F. (Weimarische Kunst-Freunde— the name adopted by Goethe, Schiller and Meyer for their anti-Romantic league). Meyer is evidently puzzled at not finding more that he can disagree with in Fuseli's art theories; he is on the look-out for specifically Romantic doctrines, and does not find them. But he is still conscious that Fuseli stands for a very different conception of art from W. K. F. 'Whether one likes Fuseli's peculiar manner or not,' Meyer says, 'he must certainly always be ranked amongst the first painters now living.' Fuseli's eminence and powers make it all the more necessary that attention should be drawn to everything in his *Lectures* that 'might disseminate error, and it is a double duty, carefully to sort out the wheat from the chaff'. Meyer bestows the highest praise on Fuseli's treatment of Raphael ('pure gold') and of Rembrandt, and almost as high praise on his accounts of Michelangelo ('on the whole exceptionally good') and of Rubens and Van Dyck. But he finds him too severe to Dürer, and his contemptuous treatment of fourteenth- and fifteenth-century Italian painting seems inexplicable on any other assumption than that he knows far too little about it. In particular Heinrich Meyer defends Mantegna, who was a favourite of Goethe's, against Fuseli's censures. Only at two points is Meyer able to find something like a real *casus belli* in the *Lectures*—these points are, however, both of considerable interest for us, showing as they both do how much the W. K. F. group suspected some hidden connexion between Fuseli and the young Romantics they were contending against at home. The first is this: 'We should have been glad to pass over unmentioned the injustice towards Winckelmann, and the German critics altogether, of which our author is guilty at the end of his first lecture—but it is not expedient to let flagrant unfairness escape scot-free. If Herr Fuseli intended thereby to pay an incidental compliment to his listeners as Englishmen, he was, to say the least of it, not acting magnanimously, for his footnotes disclose something, indeed, but by no means the whole of what he owes to German authors. Should he belong, however, to the sect of those who lose no opportunity to cavil at Winckelmann, we can only pity him.' The other point turns on the questions raised by Fuseli, whether a painter may represent 'what is strictly speaking impossible' and whether he may invent his own subjects, instead of always taking them over from poets or from existing traditions. 'As is to be expected, the answer is in the affirmative', writes Meyer. 'But in his efforts to demonstrate that free invention is permissible, Herr Fuseli reveals to us on the one hand the rightness of his feeling, on the other the instability and equivocalness of his notions.' Meyer concludes his review with the hope that Fuseli will go on with and complete the *Lectures*, because 'the whole will contain a multitude of brilliant and sound observations, which, when once freed from the encumbering dross, must prove truly profitable to the lovers of art'.

INDEX (selected)

367

A A